The
Book
of
Samuel

Also by Mark Rudman

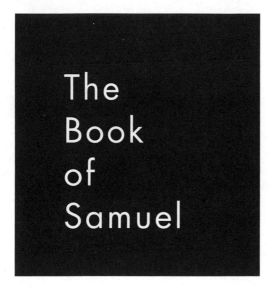

The Book of Samuel

Essays on Poetry and Imagination

MARK RUDMAN

NORTHWESTERN UNIVERSITY PRESS

EVANSTON, ILLINOIS

Northwestern University Press
www.nupress.northwestern.edu

Printed in the United States of America

10   9   8   7   6   5   4   3   2   1

Library of Congress Cataloging-in-Publication Data

Rudman, Mark.
    The book of Samuel : essays on poetry and imagination / Mark Rudman.
       p. cm.
    Includes bibliographical references.
    ISBN 978-0-8101-2538-4 (pbk. : alk. paper)
       1. Rudman, Mark. 2. Poets—20th century. 3. Poetry—Themes, motives. I. Title.
    PS3568.U329B66 2009
    814.54—DC22

                                                                    2008048265

To succeed in not distorting the source of life which resounds within us.

—BORIS PASTERNAK

Contents

Acknowledgments

Thanks to the editors of these publications for allotting earlier versions of these essays the space they needed.

American Poetry Review: "Reading T. S. Eliot on My Cousin's Farm in the Gatineau," "On the Road, Touch and Go, with D. H. Lawrence," "The Voyage That Never Ends: Hart Crane, Malcolm Lowry" (earlier title, "Mexican Mosaic"), "William Carlos Williams in America"; *Kenyon Review:* "The Milosz File, and Choruses of Ghosts (II)"; *New England Review:* "The Book of Samuel" (excerpts), "A Garland for Nicanor Parra at Ninety"; *TLS:* "First Glimpse of Cimabue's Crucifix Reconstructed."

Further thanks to my wife Madelaine Bates, my son Samuel, Karen Bender, Matt Corey, Stephen Donadio, Denis Donoghue, Michael Hofmann, Shelby Girard, Edwin Frank, the late Paul Magnuson, Alexander Nemser, Daniel Soare, Mike Wexler, and Erica Wright, for various forms of contributions and support along the road. And special thanks to Barbara Epler.

Part of a Preface,
Part of an Introduction,
Part of an Afterword

". . . our love has just begun,
but that was yesterday and yesterday's gone"
—CHAD AND JEREMY, "YESTERDAY'S GONE"

Suspicion of Memory

Dante sets the boundaries of my journey, both quandary and quarry, in of all places, this unreachable, ungraspable, breathtaking opening passage of his *Paradiso,* where he reminds us that arrival is illusory, that departure is desired even in the empyrean; which leaves everything vibrating but still irresolute: unresolved. And the teen muse of the nineteen sixties duo fades away like Beatrice. Memory will take his utmost effort to retrieve, and he vows to search for these lost treasures and make his future songs out of them. Awareness of the environment is still the prerequisite for the journey. Rising and falling, vacillation, running his course "between extremities," as Yeats put it indelibly five hundred years later.

A balance in the way the prime mover distributes
the crepuscular in that valley, and sheer radiance over here
where I fall upward toward the light, undiluted, blinding,

yet glimmerings signal what he who comes down from the heights,
intellect rattled, speech impeded, can still see:
even in paradise—the closer we get to where we want to go the more

the mind's capacities are drawn down—
the ravine bottomless, profound, still unknown as now
divests itself of what it had taken for its own.

(DANTE, *PARADISO,* LINES 1–9, MY TRANSLATION)

There is only one viable attitude towards memory, and that is suspicion. In 1984, Madelaine and I stood before a wooden crucifix by Cimabue in the Basilica of St. Francis in Assisi. We gasped with awe and relief. Cimabue's name had seemed so lonely in relation to the painters about whom more is known and available to see. The great blackened cross, its wings outstretched, pressed down on me. It was an indelible moment, and very unlike seeing something tamed by the ambience of a museum. Madelaine and I, mathematician and poet—people of entirely different casts of mind—have an identical memory of this day; we encountered the crucifix after the train ride from Perugia to Assisi. When I told a friend of this encounter, he informed me that Cimabue's crucifix wasn't in the basilica of Assisi. I argued that was impossible. Madelaine agreed. We would set this friend right. I leafed through a book of Cimabue's complete works and, with mounting panic, discovered there was never any such wooden crucifix in Assisi. How curious that this demotion should occur with regard to the first great painter who was not anonymous, and whose reputation, as Dante claims in the *Purgatorio,* was quickly eclipsed by his student, Giotto.

Cimabue's crucifix is painted on wood, but the wood isn't shaped like a crucifix, as I remembered it to be. And it's the first thing you see as you enter the Basilica of Santa Croce, in Florence, a far more accessible place than Assisi.

Giorgio Vasari—writing about the same time that Marlowe and Shakespeare were being delivered out of their mother's wombs, 1560 (all dates and facts in addition to the details of the individual lives themselves are thought to be no more reliable as history than Thomas Carlyle's *History of the French Revolution*)—reports that Cimabue's works were in dubious condition even then. I find that in itself distressing. It's one thing to think about the ancient world, Gilgamesh, Homer, the pre-Socratics, the fragments of Sappho—and of course the biblical books of Samuel 1 and 2—and even the B.C./A.D. world of Horace and Ovid, but 1560 seems a long way off in its own way, and I find it hard to take in that when the antique Vasari wrote his *Lives of the Painters* it was already some three hundred years after Cimabue. Once again, echoing Pound, Dante's *Commedia* is news that stays news:

> Cimabue bought the showered hype until news
> of his former pupil's perfect circle grew and the crowd
> chanted "Giotto!," and the renowned was now unknown.

Part of a Preface, Part of an Introduction, Part of an Afterword

Our supple tongue glides from Guido to Guido,
someone at this moment is being born who's destined to bring down
those who coveted reputation and yesterday's throne.

So no, it's not the number of years, it's that we tend to further conflate the remove of these figures (especially those who painted before perspective): Cimabue is further removed from Vasari than George Washington is from us. I can't be alone in thinking that Alexander Pope lived a very long time ago, in another world, pre-industrial; I could easily conflate Pope and Shakespeare, but the moment I go further back, in addition to hitting ANONYMOUS, time seems to collapse. It's connected to the concept of "dated." But take heart; silent films, even black-and-white films, are as or more dated to today's students than these mysterious works they see at firsthand on their "junior year abroad," which is becoming "a series of years before I want to decide what I want to do" after graduating college. And they aren't going to Florence. They flock to Africa, Berlin, India, Russia: anywhere that was not familiar to the previous two generations—a positive sign. They know that the European museum is wonderful to visit, but unlikely to generate anything unforeseen. And this connects to my distinction between D. H. Lawrence and T. S. Eliot as "generative" as against the numerous words that convey the opposite impulse.

The best I can do, to give this memory some legitimacy, is to say that what I saw in Assisi was a badly damaged fresco: what I thought were wings that Cimabue had painted black, were simply signatures of its ruined condition. Perhaps what floored me was the sadness that a work by a painter whose works are so scarce and whose reputation was eclipsed in his own time by Giotto should be ruined beyond any hope of restoration. It could be reduced to the condition of memory, a mere approximation of a reality, forever undependable, unknowable.

This appears to be a statement. It probably was when I first set it down. But more likely it helped create the conditions under which I undertook the prose in *The Book of Samuel*.

I've done my best, with as little elaboration as possible, and a decision to quote only when absolutely necessary and only the necessary lines—a reversal of my early approach to writing about poetry, which was to get in as many quotes I valued as I could.

But this short poem, wrung from the same conception, may help prepare the reader for the twists, turnings, and reversals that arise in the essays that compose this book.

First View of Cimabue's Crucifix Reconstructed

I
didn't just look up at the blackened crucifix:
it looked back, pressed down,

like an immense wing, dark and charred;
impinged, with all the weight it had borne.

The inertial pull of the burden itself is invisible,
though we could swear at times that the cross

was actually on our backs, as in the innumerable images
rendered by the anonymous and the known.

And the artist was the first to sign his work.
It goes like this: anonymous, then Cimabue, then—

The
Book
of
Samuel

Are You Basque?

For Kirmen Uribe

"Are you Basque?" it struck so hard, the concept, tacit, of someone who was and wasn't
part of the countries that surround the natural fortress where the inhabitants can pick
and choose where they want to be in time, the latest portable technological advances
sold in a stone house built in the 14th century.

I think something terrible happens in Sartre's story "The Wall" I devoured
at nineteen, or twenty, nowhere near twenty-one, and the question that stuck is still
audible: "Are you Basque?" I hope they didn't line them up against that wall,
where they handed out blindfolds in a grotesque parody of old world

manners, forcing a blind man to take off his sunglasses in order to be executed
according to the updated Executioner's Handbook,
to wrap a sterilized blindfold—that doesn't have the wonderful tree smell that imbues
cotton and wool in the high country—around his head and tie a secure knot, "Is it secure?

Are you sure?" in order to convenience the squad of tetchy boredom-stricken
sharpshooters, infallibly accurate at a distance of six feet or under.
If we could divide our 21st-century world into Loyalists and Fascists, who would be who?
It doesn't help that I adapted the story as a play when, mountainously alone one summer

in Colorado Springs, where I'd gone to recover from the aftershock of the machete
incident, while my mother and stepfather were packing for yet another summer's
three-week ritual stint in hell in another "top vacation spot," leaving me with wheels
and the view of Pike's Peak from the terrace.

Alone, knowing no one—ok one girl my age—I drove around in air as clear
as the superfluous billboards that bordered the sites they advertised.
And what's more antithetical to beauty than too many mentions of it
when silence is key and a detour needed to prepare:

what could take away my love of driving before night through the subdued
glow that burnished red rock canyons and boulders that loomed over bends in the road
and the dwindling one-horse towns that retained indelible elements of charm
before the next barrage of signs blotting out precious distances

announcing bargains on imitation authentic Western stuff that roused savvy kids
to insist they be "taken away from here!" which, translated into my situation meant—
turn around!—and get back to the smoky strobe-equipped bar on Main or State,
cadge a black and tan on tap and get in tune with the local rockers whose takes

on Beatles Byrds and the Lovin' Spoonful "for the great relief of having you to talk to"
vanquished isolation and made visible the presence of one girl—intriguingly
quiet kept her distance but was known by everyone and got so many nods
I figured she'd lived in the Springs since before she was born—who grabbed my eye,

and would have anywhere despite the post-hippie suede pants the color of wet sand
and sandals she'd alternate with the turquoise-beaded moccasins she wore with loose-
around-the-waist Levi 501s. And no belt, which made my heart beat.
When I see photos of my family, my friends, and myself in successive decades, all our

clothes have a tinge of the absurd. But no worse than togas, corsets, Elizabethan ruff.
What was played out in "The Wall" was squeezed into a slender book called Intimacy.
The girl brought it back to me along with the truth behind the truth,
that consciousness comes into being at the sight of a memory trace. Best

located on foot. "But I'm a stranger, where to walk around here?" "O, I'll show you.
Hiking can keep you sane, once removed from the town's contagion: image."
It exuded vapor it would be my part to recover, restore, recreate, so think:
en soi and pour soi, the waiter, one who waits and waits on good faith and bad faith,

played out in a story as inevitable as a road the obscure alphabet leads me down. Enemy
infantries passed over Basque country, over and over,
because the distances, insular, soaked up sound, commands were wasted
in the Pyrenees, vanishing point and periphery, curiously aligned,

and every Fascist soldier stood out in uniforms a shade too green—
unaware that sights were fixed on them by well-hidden men and women,
crack shots who learned to kill quickly moving small animals
as little children.

On the Road,
Touch and Go,
with D. H. Lawrence

There are blows in life, so powerful . . .
I don't know!

—CÉSAR VALLEJO, TRANS. CLAYTON ESHLEMAN

I didn't want to, but for reasons that will become abundantly clear, I'm forced
to begin at the beginning, at the sources that gave rise to this writing. In the
summer following my mother's death, with my son for the first time, at the age
of sixteen, safely stowed in a summer camp, my wife and I headed to Italy for
a breather. Other losses had also occurred. At some point, we were staying in
Lazio to be within proximity of both Rome and several Etruscan sites. I began
to feel a thickness in my lungs building up. Cats in the courtyard? Except for
one respiratory flu in my mid-twenties, I hadn't had an asthma attack since I
was eleven when we moved from Illinois to Utah, and I lingered—and malin-
gered—in the West long enough, as they say, to outgrow it. Outgrow it, but
not without fear of its reoccurrence. Everyone has a defining fear having to
do with their own mortality, usually connected to childhood illness, and mine
is suffocation: not getting enough air in my lungs. After Lazio we headed into
the Abruzzi, to a town called Abateggio, as far as possible from "culture" and
where the most wonderful dishes were made from rabbits and boars and could
be had for less than it cost to eat at the local Cuban-Chinese restaurant in New
York City. Pretty soon I would be out hunting rabbits with a bow and arrow
like figures in a painting by Paolo Uccello. As night came on, my voice lowered
several octaves, my lungs began to thicken, my breathing grew heavy. What
could it be? What could have followed me from Lazio to Abateggio?

I feel imperiled by the heat and the toxic smoke from the cement factory in
Scafa, yet too restless and curious to imitate the lizard's stillness. The heat of the
day is trapped in the valley of Scafa. Turns the port of Pescara into a dead zone.

I found the following passage in Lawrence's novel *The Lost Girl* on November 4, 2004: "It seems that there are places which resist us, which have the power to overthrow our psychic being. It seems as if every country has its potent negative centers, localities that savagely and triumphantly refuse our living culture. And Alvinia had struck one of them, here on the edge of the Abruzzi."

The light pattern in the scattered villages reaching from these mountain heights to Pescara is reminiscent of what it looks like from the hills in miniature above Los Angeles, Salt Lake City, or Albuquerque; the distance between sustained bands of segments, the abrupt break off into hilly darkness, the disbanding of illumination, is as much an impression, a healing vapor.

And the mystery of the scattered zigzag ablaze in the night is resolved, if not solved, in the twilight: it was like a runway to Pescara, like an unlit pinball machine.

The heat trapped in the Apennines. The refracted possibility that the scarce coolness from the snow-covered peaks will blow over and down. The heat made twilight come early in the Abruzzi one night. The young woman who runs the *herboristica* in Scafa was tugging on her T-shirt to emphasize the heat. She was amused at my requests for multiple products containing green tea, and when I commented on its proximity to eucalyptus she said she'd been thirteen times to Australia to visit her brother, a professional soccer player, who lived there with his Australian wife, and handed me a koala with an Australian flag. When she learned why I was so avid about green tea, she told me of a secret place "where the mothers take their babies to breathe the vapors."

Where will this lead lead?

➤

No one around, except history. Plaques that inform how this river has provided hydraulic power for five hundred years. I wade into turquoise shallows. Softer than belief, they grab my feet. And now with quicksand between my ankles and knees, I grip a log. Test my weight, haul myself on like mounting a mule, edge onto my back, sit down. Safe, for the time being. It's an effort to maintain equilibrium: to stay on the log and have my ankles in the water at the same time, shoulders aching from the balancing act—left foot braced against solid, sensuous and mossy rock, right foot embraced by the milky sand.

I lie across the log and try to dip my head into the curative waters. To dip my head and not crack my skull. Impossible. And so to splash *acqua fredda* on my head I am forced to fill my baseball cap with this sulfurous water—murky and clear and way colder than the legendary waters that assail, jab, and pound Schoodic Point's imperious granite, far enough north on the Maine coast to know you're somewhere else, unfamiliar, and real.

One night in Pescara, we got the scuttlebutt from a pharmacist. (Pharmacists in Italy are often like what doctors used to be like in the U.S.A., serious, thoughtful, empathetic human beings.) "It is a late spring this year," he said. His daughter, a girl of thirteen, had been so choked up that they closed all the shutters of the house, and for days she couldn't leave because she couldn't breathe, and as far as he knew, she had no history of asthma or allergies. "It's the late spring," he said. "The trees are blooming in July when they ought to have bloomed in May, so the entire climate is altered." He recommended a new drug, a tawny allergy pill the size of a bullet. His main warning about taking it was: wait until night. (I did what he said, and it helped a bit, and when I later showed it to a pharmacist in the U.S.A. she recognized it instantly as our mega-advertised Allegra.) I sought other remedies, including cortisone shots, which, once again, pharmacists can administer in emergencies in Italy, but this led to insomnia. . . .

We left Italy a week early, reluctantly. Waiting in the mail was a letter from a professor at the University of Illinois named Gary Adelman. It told of how when he tried to give a course on D. H. Lawrence, his students rebelled. (But did they muster a loathing and detestation worthy of a character in a work by Lawrence?) Now that Lawrence's reputation, as a novelist, had fallen, in what "they" call the "canon," he wanted to compile a book called *Reclaiming D. H. Lawrence* around the responses of poets and novelists to Lawrence's work. How strange, having just lost myself in wonder at *Sketches of Etruscan Places,* to have received such a letter at that moment. The next day I fired off a response. Lawrence has been much on my mind ever since.

To read D. H. Lawrence is to be revived by the electric current of energy that flows through his words. Lawrence was a living conduit, an electrical force whose existence took the form of a man. I'm sure that others have also noted a certain resemblance of his to Van Gogh, the red hair, the beard, the piercing eyes, the spectral intensity—their longing for connectedness.

I think the reason that most of his novels after *Women in Love,* with the exception of *Saint Mawr,* fall apart for me is that the electrical current of the poetic impulse is so powerful that it dismantles the narrative and the concept. And yet when I open *The Plumed Serpent* at the page where I gave up reading it, I feel as if the next paragraph were overhearing my thoughts, offering a silent reproach, and I catch my breath.

> The electric light in Sayula was as inconstant as everything else. It would come on at half-past six in the evening, and it *might* bravely burn till ten at night, when the village went dark with a click. But usually it did no such thing. Often it refused to sputter into being till seven, or half-past, or even eight o'clock. But its worst trick was that of popping out just in the middle of supper, or just when you were writing a letter. All of a sudden, the black Mexican night came down on you with a thud. And then everybody running blindly for matches and candles, with a calling of frightened voices. Why were they always frightened? Then the electric light, like a wounded thing, would try to revive, and a red glow would burn in the bulbs, sinister. All held their breath—was it coming or not? Sometimes it expired for good, sometimes it got its breath back and shone, rather dully, but better than nothing.

Maybe it's this flickering, as inconstant as everything else, that is more conducive, finally, to a poetry of the present and the Etruscan essays, where his impatience doesn't impinge on his underdeveloping characters, than to fiction. Lawrence pressed language to its limit to convey instantaneous occurrences. Is Lawrence's imagination prophetic of Teilhard de Chardin's fantasy that if instantaneous communication were to occur globally, through technology, we would have found God? Lawrence's writings trace the transformation of coal through hydroelectric power. This is reflected in the change from his early rhymed poems to the controlled style of *Sons and Lovers* to the charged, hyperkinetic prose of *Women in Love* and many poems in *Birds, Beasts, and Flowers*—works which exhibit an almost unprecedented charge. In *Women in Love,* Lawrence clues the reader in to the fate of the inheritor of this "mechanicalness," Gerald Crich.

> An enormous electric plant was installed, both for lighting and for haulage underground, and for power. The electricity was carried into every mine.

New machinery was brought from America, such as the miners had never seen before, great iron men, as the cutting machines were called, and unusual appliances. The working of the pits was thoroughly changed, all the control was taken out of the hands of the miners, the butty system was abolished. [Prior to the Mining Act of 1872, the coal miners were hired by and worked for a contractor, known as a "Butty."] Everything was run on the most accurate and delicate scientific method, educated and expert men were in control everywhere, the miners were reduced to mere mechanical instruments. They had to work hard, much harder than before, the work was terrible and heart-breaking in its mechanicalness.

There are electrical analogies strewn throughout Lawrence's work like a system of signs. In "Bare Almond-Trees" he asks,

What are you doing in the December rain?
Have you a strange electric sensitiveness in your steel tips?
Do you feel the air for electric influences
Like some strange magnetic apparatus?
Do you take in messages, in some strange code,
From heaven's wolfish, wandering electricity, that prowls so constantly
    round Etna?

Lawrence is a coal miner's son. Every day his father, grimy with soot, carbonized, emerged from the underworld. In other words, his whole existence had been forged from within by an energizing principle, whose palpable form was his family. His mother wanted to curtail his energy: "Don't go into the mines! You were made for better things!" But he knew to follow the nonverbal message transmitted by his father, that this descent into the underworld was the necessary prerequisite to creation. Wherever he is he obsesses about the condition of coal in England. On the twenty-fourth of June 1926, he posts a letter to Margeret King written at Villa Mirenda, Scandicci, Florence: "That beastly coal strike, it sounds too dreary for words. Coal was the making of England, and it looks as if coal were to be the breaking of her too. But one can do nothing, so it's no good fuming."

The fiercely Oedipal construction of *Sons and Lovers* was as new at that moment as the raw and open sexuality of *Lady Chatterley's Lover* would be later. But there were also farms and open fields rife with flowers and animals around Nottingham that provided a critical counterpoint to squalor and left Lawrence unabashed to name his great book of unrhyming poems *Birds, Beasts, and Flowers.*

But he left out fruits! And fruits give rise to his most explicitly sexual, usually female, images.

> Now in Tuscany,
> Pomegranates to warm your hands at;
> And crowns, kingly, generous, tilting crowns
> Over the left eyebrow.
>
> And, if you dare, the fissure!
>
> Do you mean to tell me you will see no fissure?
> Do you prefer to look on the plain side?
>
> For all that, the setting suns are open.
> The end cracks open with the beginning:
> Rosy, tender, glittering within the fissure.
>
> ("POMEGRANATE," *BIRDS, BEASTS, AND FLOWERS*)

Everything conspires to lead him to the Etruscans and the underworld. The descent into the Etruscan tombs must have let him feel he was commingling with his father, father and son consubstantial.

Lawrence was a master at making a mess of things, and out of this mess, he forged his imperfect works. He had before him Joseph Joubert's wisdom: "Everything beautiful is indeterminate." Before he took on the assignment of writing *Sketches of Etruscan Places,* he had written a poem that already contained many of the revelations that he had several years afterwards. He was moved to write "Cypresses" after he viewed some fragmentary Etruscan walls in Fiesole. He asks if the Etruscan cypresses contain "the secret of the long-nosed Etruscans / The long-nosed, sensitive-footed, subtly-smiling Etruscans, / Who made so little noise outside the cypress grove?" The Etruscans, the "slender, flickering men of Etruria / Whom Rome called vicious."

They say the fit survive,
But I invoke the spirits of the lost.
Those that have not survived, the darkly lost,
To bring their meaning back into life again,
Which they have taken away
And wrapt inviolable in soft cypress-trees,
Etruscan cypresses.

Even though he was a coal miner's son, Lawrence was under no ordinance to make Gerald Crich in *Women in Love* the son of the coal baron and a man whose desperate energy and violence would allow him to enact fantastically dramatic scenes and also register his withering. His "way" wears out and when he wanders out into the snowy wastes to die, it is to kill what is already dead inside. Crich can't change, can't make the transformation, the leap. His death drive proceeds on a similar course as would his inherited industry, coal mining— though his father had the foresight to use hydroelectric power to light their own house. Gerald Crich's steely bloody-mindedness makes him an unforgettable character.

So many poets and writers have taken an essential impulse from Lawrence. A short list would include Henry Miller (who would never finish his tome on Lawrence, who would never finish his *Study of Thomas Hardy ...*), then his friends and co-conspirators Lawrence Durrell and Anaïs Nin (who did complete her elegant study of Lawrence), William Carlos Williams, Theodore Roethke, Ted Hughes, Sylvia Plath, and Galway Kinnell. (If I leave out Marianne Moore and Elizabeth Bishop, it is because their copious use of animals is more specific and doesn't have a trace of a Lawrence-like energy.) And Lawrence himself comes out of a rural English tradition of which an exemplar is John Clare. And there's an entirely other domain that I won't attempt to enter at all, the "working-class hero" novel, which flourished in the late fifties and early sixties, like Allan Sillitoe's *The Loneliness of the Long-Distance Runner* and *Saturday Night and Sunday Morning* and David Storey's *This Sporting Life*. All of these novels were trans-lated into breakout films; here Lawrence ignited the radical transformation that occurred in British filmmaking at that time. (I don't remember anyone who, like me, saw these films in revival houses or on TV a decade or more after they appeared, who felt moved to read the novels. Though we mustn't lose hope;

there may come a time; film is an ephemeral medium. . . .) John Boorman—in my view the most resourceful of the British postwar film directors—on the first page of his autobiography *Adventures of a Suburban Boy,* speaks of Lawrence and *The Lost Girl* as an initial source: "In *The Lost Girl,* D.H. Lawrence describes Nottingham miners watching those early films: while they looked at the live music acts out of the corners of their eyes, embarrassed, uneasy, they *stared* at the movies, unblinking, mouths agape, like men in a trance, mesmerized."

There is a striking parallelism between Boorman's *The Emerald Forest,* filmed on the Amazon and in the rain forest, and Lawrence's Nottingham, which isn't far from Sherwood Forest. The film has aspects of *Sons and Lovers* and recaptures some of the dynamic between Lawrence and his father, Walter. *The Emerald Forest* is about an engineer who goes into the Amazon to build a dam to harness hydroelectric power to accommodate the usual—industry, urban sprawl, capital. The project spills into the rain forest, and along with it, he and his wife, daughter, and five-year-old son. The boy wanders off, is kidnapped by the Invisible Tribe—it's based on a true story—and the engineer spends every available moment over the next ten years returning to search for him. Finally he succeeds, but his son, played by the director's son, Charlie Boorman, loves living in the forest with the Invisible Tribe. His father warns that the dam will bring men who will further impinge on the Emerald Forest and destroy everything. His son calls the dam a "logjam"; he will chant a rainstorm out of the sky strong enough to break through the dam. And he does. Father and son are reconciled, though they will never see each other again. The extermination of these Indian tribes—down to a hundred thousand from four million— along with the thoughtless and insidious deconstruction of the forest, is the link between Boorman's film and Lawrence's ideas about the genocide of the American Indians in *Studies in Classic American Literature.*

Inevitably, Boorman arrives in Hollywood. Worn down by the post–election day blues, I stare in disbelief at the page as Boorman's reflections on Christopher Isherwood slide inexorably into my thoughtstream.

> Like a crackle of electricity he seems to jump the terminals, short-circuit the mysterious process by which a great writer subsumes his raw material, passes it through the murky acids and leaden depths of the unconscious before it flows out again at an even voltage on to the page.

➤

Poets admire Lawrence for all sorts of reasons. Poets, more than novelists, have found in Lawrence's brilliant and protracted use of birds, beasts, and flowers a counterpoint to the forces of technology and mechanization that threaten the poetic imagination as well as the earth—and the two are inseparable. Poetry must be autochthonous. Thomas Pynchon in *Gravity's Rainbow* and Don DeLillo in *Underworld* can respond to the global predicament with a critical, ironic, satirical edge ideally suited to the novel as a form. Poets are more involved in a salvage operation. Take Theodore Roethke. Roethke has always been identified with John Berryman, Elizabeth Bishop, and Robert Lowell, but vastly more has been written about these other poets than about Roethke, and for the simple reason that critics, deaf to the music of poetry, to what makes a poem a poem, find him limited in range. Once again, how much can be said about birds, beasts, and flowers, and in Roethke's case, his father's greenhouse? More than might be imagined, as in "The Lost Son."

> What a small song. What slow clouds. What dark water.
> Hath the rain a father? All the caves are ice. Only the snow's here.
> I'm cold. I'm cold all over. Rub me in father and mother.
> Fear was my father, Father Fear.
> His look drained the stones.
>
> What gliding shape
> Beckoning through halls,
> Stood poised on the stair,
> Fell dreamily down?
>
> From the mouths of jugs
> Perched on many shelves,
> I saw substance flowing
> That cold morning.
>
> Like a slither of eels
> That watery cheek
> As my own tongue kissed
> My lips awake.

Sylvia Plath took flight from Roethke's miraculously condensed and staccato lines. It accounts for the decisive flick of the wrist of her later poems: "Barehanded, I hand the combs" ("Stings"). In the twentieth century, when global awareness has become instantaneous, a poet's work has to be read in light of what it leaves out as much as what it leaves in. Lawrence's animals are expressions of a life-force shorn of the inhibitions, attitudes, and neuroses that infect his characters so often thwarted by willfulness and, to use a word Lawrence favored, perversities, unsuccessful attempts to experience being. The author of "Tortoise Shout" and "Tortoise Family Connections" knew that tortoises are not known for spending too many hours on the psychoanalyst's couch (and probably had not read either of Lawrence's treatises on the subject, *Psychoanalysis and the Unconscious* and *Fantasia of the Unconscious*), but the very act of confronting and imagining what it is like to be these creatures is a move toward enlightenment. God knows they have a lot to say and can free-associate with the best of us.

> His mother deposited him on the soil as if he were no more than droppings,
> And now he scuffles tinily past her as if she were an old rusty tin.
>
> A mere obstacle,
> He veers round the slow great mound of her—
> Tortoises always foresee obstacles.
>
> It is no use my saying to him in an emotional voice:
> "This is your Mother, she laid you when you were an egg."
>
> He does not even trouble to answer: "Woman, what have I to do with thee?"
> He wearily looks the other way,
> And she even more wearily looks another way still,
> Each with the utmost apathy,
> Incognisant,
> Unaware,
> Nothing.

("TORTOISE FAMILY CONNECTIONS")

The creatures behave according to their natures, and if you were to put them all together, all their natures into one human being, you would have characters as tortured and ambivalent as those who populate Lawrence's novels and whose contradictions overwhelm his narratives. In "Man and Bat," Lawrence endures a confrontation that would drive other people to murder, but he is able to limit his exasperation at the bat to its inappropriate invasion of his working space. The bat drives him batty, but Lawrence never forgets that it is a bat, and that in ways difficult for a man to fathom, it is behaving according to its nature, staying inside because it hasn't got sunglasses, much less a sleep-mask.

Something seemed to blow him back from the window
Every time he swerved at it;
Back on a strange parabola, then round, round, dizzy in my room.

He *could* not go out,
I also realized. . . .
It was the light of day which he could not enter,
Any more than I could enter the white-hot door of a blast furnace.

He could not plunge into the daylight that streamed at the window.
It was asking too much of his nature.

Worse even than the hideous terror of me with my handkerchief
Saying: *Out, go out!* . . .
Was the horror of the white daylight in the window!

So I switched on the electric light, thinking: *Now*
The outside will seem brown. . . .

But no,
The outside did not seem brown.
And he did not mind the yellow electric light.

Silent!
He was having a silent rest.
But never!
Not in my room.

➤

Lawrence's sensitivity was such that he almost always in the end polarized other people. One illustration of this is Aldous Huxley's portrait of him in his novel *Point Counterpoint.* Unfortunately for me, Huxley's name for the Lawrence character in the novel is Mark Rampian (but this is not nearly as bad as the little boy's repetition of "redrum" in *The Shining,* which shivers my spine). Huxley could do no more than portray Lawrence as thin-skinned, irritable, and argumentative, all of which is true, but just scratches the surface. He was Lawrence's loyal friend and advocate, but his Lawrence is almost a cartoon of the man, just as his novel *Point Counterpoint* is a skeletal rip-off of André Gide's wonderfully weird and innovative novel within the novel *Les Faux Monnayeurs* (*The Counterfeiters*).

Lawrence found it hard to be around himself—one reason he was always moving around. He was also moving around when he was still, and the world moved around him. Lawrence illustrates Osip Mandelstam's assertion that "standing still is a variety of accumulated motion." In his poem "Snake," it is the snake who seeks out the man, who is lured there by his energy. Even snakes know a receptive and empathetic witness when they sense one. (Scratch "even. . . .")

> A snake came to my water-trough
> On a hot, hot day, and I in pyjamas for the heat,
> To drink there.
>
> In the deep, strange-scented shade of the great dark carob-tree
> I came down the steps with my pitcher
> And must wait, must stand and wait, for there he was at the trough before me.

Creatures find him because he is one of them. He is fully human, but somehow he escaped desensitization. This is what makes Lawrence so popular with creatures often feared and disdained by people.

The Etruscans behaved according to their own nature as well. And then the Romans, the real barbarians, arrived. And the power drive became predominant. Lawrence probes this in *Sketches for Etruscan Places,* which stands among his finest prose works.

> But in the bewildering experience of searching for the Etruscans there is the one steady clue that we can follow: or rather, there are two clues. The first is the peculiar physical or *bodily,* lively quality of all the art. And this, I take it, is Italian, the result of the Italian soil itself. The Romans got a great deal of their power from *resisting* this curious Italian physical expressiveness: and for the same reason, in the Roman the salt soon lost its savour, in the true Etruscan, never.

The copper-skinned woman in the rust-colored dress with her hair still wet who materializes at the bus stop at Largo Argentina: a message from Etruscan Central.

I knew that I had to get to the Etruscan sites, and this had very little to do with Lawrence. When I visited my first Etruscan site, Veio, I hadn't read a word of what Lawrence had written on the Etruscans. I took it for granted that whatever he wrote would be interesting, though more about Lawrence than the Etruscans. What I remember of the trip to Veio was, as is so often the case, the trip, the long, hot, rackety, hydraulic give-and-go bus ride and the interminable wait for the return bus that led to a fight between my wife and me on the subject of public transportation and another hour in the brutal heat without water. There really wasn't much to see in Veio other than the bare foundations of dwellings. No city, no painted tombs. And this, combined with our ignorance, led to frustration.

What I remember the most about Veio was the flickering tongue of a lizard perched on a rock above the torrent, the rush of water, below. The Tiber took a shortcut. We should have rented a boat.

We must have gone to Veio first, on our first trip to Italy, because it was closest to Rome and reachable by public bus. I began to dream about the Villa Giulia, then closed, where the real treasures that were once in Veio are kept.

Lawrence's Etruscan period coincides with his being diagnosed with tuberculosis. But if his Etruscan period gave him a second life in light of his impending death, it also lent some resolution to certain inconclusive aspects of *Women in Love,* and to the poetic gesture that defined him. At the end of *Women in Love,* Birkin/ Lawrence presses on in his persistence that in order to be wholly complete he needs more than the love of a woman; he also needs a man friend with whom he is on intimate terms. Lawrence's propensity for arguments was useful for dialogical purposes, as part of the novelist's palate; but as he has cautioned us indelibly: "Never trust the teller, trust the tale." This constant sense of incompleteness, his almost perverse tweaking of existence, is somehow resolved in the cathartic moment when he sees the men and the women entwined forever on the lids of the sarcophagi in the Guarnacci Museum in Volterra.

Lawrence was gifted with this immeasurably deep sensitivity, which delivered deep truths to him suddenly and instantaneously and never flowed over into a concern for whomever he battered in the high-pitched unstoppable intensity of his attacks, which though they weren't directed at others personally, still left the majority of those who were utter strangers to a blaze such as one Lawrence possessed with the task of not letting on that he had gotten to them—to save face. Eighty some years prior a duel would have been inevitable. And maybe the fact that he knew no one could retaliate with an equivalent force, in a manner either sober, balanced, or inept, led his language and imagination to ferment even more in the depths which made him both more profound and impatient of his own imprecision in a way that would actually fuel his utter lack of consideration for the other—the other person across the table that is. His patience for human hesitation had long ago run out and he wanted, like Whitman, to go and live with the animals: and so he did. But underneath his irascibility there was always the horror of his impending death which he also rebutted, it must be said, with fantastic success, managing his journey to Etruscan places as the end approached far more swiftly than he could struggle up the steep hills that led to the hilltop fortresses.

➡

It was with great anticipation and trembling that we drove to Cerveteri one morning in July of 2001. I think that people sometimes go to ruins like this with the subconscious hope of being transformed. They are right to feel this way. On the way to Cerveteri, I noticed the turnoff for the town of Civitavecchia, off the turnoff for Leonardo da Vinci airport. There is also a beach at Civitavecchia, and that's where I wanted to go on the way to Cerveteri. My wife dismissed this as madness. Everyone knew that the beach at Civitavecchia was crowded and corrupt. There was no reason on earth to go there. But there was, I argued, in my unfailing battle with reality. The beach at Civitavecchia is where Michel Foucault first read Nietzsche's *The Birth of Tragedy* in a downpour of light. I sighed, realizing that fifty years ago Civitavecchia might have been a different place altogether, and I let it go. I would spare myself what John Boorman encountered on his first visit to Los Angeles in 1965.

> After my work with Everson, I went on to LA to meet Christopher Isherwood. I rented a car at the airport and drove down the length of Sunset Boulevard until I came to the Pacific. And there was the promised sunset in the promised land, sitting in its smog-enhanced glory on the flat oily ocean. I stared at it in lonely wonder. No one to tell. LA caught me unawares: the flimsy facades, the absence of architecture, its shape defined only by neon signs and vast hoardings, tangles of power cables looping across the sky—it all looked so insubstantial and temporary. I could find no purchase, no point of reference. I stayed at the Bow and Arrow Motel in Santa Monica. In the Robin Hood Bar I drank beer and . . .

As I walked around the Etruscan burial mounds at Cerveteri, I thought of how forward they were in so many ways, in their vision. The stimulation was almost

too much, as if it would turn or churn the mind into a volcano, bubbling, percolating, crashing against the barricades of the brain, the skull. They were highly
developed in so many ways, subtle, delicate, strong, informed about Greek
myths; okay, they traded with the Greeks, there was an Aegean connection, but
it's too much to take in. . . . I stand there—dust stinging my eyes, in a time warp.
It's 700 B.C., and the Etruscans are drawing the labors of Hercules and Odysseus
putting out the Cyclops's eye, and there among the tombs, green-headed snakes
slither along the sides of the tufa—and I'm blown apart by the thought that the
Etruscan artists and Bernini, with two thousand years between them, worked
with the same underworld image: Persephone, Cerberus, Bernini's three-
headed marble dog and this tufa-sculpted three-headed dog who resides in the
actual imaginary real underworld of Cerveteri. I realize that Ovid wasn't exiled
because *The Metamorphoses* was too this or that, too erotic or pornographic
or political in the wrong way for the regime who sent him off to Tomis, but
because he forced the Romans to think hard about these myths again, and their
origins, and the destruction of the Etruscans. I realize that the Romans' attitude
to the Etruscans is parallel to ours with regard to the American Indians, and that
we carry this oblique, shadowy, invidious guilt about these genocides. Maybe
it's the guilt about the genocides that leads empires to ruin, to slacken, grow fat,
and die. The idea comes spontaneously. But how can I escape the truth—that
a reading of Lawrence's *Studies in Classic American Literature* when I was twenty
went straight to my unconscious.

Lawrence's attraction to the Etruscans has an instinctive quality, as if he were
beguiled by his unconscious—or the gods—to a world where death is part
of a passage, an active force that is consonant with the value of living in the
moment, where the moment is everything because in reality existence offers
nothing more. This is exemplified by the dance. And what does this dance do if
not kindle the quick, electrical connection between people? It is time to study
the ways in which people come alive. I wish it would be possible to see what the
energy itself looked like between people who are attracted to each other, like
those white lines on some of Tintoretto's paintings that were visible during the
time of day when the painting wasn't meant to be seen.

As we get older, as we approach that weighty, nebulous period called "middle
age" (which Lawrence didn't live beyond), our job is to transform ourselves, to

reconnect to the energies that came thoughtlessly and spontaneously in youth (and are often eradicated, as if a wall had come down long before people reached thirty). And this accounts for Lawrence's appeal; his alertness was so acute that he was able to change, to metamorphose, continually, with a rapidity which would have awed Ovid, whose metamorphoses were—I often must remind myself—imaginary. Every time Lawrence transformed himself into a horse or a swan, he metamorphosed, became someone who was no longer commensurate with the person he had been before (and who had written those books that only *partially* revealed what he had to reveal), amidst a circle of friends who were always the same, condemned to consistency, repetition, death-in-life— only they weren't aware of it; they were literally creatures of habit like those rendered by Ovid and condemned by Dante. He appeared to quarrel often with people, with almost every friend he made, many of whom were among the best minds of their generation; but what made him so restless, tetchy, and irritable was the stasis they had embraced for the simple reason that it made their lives easier, less conflicted, less fraught, a spiritual equivalent of tenure. One wonders what stance Lawrence would have taken toward entropy and erosion, all the numerous, negative "facts" about the universe that have put a damper on hope since the time of his death. But how he would have fumed and foamed over the innumerable thoughtless and avoidable disasters that have maimed the planet, from the exhaustion of the earth's oil to the depletion of the ozone, to a short-sightedness that fueled stasis and short-changed change, and bred something we call terror but is really about power, energy, oil—that which Lawrence, through imagination, transformed, as I have said, into electricity as he followed Whitman's road and sang the body electric. Poetry has always known this and seems to favor exiles like Ovid, Dante, Lawrence, and Milosz—where there's a constant external pressure to be alert, attentive, especially to those things that have no inherent "poetic qualities."

How do I really know that I was "twenty"? I have an answer. I can see myself absorbed and riveted by library editions of D. H. Lawrence's letters in two (finite!) volumes. I returned to them as a guilty pleasure. Here's why: a single letter by Lawrence often contains nascent poems in casual observations, updates on his physical condition (often severely affected by the weather, especially the cold and rain), reflections on what he's struggling with as a writer in the practical sense, aesthetic judgments, and announcements of future projects. When he wrote the following letter to Else Jaffe on the twenty-sixth of May 1926,

The Book of Samuel

he had taken the top half of an old villa about seven miles out of Florence that he might use as a center from which to travel to "Bologna and Cortona and Volterra and down to the Maremma to Tarquinia—quite a number of places in Tuscany and Umbria, where the best remains are."

My dear Else

The Schwiegermutter wrote from Baden that you aren't well, and had a little operation. That's bad luck! I do hope you're better.

It isn't a good year, anyhow. Here it has rained and rained, till the country is turning yellow with wetness. But these last two days are sunny and warm: but not hot, as it should be. . . .

The country around is pretty—all poderi and pine-woods, and no *walls* at all. I hope in the autumn, really, you'll come and stay a while: unless everything goes muddled again. For myself, I struggle to get back into a good humour, but don't succeed very well. . . .

Myself, I am labouring at the moment to type out Frieda's MS of the play *David*. It's a slowness, I'm no typist. But it is just as well for me to go through the MS myself, and it is good for me to learn some German, I suppose. Frieda's daughter Else typed up the first 26 pages—and there are a fair number of alterations. But I shall send you the typescript as soon as it is finished: within a month, pray God!—I am interested, really, to see the play go into German, so much simpler and more direct than in English. English is really very complicated in its *meanings*. Perhaps the simpler a language becomes in its grammar and syntax, the more subtle and complex it becomes in its suggestions. Anyhow this play seems to me much more direct and dramatic in German, much less poetic and suggestive than in English. I shall be interested to know what you think of it.

I said to myself I would write perhaps a book about the Etruscans: nothing pretentious, but a sort of book for people who will actually be going to Florence and Cortona and Perugia and Volterra and those places, to look at the Etruscan things. They have a great attraction for me: there are lovely things in the Etruscan Museum here. . . . Mommsen [author of *The History of Rome*] hated everything Etruscan, said the germ of all degeneracy was in the race. But the bronzes and terra cottas are fascinating, so alive with physical life, with a powerful physicality which surely is as great, or sacred, ultimately, as the *ideal* of the Greeks and Germans. Anyhow, the real strength of Italy seems to me in this physicality, which is not at all Roman. . . . As for the text, I've read one or two books, and they're very dreary, repetition and surmise. It seems amazing that we should know so very very little about a race that lived alongside the Romans. But I can find very little *fact*. . . . Italy is so wildly nationalistic, that I think Tuscany feels she may as well go one further back than Rome, and derive herself from Etruria. But they all feel scared, because Etruria was so luxurious and "merely physical." . . .

Remember me to Marianne. She's a young woman now, no longer a mere girl. It's a strange thing to have a grown-up family: other people! . . . I hope Alfred is well—The longer I live the more I realize it would shatter the nerves of an Aristotle or a Socrates, to have to think deeply about this world we've gotten ourselves into. It's no good taking long views: it's like looking down the crater of Vesuvius, you see nothing and you asphyxiate yourself. Best only tackle little problems and tidy up small corners. A man tears himself to bits grappling with the whole machine. That miserable strike in England looks like the beginning of another end!

But there, why think about it! Best go down to Scandicci and buy paint to paint these old doors and window-frames. Carpe diem, quam minimum etc. No good thinking about what's coming after!

It is slightly staggering, on reflection, to consider how this letter, in its rhythm, phrasing, and constructions, and other subtle and probably unintentional ways, approaches the condition of a work of art. The kid can't help it. In one letter he recapitulates so many of the issues that formed him and the themes that obsess him and then returns to the blessing of chores. A little fresh paint can't hurt! It shows how good Lawrence is when he isn't trying and the note of stridency, his hysteria that no one will understand, is reduced by the intimacy—real or imagined but very much part of the act of letter writing—with the addressee.

Cerveteri was fascinating if your idea of heaven is to walk in the wind with the dust blowing in your eyes and mouth while you scramble over mounds and poorly marked paths and clamber down steps to gaze into tombs that house sometimes barely discernible drawings and other relics. This was real work, and I loved it. I loved kneeling and squinting to discern the shapes of horses and ships. It was exhilarating being out in the open air, exploring these burial mounds, which really had earned their name as a ruin. There is no better instance of Lawrence's assertion that our experience is vastly diminished when we see things torn out of their settings.

What one wants is to be aware. If one looks at an etruscan helmet, then it is better to be fully aware of that helmet, in its own setting, in its own complex of associations, than it is to "look over" a thousand museums of stuff. Any one impression that goes really down into the soul, it is worth a million hasty impressions of a million important things.

And much of the charm of *Sketches of Etruscan Places* comes from Lawrence's recounting of how he got there and the people he encountered. It gives credibility to a book whose subject is being fully alive.

There were few other people visiting the site that day, among them a couple: an older, thickly set man with close-cropped, thinning gray hair wearing a black polo shirt and cargo shorts, and a spry and shapely woman in her mid-thirties with sandy-brown, shoulder-length hair wearing a T-shirt and shorts and hiking shoes. So yes, they could have been father and daughter, but clearly they were partners with a twenty-year age difference. And from overhearing a bit of their conversation, they shared an obsession, interest, and knowledge in Etruscan burial sites; they turned out to be archeologists who intended to visit every known and hopefully unknown Etruscan site on this trip.

As the conversation ensued, the man offered that it was now thought that what Lawrence had written about the Etruscans was more accurate than what the historians had been able to decipher with their measuring rods and aerial radar photographs of remains that were buried under the earth. Yes, the man said, it turned out that Lawrence's intuitions were amazingly on the mark. I told him that despite my admiration for Lawrence's other work, I had never considered reading *Sketches of Etruscan Places* because I had assumed that they would be impressionistic travel sketches, approximations, and it wasn't my preferred way of reading Lawrence. At this point, the man gave very precise instructions on what edition of Lawrence's Etruscan writings to get, to stay clear of editions of Lawrence's work that mixed up a lot of his different writings on Italy. Don't worry, I didn't take his advice too soon. I already owned *Twilight in Italy* and *Sea in Sardinia* and had never gotten past a chapter of either. The last thing I wanted was to look at Etruscan places through Lawrence's eyes.

Enlightenment for Lawrence begins by looking down into the depths of the earth, as his father descended every day into the mine. In *Sketches of Etruscan Places,* he is shown a nonmorbid, even a joyous, entrance into the underworld;

the underworld of a people to whom the quick of life, transience, was of paramount importance. That's why they burned down their straw shelters and left no trace of their dwellings, only their sarcophagi and burial mounds. The Etruscans were aficionados of the afterlife, and this freed them to live in the moment.

> There are no Etruscans out-and-out, and there never were any. There were different prehistoric tribes stimulated by contact with different peoples from the eastern Mediterranean, and lifted on the last wave of a dying conception of the living cosmos.

Rereading Lawrence's Italian poems upon returning from Italy, I was of course once again astonished at how he connects the landscape, the trees, animals, and flowers with the history of the people who lived there. Then I came across a passage in "Sicilian Cyclamens," stunning in its use of inversion, apposition, and line breaks.

> Slow toads, and cyclamen leaves
> Stickily glistening with eternal shadow
> Keeping to earth.
> Cyclamen leaves
> Toad-slimy, earth-iridescent
> Beautiful
> Frost-filigreed
> Spumed with mud
> Snail-nacreous
> Low down.

This shows how much Roethke derived from Lawrence's use of form as his use of nature. The difference is that Lawrence allows himself some broad strokes that Roethke would have nixed to keep his poem neo-critical. Lawrence makes a beautiful mess.

And then there is William Carlos Williams, the American poet who was closest to Lawrence in temperament and not quite as impermeable to his influence as his good friend Marianne Moore. And what do the "falls" stand for in *Paterson*—beyond the actions of that daredevil who goes down them in a barrel, Sam Patch—if not hydroelectric power?

Williams is the American writer whose connectedness was closest to that of Lawrence. My conjecture is that Williams owes his restlessness and volatility and receptiveness to his Spanish blood from his mother's side. Were two books ever more beautifully aligned than Lawrence's *Studies in Classic American Literature* and Williams's *In the American Grain?* They are both priests of imperfection, but for different reasons: Lawrence because he knew he wouldn't live long, Williams because his doctor job consumed so much of his time that he was forced to write on the run, jotting down notes between house calls. And if Williams was liberated from earlier constraints by Lawrence's essays, he also took Lawrence's impulses to another plane with regard to the elasticity of this prose. Williams, unlike Lawrence, never really had to leave his continent to revive his poetic energies; and perhaps it is his Spanish blood that allowed him to continue to find America exotic. It was in Williams's nature, as it was in Lawrence's, to write a poetry of the senses, of the present tense, as in his elegy to Lawrence.

> Greep, greep, greep the cricket
> chants where the snake
> with agate eyes leaned to the water.
> Sorrow to the young
> that Lawrence has passed
> unwanted from England.
> And in the gardens forsythia
> and in the woods
> now the crinkled spice-bush
> in flower.

Lawrence places a deliberate emphasis on "the lingering of the voice according to the feeling—*it is the hidden emotional pattern that makes poetry, not the obvious form.*" Unlike Williams, many American writers have been inflicted with a Puritanical streak that acts like an impediment against which they choose to do battle. A cold focus on sex divorced from passion in fiction is a demonstration of this. Doing battle is exactly what Lawrence warns against in his Etruscan essays. What makes him warm to the Etruscans is their sensitivity.

Tarquinia is a site of jubilation: the images in the tombs come alive with banquets, dancers, horse races, don't play one flute when you can play two and remember now is forever, tomorrow contained within today, paint your skin vermilion, keep it up, up, the joyful sound, the tambourine, a symposium, wine and dancers, thoughts circulating like blood. Looking at the tomb of the painted vases in Tarquinia, Lawrence muses:

> Rather gentle and lovely is the way he touches the woman under the chin, with a delicate caress. That again is one of the charms of the etruscan paintings: they really have the sense of touch; the people and the creatures are all really in touch. It is one of the rarest qualities, in life as well as in art. There is plenty of pawing and laying hold, but no real touch. In pictures especially, the people may be in contact, embracing or laying hands on one another. But there is no soft flow of touch. The touch does not come from the middle of the human being. It is merely surfaces, and a juxtaposition of objects. This is what makes so many of the great masters boring, in spite of all their clever composition. Here, in this faded etruscan painting, there is a quiet flow of touch that unites the man and the woman on the couch, the timid boy behind, the dog that lifts his nose, even the garlands that hang from the wall.

This is what attracted him to the Etruscans: what is generated by touch; touch as generator. This is what Mellors in *Lady Chatterley's Lover* teaches Connie Chatterley: touch. And one of the songs that has helped me override the supervenient thoughts that crowd in as the war in Iraq escalates and the election nears through the drafts of this essay is "Wild as the Wind" sung by Chan Marshall in a way that throws stress on the torch singer's caressing and drawing out of the phrase: "you touched me." Tennessee Williams was so affected by Lawrence's story "You Touched Me" that his response was to adapt it for the stage. And touch is what Gudrun in *Women in Love* objects to most about Gerald; she doesn't like the way he touches her. She certainly for a time likes the way he fucks her, especially on the night of his father's death. Death is the mother of self-abandonment.

Later, when their relationship is at the point of breaking, this brutal exchange:

> "Try to love me a little more, and to want me a little less," she said, in a half contemptuous, half coaxing tone.
>
> The darkness seemed to be swaying in waves across his mind, great waves of darkness plunging across his mind. It seemed to him he was degraded at the very quick, made of no account.
>
> "You mean you don't want me?" he said.
>
> "You are so insistent, and there is so little grace in you, so little fineness. You are so crude. You break me—you only waste me—it is horrible to me."

The actor Oliver Reed who played Gerald in the 1969 film had an implosive on-screen presence. He is effective even though he is almost the polar opposite of the emphatically blonde Gerald Crich in the novel. One of the most piercing moments in Lawrence's writing occurs after this exchange when Gerald forces himself on Gudrun. "Shall I die," she asks herself. But in the film version of *Women in Love,* the actress Glenda Jackson, playing Gudrun, utters this line aloud with an emphasis on the last word; she could project an overpowering emotion that went beyond the words themselves, something she may have learned when acting in countries as part of Peter Brook's troupe where no one in the audience knew English.

During the last moments of her performance as Vittoria in Edward Bond's cruelly stylized 1976 adaptation of John Webster's *The White Divel,* she delivered her last lines in a way that brought me back to the earlier explosion in the film.

LODOVICO: Strike, strike,
    With a Joint motion.

VITTORIA: 'Twas a manly blow,
    The next thou giv'st, murder some sucking Infant,
    And then thou wilt be famous.

FLAMINEO: O what blade is't?
    A Toledo, or an English Fox?
    I ever thought a Cutler should distinguish
    The cause of my death, rather than a Doctor.
    Search my wound deeper: tent it with the steele
    That made it.

VITTORIA: O my greatest sinne lay in my blood.
    Now my blood paies for't.

She cries out as the sword is thrust between her legs, under her skirt, less we should miss the point, with a violence that immediately brought to mind Gerald/Oliver Reed's rape of her in the scene in *Women in Love* when she says, "Shall I die?"

I'd always felt guilty about being subject to extreme vacillations in mood, which shift so much within the smallest sections of time, minutes, seconds, not hours, not days, and *Women in Love* is the only novel I know that provides relief and reminds me that it is all too human to feel this way. As Lawrence tries to create and define what it is to be a fully alive human being, the creation of Gerald Crich presents the difficulties, the obstacles. In *Women in Love,* in addition to the hyper-real intensity of certain scenes, set pieces, Lawrence renders the full violence of people's shifting feelings toward each other from warmth to revulsion within moments. It is as "electric," as instantaneous, as the interaction between man and bat. This capacity is what made him in the end more of a poet than a novelist, even though he had sufficient gifts and discipline to lead F. R. Leavis, a dominant British critic of his time, to write the book—with what to me was always a mysterious, inscrutable title—*D. H. Lawrence: Novelist.* Leavis's book lived in my apartment for many years, and from time to time, I would scrutinize it with a kind of nervousness that this peculiar emphasis on Lawrence as the inheritor of *The Great Tradition* (another Leavis title) could have back-fired and provoked negative responses. Leavis, Lawrence's most rousing and convincing advocate, still manages to sidestep the poems and nonfiction entirely, willing to hang his entire argument on Lawrence's greatness as a novelist and short-story writer. The attacks on Lawrence are almost all fueled in response to his fiction by people who must have thrilled to pass judgment on fiction that doesn't aspire to meet prior received ideas. It's creepy to think of Lawrence being dismissed by politically correct readers who were hardly if at all familiar with his great work in other genres.

In *Women in Love* it's crash and burn in every paragraph; the animals still leap out with such ferocity and maniacal fervor that it seems almost inconceivable anyone could render this in prose.

> And suddenly the rabbit, which had been crouching as if it were a flower, so still and soft, suddenly burst into life. Round and round the court it went, as if shot from a gun, round and round like a furry meteorite, in a tense hard circle that seemed to bind their brains.

And not to be outdone, in a heightened, rapturous passage Rupert Birkin stones the moon's reflection in the pond; it scatters; it doesn't disappear.

Lawrence's change in style didn't come easily. He felt thwarted and restricted when reworking *Sons and Lovers,* and during that time he was still shouldering the harness of rhymed poems. He claimed that *Sons and Lovers* would be the last book that he would attempt in what he called the Flaubertian mode; he had grown impatient with an emphasis on objectivity, precision, and the invisibility of the author. It was like a yoke, a job, a service to be performed. He knew that his readers would resist being shaken up. And he lived mostly on the income from his prose. The economic prerogative is another constant pressure that gives Lawrence's work its urgency. The only "tenure" he had was the lease to write about a book a year. Necessity is something that Gary Adelman's students at the University of Illinois, along with others who from their high chairs deign to pass judgment, might have considered. In his "Foreword" to *Women in Love,* Lawrence identifies his intention, which is often criticized as if he did it carelessly.

> In point of style, fault is often found with the continual, slightly modified repetition. The only answer is that it is natural to the author; and that every natural crisis in emotion or passion or understanding comes from this pulsing, frictional to-and-fro which work up to culmination.

I would like to add: some points bear repeating. It's not for any stylistic reasons that Lawrence usually repeats the same ideas in everything that flowed from his pen: his poems, essays, stories, novels, and letters.

Curiously, for W. H. Auden, Lawrence was neither so much the poet nor the novelist as the author of treatises. (One wonders, would W. H. Auden have chosen to use initials instead of his beautiful first name, Wystan, were it not for the example of Lawrence?)

> When I first read Lawrence in the late Twenties, it was his message which made the greatest impression on me, so that it was his "think" books like *Fantasia on the Unconscious* rather than his fiction which I read most avidly. As for his poetry, when I first tried to read it, I did not like it; despite my admiration for him, it offended my notions of what poetry should be.

Auden reminds me of just how many "Lawrences" there are—he's unique in having been a great writer (and I use the word "great" always with trepidation) in every genre he practiced: novel, short story, poetry, criticism, travel book, letters, and the essay. As late as 1983, Anthony Burgess would write that "Lawrence, or Lorenzo, is mainly known as the author of *Lady Chatterley's Lover* and not as the great poet and original thinker he really was" (*One Man's Chorus*).

Lawrence was mistaken as a man of ideas, when ideas for him were just another way to approach the matters that concerned him, and ward off misinterpretation. He felt obliged to intercede once he sensed that his readers had lost sight of the unity behind the variety of forms he put his hand to. If someone as brilliant and sympathetic as W. H. Auden could cordon off Lawrence the prophet from Lawrence the creator of imaginative works—though Auden chides himself for this mistake in an appreciative later essay on his poetry—we can see the reason for his anxiety. What we can't really see is something far more brutal: the embattled conversations—arguments—with the very people who he thought were most capable of absorbing the implications of the writings that converged at them from all angles, novels, stories, poems, essays, travel books. Was not the Lawrence who they say quarreled with everyone and broke with most of his friends—many of whom, like Constance Garnett and Katherine Mansfield, are legendary figures to us—not also short-tempered and contentious? Not in his work, usually, except when he set out to argue a point and then hammered it to death. Then there are books in which he took that impulse to almost bludgeon the reader into submission and transformed it into an approach that took on a rhythmic, ritualistic quality, like *Women in Love* and *Studies in Classic American Literature*. Maybe he derived some of that nearly hysterical, hyperbolic tone from Dostoyevsky. Why so? Because Dostoyevsky did not only revolt him; he was also put off by his editor Edward Garnett's wife and his own former friend, Constance.

What Lawrence had was vision: he could make us see, like Van Gogh, vividly—far more vividly than the camera! But this form of seeing is an instantaneous indwelling that engages all the senses.

> At a wavering instant the swallows give way to bats
> By the Ponte Vecchio . . .
> Changing guard.
>
> Bats, and an uneasy creeping in one's scalp
> As the bats swoop overhead!
> Flying madly.
>
> Pipistrello!
> Black piper on an infinitesimal pipe.
> Little lumps that fly in air and have voices indefinite, wildly vindictive;
>
> Wings like bits of umbrella.
>
> Bats!

Creatures that hang themselves up like an old rag, to sleep;
And disgustingly upside down.
Hanging upside down like rows of disgusting old rags
And grinning in their sleep.
Bats!

In China the bat is symbol of happiness.

Not for me!

("BAT")

Lawrence's urgency, like that of the boys from Liverpool, is inseparable from growing up poor as a coal miner's son in northern England. Money was always a sore spot: a man is worth only what he is worth. And one theme, one tune, served him well through all his vacillations: "Can't Buy Me Love."

> Why isn't anything free, why is it always pay, pay, pay?

> A man can't get any fun out of wife, sweetheart or tart
> because of the beastly expense.

> Why don't we do something about the money system?

("ALWAYS THIS PAYING")

I have always assumed that Lawrence's intensity in focus was also connected to tuberculosis. Passage after passage in his books and his letters would appear to confirm this:

> Birkin smiled to himself as he sat by the fire. When Ursula came down
> he sat motionless, with his arms on his knees. She saw him, how he was
> motionless and ageless, like some crouching idol, some image of a deathly
> religion. He looked round at her, and his face, very pale and unreal, seemed
> to gleam with a whiteness almost phosphorescent.
> "Don't you feel well?" she asked, in indefinable repulsion.
> "I hadn't thought about it."
> "But don't you know whether you are unwell or not, without thinking
> about it?" she persisted.
> "Not always," he said coldly.

(WOMEN IN LOVE)

While writing this essay I began to feel queasy about this assumption, and once I began to look into the facts of his life I found it strangely difficult to ascertain whether he was tubercular or not until he was given a "condition terminal" diagnosis in 1925, right before his Etruscan period. Before that he in all likelihood had carried "the tubercle," and it had made him exceedingly susceptible to illness, with much coughing of blood into his handkerchief. He fervently denied that he had tuberculosis, but I'm sure that the ultimate fragility of his health, despite the stamina that allowed him to walk immense distances, contributed to his low boiling point and consummate irritability. No matter what facts are presented, with regard to illness I will always think of Lawrence much as I do of the equally adventurous, intensely focused, and productive poets and novelists Robert Louis Stevenson and Stephen Crane, because this is how he appears to me.

In a review of *Death in Venice,* Lawrence shows his repugnance for the amount of repression involved in the Flaubert/Mann method of composition. He has disdain for Mann's character Aschenbach who "forced himself to write, and kept himself to the work." As one of the few people I'm aware of who also feels an antipathy toward *Death in Venice,* I felt strangely vindicated when I read Lawrence's review. In Mann's other books he deals with physical sickness, soul-sickness, and madness, but with *Death in Venice* there is something sick about the book itself. It sounds almost treasonable to dislike a work—*The Great Gatsby* would be another example—about which there seems to be a consensus that it is beyond reproach, a masterpiece, a classic.

> Thomas Mann seems to me the last sick sufferer from the complaint of Flaubert. The latter stood away from life as from a leprosy. And Thomas Mann, like Flaubert, feels vaguely that he has in him something finer than ever physical life revealed. Physical life is a disordered corruption, against which he can fight with only one weapon, his fine aesthetic sense, his feeling for beauty, for perfection, for a certain fineness which soothes him, and gives him an inner pleasure, however corrupt the stuff of life may be. . . . Already I find Thomas Mann, who, as he says, fights so hard against the banal in his work, somewhat banal. His expression may be very fine. But by now what he expresses is stale. I think we have learned our lesson, to be sufficiently aware of the fulsomeness of life. And even while he has a rhythm in style, yet his work has none of the rhythm of a living thing, the rise of a poppy, then the after uplift of the bud, the shedding of the calyx and the spreading wide of the petals, the falling of the flower and the pride of the seed-head.

I taught a graduate class on the idea of "sources," and one week used F. Scott Fitzgerald's "The Afternoon of the Writer" and Peter Handke's *Afternoon of the Writer.* (Handke admits to his fascination with Fitzgerald's modest short story.) At some point in the class, a student introduced a comparison between Handke's modest novella and Mann's magisterial *Death in Venice,* bristling with resentment at being introduced to a book that everyone *hadn't* already read. I said that I preferred the Handke to the Mann, at which point he went berserk (others were merely unsettled) and became outraged that I could compare something as casual, as modest and fragile—though I would add subtle, lyrical, open—as Handke's book to a work as unimpeachable, as immortal, as canonized, as *Death in Venice* (which by the way I once taught using Kenneth Burke's translation from an issue of *The Dial*). This led to a lively discussion about questions of the will and ambition in imaginative writing. As one who loves several works by Thomas Mann, a number of the stories (including ones that Lawrence detests), *The Magic Mountain,* and most of all *Doctor Faustus,* I felt vaguely guilty about my stance toward *Death in Venice* until I realized I wasn't alone. If you think that Lawrence has gone off his head here, let me add that he was just as responsive to a book called *In Our Time* by an unknown twenty-three-year-old American writer as he was antipathetic to *Death in Venice.*

> Nothing matters. Everything happens. . . . Mr. Hemingway's sketches, for this reason, are excellent: so short, like striking a match, lighting a brief sensational cigarette, and it's over. . . . It is really honest. And it explains a great deal of sentimentality. When a thing has gone to hell inside you, your sentimentalism tries to pretend it hasn't. But Mr. Hemingway is through with the sentimentalism. "It isn't fun any more. I guess I'll beat it." And he beats it, to somewhere else.

In a graduate class at NYU, I once instructed the students to read *Look! We Have Come Through!* and *Birds, Beasts, and Flowers* in a week; to read each separately, in one sitting. I read along with the students and found myself transported, my brain waves altered and alerted as I fell into a hypnagogic trance. The students reported a similar out-of-body experience. They were lifted up without a deus ex machina or a drug to assist them. Many of the individual poems are great, but the books also trace the working out of love against the odds. The two books have both an intensity of focus and a totality that make them among the best by an English poet, and an equivalent to the books, such as César Vallejo's *Trilce* and

Pablo Neruda's *Residence on Earth,* that were waiting to be written, waiting for Lawrence to show them the way to go all out, pull out all the stops, in his earlier appropriations of Whitman. When I opened a recent issue of the *American Poetry Review* it was as if life was imitating literature: the very quintessence of what I meant in the previous sentence was in the poems by César Vallejo that Clayton Eshleman has translated. This is what I would call a direct hit:

> It is an enormous spider that now cannot move;
> a colorless spider, whose body,
> a head and an abdomen, bleeds.
>
> Today I watched it up close. With what effort
> toward every side
> it extended its innumerable legs.
>
> . . .
>
> And I have thought about its eyes
> And about its numerous legs . . .
> And I have felt such sorrow for that traveler.
>
> ("THE SPIDER")

Both Lawrence and William Carlos Williams found themselves confronting what we could call the post–*Waste Land* sterility in literature, with its maniacal emphasis on form, which rhymed with progress and the accelerating emphasis on technology and Auden's metrics. The writers who allow themselves to be enthusiastic about Lawrence, rather than hypercritical to defects to which Lawrence often readily admitted, are writers who allow themselves to be passionate, necessarily imperfect. Lawrence, in his quest to be fully alive, like the Etruscans, rejected the poetry that strove for "all that is complete and consummate . . . exquisite form: the perfect symmetry, the rhythm which returns upon itself like a dance where the hands link and loosen and link for the supreme moment of the end." As we say today: closure. R. P. Blackmur thought: "I will give that brat a piece of my mind." And he did in "D. H. Lawrence and Expressive Form." Auden and Blackmur may be right, but perhaps there is more to things than being right. Lawrence's apprenticeship to error always allowed him to move on.

Lawrence wanted nothing less than "the poetry of that which is at hand: the immediate present," in which there is "no perfection, no consummation, nothing finished." In his essay "Poetry of the Present," which served as his introduction to the American edition of *New Poems* (1918), he called for

> mutation, swifter than iridescence, haste, not rest, come-and-go, not fixity, inconclusiveness, immediacy, the quality of life itself, without dénouement or close. There must be the rapid momentaneous association of things which meet and pass on the forever incalculable journey of creation: everything left in its own rapid, fluid relationship with the rest of things.
>
> This is the unrestful, ungraspable poetry of the sheer present, poetry whose very permanency lies in its wind-like transit. Whitman's is the best poetry of this kind.

But Lawrence isn't so much a poet of the present as he is of the instantaneous. Lawrence's ambitions expressed in this essay would later be echoed by such farsighted practitioners as Osip Mandelstam and Charles Olson, but to ask for something as elemental as awareness in the mid-twentieth century is easier said than done. It is hard to emphasize without Lawrentian! exclamation points how remote this is from analytical Anglo-American criticism and how closely it approaches what Mandelstam would say fifteen years later in "Conversation About Dante" (finally back in print in Clarence Brown's translation in the *Selected Poems of Osip Mandelstam* in the New York Review Books reprint of Merwin and Brown's superlative and shattering versions).

> In poetry only the executory understanding has any importance, and not the passive, the reproducing, the paraphrasing understanding. Semantic satisfaction is equivalent to the feeling of having carried out a command.
>
> The wave signals of meaning disappear once they have done their work: the more powerful they are, the more yielding, and the less prone to linger. . . .
>
> The quality of poetry is determined by the rapidity and decisiveness with which it instills its command, its plan of action, into the instrumentless, dictionary, purely qualitative nature of word formation. One has to run across the whole width of the river, jammed with mobile Chinese junks sailing in various directions. This is how the meaning of poetic speech is created. Its route cannot be reconstructed by interrogating the boatmen: they will not tell us how and why we were leaping from junk to junk.

I ask myself why Lawrence would share his poetics with a Russian poet; I am reminded that he counted among his closest associates (the word *friends* with Lawrence can too easily convey a more agreeable relationship than the fraught one that usually existed—Lawrence was a world-class quarreler!) his editor Edward Garnett and the latter's wife Constance, who was then actively engaged in bringing the works of the Russians into English. If there is something Dostoyevskian in Lawrence's polarities, he not only read Dostoyevsky and the other Russians, he was plugged into the source. His dislike of Dostoyevsky, "a reptile" (which misfires as an insult from the snake-and-turtle-loving Lawrence), was so intense it borders on the comical. I wish Lawrence had lived to absorb Mandelstam's essay.

To look at it from the most extreme point of view, the poet who was most responsive to Lawrence's call was Sylvia Plath. Even the title of her book, *Ariel,* recalls Lawrence and his beloved horses. It was as if he had Plath in mind when he wrote this passage in *Women in Love:*

> Her whole nature seemed sharpened and intensified into a pure dart of hate. She could not imagine what it was. It merely took hold of her, the most poignant and ultimate hatred, pure and clear and beyond thought. She could not think of it at all, she was translated beyond herself. It was like a possession. She felt she was possessed. And for several days she went about possessed by this exquisite force of hatred against him. It surpassed anything she had ever known before, it seemed to throw her out of the world into some terrible region where nothing of her old life held good. She was quite lost and dazed, really dead to her own life.

But in order to accomplish this, to throw off all her restraints, Plath had to die and unfortunately, it was not the kind of symbolic death that Lawrence's characters, like Birkin in *Women in Love,* are often allowed, as a form of regeneration.

> He lay sick and unmoved, in pure opposition to everything. He knew how near to breaking was the vessel that held his life. He also knew how strong and durable it was. And he did not care. Better a thousand times take one's chance with death, than accept a life one did not want.

Plath's response to Lawrence, like Roethke's, was imbued, even infected with a desire for perfection, for a consummate expression of that which was in flux. Here we enter a field riddled with paradoxes. Roethke and Plath wrote Lawrentian poems, but they wrote them better—with greater concision—than

Lawrence. The drawback was that they limited the range of material that could be deployed within the poem. What separates Lawrence from poets and novelists he influenced and who, it could be said, improved upon aspects of his work, is that they had a far narrower focus. Lawrence was open to anything that might fly into his poem.

> When I went into my room, at mid-morning,
> Say ten o'clock . . .
> My room, a crash-box over that great stone rattle
> The Via de' Bardi. . . .
>
> When I went into my room at mid-morning,
> *Why? . . . a bird!*
>
> A bird
> Flying round the room in insane circles.
>
> In insane circles!
> *. . . A bat!*

("MAN AND BAT")

So, does the built-in imperfection of Lawrence's poetry diminish it as art? He is among the most generative of writers in every form that he wrote in. The only response to reading a novel or story or poem or essay by D. H. Lawrence, since his works deconstruct themselves as they go along, is to use this heightened awareness to live, love, and create, with renewed vigor—or if you're Tennessee Williams, to write a play based on his story "You Touched Me." And of course to have heightened awareness, feel more intensely alive. Lawrence lived his life as an adventure in accordance with Keats's dictum, "That which is creative must create itself."

I gave in to my wife Madelaine's rejection of my impulse to turn off and check out the beach at Civitavecchia. I had gotten my way in another place, and the result—since I hadn't yet read *Sketches of Etruscan Places* and been forewarned by Lawrence—wasn't what I hoped. Unwilling to forgo suffering, we had taken our son with us to Italy in the summer of 1995 when he was ten, and on our second day in Rome, giving in to his insistence to go to the nearest McDonald's just off the Spanish Steps, we met an attractive, blonde American woman with two boys in tow, and we all got to talking; I with the woman and my son with her son who was the same age. It turned out that she was living in Rome reluctantly. She said she was here because her husband was an Italian film producer who specialized in low-budget spectaculars of some sort, and though he was a mere ten years older than she was, he was at that moment lying in the hospital with his heart giving out. His death was imminent. In any case, she warned us against gangs of marauding youths who were experts at severing purses and shoulder bags and running off with your identity if you were willing to risk taking public transportation to various sites. She offered to drive us anywhere we wanted to go, and in this way, her older son and Sam would be entertained. One afternoon we drove to Ostia Antica. The three boys did their best to ruin this trip to this marvelous and meditative ruin, and it closed just in time, but not before I had a few moments to myself in the well-preserved amphitheater. The boys were really desperate at this point, and Miranda pointed out that we weren't far from the beach at Ostia, where we could all cool off. This seemed like a fabulous idea, and the charming seaside town of Ostia gave rise to great hopes for a wonderful experience. I had no idea that the beach at Ostia would be so commercialized and was surprised to find that this had been the case seventy years prior to our plunge, as noted by Lawrence in *Sketches:* "The flowers of the new coast-line are miserable bathing places such as Ladispoli and sea-side Ostia, desecration put upon desolation, to the triumphant trump of the mosquito.") It wasn't the sand or sea that was hideous; it was the cabanas and the boardwalk and the concessions and, worst of all, the chips. In addition to screaming that they were "burning" before we arrived at the sea, the boys were now "starving," and the concession was about to close. Everything in Italy is always about to close. (The next day our crew arrived at the Baths of Caracalla the very instant that it closed, and had the door shut in our faces with a chilling finality, the one day of the week that it closed at noon instead of dusk.) We paid an outrageous entrance fee in order to just be able to sit on our towels. The boys changed into their suits in the car; the women rolled up their skirts and I my pants, so that we could wade in the shallows. It was beautiful to see the three boys run at breakneck speed and jump into the water and grow delirious with joy, and their shouts rang out as they hurled their bodies against each coming wave. There was a family next to us. Young children played in the sand. The mother wore a gold two-piece that rhymed with her gilded hair and showed her buxom breasts and prodigious hips as if she had been the double or stand-in for Anita Ekberg in *La Dolce Vita.* She had an expression of absent disdain. I couldn't help but wonder what informed her consciousness. And after listening to her and her kids eat from a crackling bag of white chips for half an hour—knowing that these chips might be the last resort for the starving boys as the concession closed—I asked her what kind of chips they were, what they were made of. She answered peremptorily, almost with a hiss, "Normalissimo." I found her self-assured obliviousness chilling while I ran off to the canteen and checked out the possibilities; as far as I could see, they were entirely made from artificial ingredients without even a smidgen of wheat or potato, or corn. This was my first experience of this sort in Italy and led us to stop at a pizzeria in Ostia before heading back to Rome in the demonical traffic, which Miranda handled masterfully, her bracelets radiant with the sun in our faces, left hand on the wheel, right hand on the cell phone, as she drove and talked rapid-fire Italian to her husband breathing his last gasps in the hospital and kept a running commentary in English to clue us in as to his situation and comment on the traffic, as cars swerved ahead of us from the left and right lanes. "The Italians all think that driving is a sport," she said. We all cracked up. I felt invulnerable in the care of this wild woman who was as adept at multitasking as an octopus.

What I had witnessed on the beach was what Lawrence would call the triumph of the Roman over the Etruscan.

I somehow felt that the quest of the Cerveteri couple mirrored my own spiritual and poetic quest, only their journey would occur in physical space and mine in imagination. On a trip into Florence, I was lucky to find *Sketches of Etruscan Places* and began to read them in a casual way with low expectations in terms of their artistic value. As Billy Strayhorn says in his immemorial song "Lush Life," "again I was wrong." The more I read *Sketches of Etruscan Places,* the more I felt that they were somehow impossibly up there with the best of Lawrence's work. I wondered how it was possible that this had been kept from me for so long, why nobody had ever mentioned it. And then I had the chance to test this revelation against something far more recalcitrant, the actual Etruscan city of Volterra. The very word sends a chill up my spine. It sounds like a fortress circled by birds of prey. I don't think I've ever entered a place before and felt so immediately transformed, transported into another, tortuous reality. As Lawrence said, "Volterra lies only 1800 feet above the sea, but it is right in the wind, and cold as any alp." The first thing that struck me on entering Volterra is that everything had changed perspective, or to put it another way, I had entered a city whose contours were those of a pre-perspective Italian painting; streets were too narrow, distances too close, heads too big. An older, heavyset woman with dyed and permed hair whose gigantic head looked far too big for the open window she leaned out of cast her eyes on the street with an ominous expression, as if in warning: don't venture too close; you're inside our fortress now, and if you don't behave, you'll never get out. More objectively, Volterra was constructed partly as a fortress; some of the arches are made so that you're sure to knock your head unless you're stooping down. Volterra was the most conclusive fortress that I've ever inhabited, and a lot of this is due to chance, to the hilltop where the Volterrans chose to build it. One of the fascinating things about Volterra, in addition to the fact that it instantly transforms the unconscious of the invader, who was now of course an unsuspecting traveler, unaware that he may be changed, is that unlike other Etruscan sites, the most interesting thing is the city itself, not the ruins. I felt my mood go down along with the sun, and now the sun was in our faces as we took a long walk down the steep decline to the unmarked, dark, moldy caves filled with lidless sarcophagi platforms and lizards who looked like they were grateful for the company.

> A lizard ran out on a rock and looked up, listening
> no doubt to the sounding of the spheres.
>
> . . .
>
> If men were as much men as lizards are lizards
> they'd be worth looking at.

("LIZARD")

I had walked many times this distance in other hilly Italian cities, but my legs had never felt so heavy. It was as if with every footstep I walked against some invisible resistance. The cliffs of Volterra may be legendary, as d'Annunzio and Borges attest, but looking out now over the hills and fields of hay bales in the luminous dusk, I felt as if I had imbibed the sadness of the hilltop town's history and what it had undergone when all the joy was removed when it was taken over by the Romans. This is possible because Volterra was unique among Etruscan towns in terms of its remoteness and the difficulties it presented in terms of getting up and down, in and out. Most of the ancient treasures had been removed from their sites and are safely stowed in the renowned Guarnacci Museum. Strangely, despite his incomparable seismograph for the slightest vacillation in the atmosphere, Lawrence was not at all spooked by Volterra, but he was making a tour with his friend Baxter of all these Etruscan sites because he was being paid to write a book. The poet in Lawrence was sublimated by the journalist in him in order to accomplish this project and get paid. Lawrence was rejuvenated by the urns in the Guarnacci Museum. He makes no mention of the gem of Volterra, a nude male youth in bronze, so skinny it's always on the brink of vanishing.

Dated as early as the third century B.C., it brings to mind a sculpture by Giacometti. D'Annunzio gave it a name that has stuck: "L'ombra de la sera," for the way it resembled the lengthening and narrowing shadows at nightfall. The art of the Etruscans gave Lawrence the energy that he thought he needed to derive from an unrealistic arrangement in real life.

Lawrence seemed almost relieved to be in a museum, rather than wandering downhill to a dark hole in a rock with a candle in an attempt to decipher barely discernible shapes. For me, the real experience of Volterra was Volterra. The fantastical existence of these rock people, who still existed. I think Lawrence is dead-on to say that today's Romans are mostly Etruscans whose direction was diverted by history, like a landslide that diverts the course of a river. People come away from Italy elated because the people are elated. They retain the Etruscan playfulness, the mad delight in living itself, even while talking demonically on cell phones, or driving like daredevils on Vespas. Lawrence enters the Guarnacci Museum:

> It is really a very attractive and pleasant museum, but we had struck such a bitter cold April morning, with icy rain falling in the courtyard, that I felt as near to being in the tomb as I have ever done. Yet very soon, in the rooms with those hundreds of little sarcophagi, ash-coffins, or urns, as they are called, the stretch of the old life began to warm one up.

And then there are the gates where three muddy brown heads, triangular, their features effaced by the weather, still watch over the city after twenty-five hundred years of wind and rain. Perhaps what I felt in Volterra looking at the heads, which it is said the Romans helped restore, was the sadness of the Roman influence, the victory of power and drive over spontaneity and sensuality.

It may be haunting me today because yesterday toward the end of an extremely draining week (and with my nerves on edge because of the gloomily looming presidential election), I forced myself to take a break from what George Eliot would call "duty" and go to the movies—*The Motorcycle Diaries*, which is not a sequel to such biker movies as *The Wild Ones, Wild Angels*, or even *Easy Rider*, but a movie drawn from the diaries of Che Guevara. And I forced myself to go early enough on this dank, gray afternoon so that I could have some empty space around me and relax, as I did in the years before my dreams became responsibilities. I thought *Diaries* would be good, but I never suspected that it would be as good as it is. And it was inspiring for me to hear Che and his friend exchange quotes of Neruda and Lorca and when they reached Peru be handed the works of César Vallejo by a doctor who befriends them. But then something terrible happens. Something as terrible as the impinging, almost strangling sensation that you get in a city like Volterra as the Roman influence and domination becomes more and more palpable. It is during a scene when the two adventurers have reached Machu Picchu, and they discuss how civilization has regressed. Their conversation in the heights runs parallel to Lawrence's discourse on the Etruscans. The Etruscans didn't have the military prowess to defeat the Roman legions. The Incas, who knew how to perform sophisticated and intricate brain surgery, lacked something that the conquistadors had—gunpowder. But what broke my heart was the next shot. One instant we're inside Machu Picchu, and the next instant the camera cuts to a view of the urban sprawl of Lima, which uncannily resembles Los Angeles. And Che comments quietly on the tragedy that civilization has gone from the "heights" of aspiration to the depths of greed and a mindless power drive.

> The fleece of the vicuña was carded here
> to clothe men's loves in gold, their tombs and mothers,
> the king, the prayers, the warriors.
>
> (PABLO NERUDA, "THE HEIGHTS OF MACHU PICCHU: VI,"
> TRANS. NATHANIEL TARN)

The Spanish did with religion what the Romans did with craving for empire, rooted out the sensual quick of the people and made them bow instead to the higher orders of a Christian God and power, acquisitions! Porsches! No more broken-down motorcycles that are worth more as scrap iron than functioning machines!

October–November 2004, New York City

Note

Clearly there was an element of theater in my exaggerated claims for Handke's novella. When I looked at it again as I prepared to send this essay in to be printed, I wondered why I had been so taken with it, unless it added another dimension—another route—to my desire to write out of, around, and about: walking.

William Carlos Williams in America

Lately I have found myself reaching for William Carlos Williams's poetry, more so than for the poems of his great peers—Marianne Moore and Wallace Stevens—who were among the first to recognize his gift. The first, who were, by miracle, his classmates at the University of Pennsylvania, were H.D. and Ezra Pound. At some point, Carlos Williams became separated in my mind from other American poets. When I asked myself what made Williams seem so different, the answer came from one of the unlikely heroes that Williams breathes new life into in one of the finest nonfiction works written by an American: *In the American Grain*. His unjaded and generous take on Poe brought to mind "The Purloined Letter," a story that gave birth to a genre that has become one of the liveliest arts, and in the blink of an eye the elusive solution to the mystery looked back with black eyes and intent gaze: Carlos.

In all these years of reading Williams, I'd never once paused over his middle name. Pound called him Carlos and "for fifteen or eighteen years" cited Williams as the sole known American-dwelling author who could be counted on to oppose the invisible barriers set up by the collective American mind-set—"the sole catalectic in whose presence some sort of modification would take place." When Williams wrote a disarmingly modest statement—"All I do is to try and understand something in its natural colors and shapes"—Pound was moved to add that "there could be no better effort underlying any literary process, or used as preparative for literary process; but it appears, it would seem, almost incomprehensible to men dwelling west of the Atlantic." The extent to which Williams stood apart is ineradicably connected to both the Spanish blood on his maternal side and his father's Dutch and English Caribbean background. The language spoken in the Williams household was mostly Spanish. To really grasp how radical a situation this was, were it not for the influence of his maternal grandmother, Emily Dickinson Wellcome, the young Carlos might never have attained mastery of the English language.

Williams's reputation is said to have been eclipsed by Eliot, Stevens, Pound, Moore, Bishop, and others. (Robert Lowell appears to be in the same slog, his reputation descending the staircase while Bishop is canonized and Berryman rehabilitated.) Why are Williams's major works not more read, considering their beautiful symmetry? Is it because, again in Pound's words, "he starts where a European would start if a European were about to write of America: America is a subject of interest, one must inspect it, analyze it, and treat it as a subject"? Am I imagining an echo of Dupin's ratiocination in Pound's lucid and concise analysis of this mystery in a country like America where the people, Pound observes, "think they 'ought' to write 'about' America" because it has inherent interest as a subject simply because it is American, and that this gives it "a dignity or value above all other possible subjects"? We think we're in hot water now; Pound knew we were in scalding water then. But to return to my earlier question, here's what I was about to say before I was graced with such a magisterial interruption. The reader who wants to enter heaven without having to die first should read *Al Que Quiere!, Kora in Hell, Spring and All,* and *The Descent of Winter,* along with Williams's three inestimable late works, *Paterson, The Desert Music,* and *Journey to Love* and such prose arias as "The Destruction of Tenochtitlan" in *In the American Grain.*

From his earliest years, Williams was aware of *différance,* Jacques Derrida's legendary concept, which made contradiction a parable for the human condition. Both men were given this theme by accident—Derrida was an Egyptian Jew who wrote in French—they were both blessed with an awareness denied to people who are never propelled to confront these questions of "who am I really?"—the kinds of questions that arise in *King Lear.* Neither Williams nor Derrida would need to ask either the Fool or Cordelia "who is it who will tell me who I am?" Williams had help in becoming steeped in contradictions, mostly from Grandma Wellcome. The dizzying changes she went through during her life were instrumental in guiding Williams to write in a way that no one had written.

This plot of ground
facing the waters of this inlet
is dedicated to the living presence of
Emily Dickinson Wellcome
who was born in England; married;
lost her husband and with
her five year old son
sailed for New York in a two-master;
was driven to the Azores;
ran adrift on Fire Island shoal,
met her second husband
in a Brooklyn boarding house,
went with him to Puerto Rico
bore three more children, lost
her second husband, lived hard
for eight years in St. Thomas,
Puerto Rico, San Domingo, followed
the oldest son to New York,
lost her daughter, lost her "baby,"
seized the two boys of
the oldest son by the second marriage
mothered them—they being
motherless—fought for them
against the other grandmother
and the aunts, brought them here
summer after summer, defended
herself here against thieves,
storms, sun, fire,
against flies, against girls
that came smelling about, against
drought, against weeds, storm-tides,
neighbors, weasels that stole her chickens,
against the weakness of her own hands,
against the growing strength of
the boys, against wind, against
the stones, against trespassers,
against rents, against her own mind.

("DEDICATION FOR A PLOT OF GROUND")

Free verse? Incantatory is more like it. Williams was steeped in Shakespeare and Keats, and yet he wrote what came to be called free verse in a dynamic way that synthesized many strains of discourse, languages, and cultures. From the start Williams is headed toward the direction that he will evolve in *Al Que Quiere!* I'd wager that that exclamation point owes itself to the English poet with whom he felt an almost preternatural connection: D. H. Lawrence.

Williams with his European upbringing found the commonplace inherently exotic—he didn't have to travel or go into exile. "At any rate, he has not in his ancestral endocrines the arid curse of our nation. None of his immediate forbearers burnt witches in Salem, or attended assemblies for producing prohibitions" (Ezra Pound). The European and Hispanic influences on Williams led to a sense of solitude (as it did with both Derrida and Lawrence) that is immeasurable and not easy to locate because of his exuberance and amiability. Ezra Pound's solidification of T. E. Hulme's attempt to define this new form, "free verse," is, I believe, made in the image of William Carlos Williams.

Despite Williams's brutal, lifelong, and unrelenting struggle for recognition and understanding, the affection that H.D. and Moore and Pound and Stevens felt for him is well documented. His likeability was contagious. But his sense of being an outsider as a poet was scarcely diminished by an abundance of prescient reviews of his books written by Kenneth Burke and Yvor Winters, and by other poets, like Moore and Pound. I wouldn't be surprised if Pound had Williams in mind while translating "To Em-Mei's 'The Unmoving Cloud'" in *Cathay:* "It is not that there are no other men / But we like this fellow the best."

The legacy of Williams's cheerfulness and brio is the belief by some that his work stays on the surface. It's quite the opposite: he argues from the inside out. He had early come to terms with an inner darkness that he intuited would never change. His first poem is almost out of a contemporary textbook on depression.

> A black, black cloud
> flew over the sun
> driven by fierce flying
>   rain.

Williams's imaginative power and production are a reaction both to the blankness of matter and to a certain personal despair that he knew would never be assuaged and to which the only remedy was work.

No one is less the stereotypical "modern artist" than William Carlos Williams. The only thing arty about the man was his art. He was nothing if not embattled all through his life when it came to aesthetics. He had a kind of detachment that enabled him to resent and despise writing that he thought would inhibit the direction he envisioned for the future of poetry, but without, as is so often the case, conflating the product and the person. This again meant holding two contradictory ideas in his mind at the same time, a rare human quality, and not one that D. H. Lawrence was blessed with. While others were looking for an aesthetic whole, Williams was saying, "Get on with it!"—an attitude informed by science as well as temperament. This allowed him to become the one poet to bridge the polarizing divide between poets writing in English who employ meter and rhyme and those who take on the challenge of organic form—as originally postulated by Coleridge. There's hardly a more thrilling sense of recognition in the history of writing than the fact that Carlos Williams became the symbolic mentor to such outwardly opposed figures as Allen Ginsberg and Robert Lowell. And Williams's effect on the great earthworks artist Robert Smithson reverberated far beyond the hospital wards where he acted as the artist's pediatrician in Rutherford. Both Ginsberg and Smithson come out of Paterson, as well as *Paterson*. Smithson retraces Williams's steps in book 3 of *Paterson,* quarrying from the quarries what would become the most far-reaching development in art since cubism.

There is no cure for the kind of despair that Williams recognized at a young age, but he used it to his advantage. This early recognition of rock bottom, of a despair that could easily have consumed him and sent him over the falls in a barrel like Sam Patch, gave him his calling: work! It's only to the point with Williams because he's famous for that jaunty manner, like "I get a kick out of / . . . delivering babies."

> Work hard all your young days
> and they'll find you too, some morning
> staring up under
> your chiffonier at its warped
> bass-wood bottom and your soul—
> out!
> —among the little sparrows
> behind the shutter.

("JANUARY MORNING")

The term *rock bottom* would become an unexpected talisman throughout Williams's twentieth-century version of the quest. "The Rock-Old Dogma":

> It had to be, of course, a rock
> over which comparatively recent ants
> crawled. When it split,
> with time, only then did the imprint
>
> of the fern reveal itself—
> And the fern, and the fish-spine or
> bird-plume—fossil botany goes
> into smaller particles.

Williams often sounds, and I don't mean to be melodramatic here, like a man, doctor or not, on the edge of a breakdown as well as a literal rocky precipice.

> Then out of the blue *The Dial* brought out *The Waste Land* and all our hilarity ended. *It wiped out our world as if an atom bomb had been dropped upon it* and our brave sallies into the unknown were turned to dust.
>
> To me especially it struck like a sardonic bullet. I felt at once that it had set me back twenty years, and I'm sure it did. Critically Eliot returned us to the classroom just at the moment when I felt that we were on the point of an escape to matters much closer to the essence of a new art form itself—rooted in the locality which should give it fruit. I knew at once that in certain ways I was most defeated.
>
> Eliot had turned his back on the possibility of reviving my world. And being an accomplished craftsman, better skilled in some ways than I could ever hope to be, I had to watch him carry my world off with him, the fool, to the enemy. [Italics mine.]

These three small paragraphs are remarkable in that they contain so many of the tensions that define modern poetry in the endless dialogue between tradition and innovation. Robert Duncan, one of the best poets to come out of the Pound/Williams tradition, phrased it with rolling *r*'s that pack a charge.

> Child of a century more skeptic than
>   unbelieving,   adrift
> between two contrary educations,
>
> that of the Revolution, which disowns
>   everything,

and that of the Reaction
which pretends to bring back the ensemble
of Christian beliefs

("PASSAGES 32")

The final line may be at the core of what made Williams so skittish in his response to *The Waste Land*. Nothing else really explains the ferocity of his response to the publication of *The Waste Land* than what he does not mention: that it is the record of a breakdown as well as a cultural collapse. It is as if the wasteland is exactly what Williams felt he could not endure (or that, as Heidegger phrases it, "the wasteland grows"). Williams's poetry represents his vigilance in overcoming, Teddy Roosevelt–style, his own limitations. When someone is consumed in a single-minded pursuit of that sort, there is little time to dismantle the engine to examine the parts for fear that it will cease to function. What we experience in reading Williams, which isn't that different from reading Keats or Rilke or Pasternak, is a release of the self, so thorough is his immersion in otherness.

How curious the bond between Stevens and Williams, two nonliterary poets who had each decided to choose a profession apart from writing, and who insisted on the primacy of the imagination. As artists they shared a certain loneliness and isolation in their daily lives as insurance executive and doctor, but this very distance forced them to draw upon inner resources they might not have otherwise tapped were it not for these pressures. A consummate tribute came from Stevens, who used an indelible short poem from Williams's breakthrough book, *Al Que Quiere!* (*To Who Wants It!*), as an epigraph:

> *El Hombre*
>
> It's a strange courage
> you give me ancient star:
>
> Shine alone in the sunrise
> toward which you lend no part!

The intractable star and the redoubtable poet in collusion share delight in independence and clarity in their separate identities that are analogous to pure existence. There is no real comfort or precise positioning in existence; and Williams insisted until the end, "Romance / plays no part in it" ("To Anthony and Cleopatra"). It's the acceptance of annihilation that allows the poet-doctor to inhale this "strange courage" from something that offers no consolation. It is this rocklike yet ultimately opaque quality that endeared the poem to Stevens. And to use the whole poem of a contemporary as an epigraph—how rare, given the competition between poets—is his interstellar way of winking to another planet with life on it. He took heart that there was someone else onto the same stress on imagination, with its capacity for synthesis, and that Williams was going after the same quarry but with different means.

The father of H.D. (Hilda Doolittle) was a prominent astronomer, and Williams's relationship with the Doolittle family—even if his visits to the house were to see the astronomer's fetching blonde daughter—may have been yet another source of his ultimate farsightedness, his capacity to take in the whole and yet present a multitude of "minute particulars": stargazing is the source of the impulse for "El Hombre." What are Williams's dicta? "Only the imagination is real." "No ideas but in things." Stevens's poetry after *Harmonium* was like philosophical discourse set to music, but that just meant he approached the same goal in the opposite way.

Williams's musings scarcely qualify as "ideas"—but he never equated anything outside the words with their "real-life" counterparts. This lent his writing its gaiety.

The particular. The general. Ideas. Things. These words have come to mean less than the coins sporting the face—"his picture in little"—of King Claudius of Denmark. But in fusion they take on a limitless potency. There must be something in the stratosphere, anything, an ungainly meteor chunk, that we can say is real outside our human conception. I think that poetry should penetrate what's real outside any imagined, imaginary frame. That the poem, whatever its material, should distract the reader, compel the reader to listen to the words in sequence, in the hope of getting through to the ineluctable modalities that Joyce identified: of the audible, of the visible. The true poem's limit is its guiding light; it brings the reader to longing—something isn't being revealed—and longing does have some relation to the infinite. And to the tall dark woman who's standing across the crowded room, quietly, distinctly uncomfortable. And that's all. No backward, no forward. Being true to the way things are. Each poem by Stevens is a totality. Each poem by Williams is, to borrow Sartre's useful and succinct concept in his search for a method, a "detotalized totality."

Walking—

> across the old swale—a dry wave in the ground
> tho' marked still by the line of Indian alders
>
> . . . they (the Indians) would weave
> in and out, unseen, among them along the stream

(PATERSON, BOOK 2)

and the music carries it through all barriers. But without that toughness, that exhausted illuminated pause, it would be friction. I believe Stevens loved the illusion of the actual thing being presented that Williams created through legerdemain, or as Kenneth Burke put it, "Williams was engaged in discovering the shortest route between object and subject." Williams's continuous creation of passages with "imaginative suspense" succeeds in getting the listener to listen, listen to how the sound and pace and placement are interlaced—and experience beauty.

➤

Williams was exceedingly conscious of the concept of register. It may be this broken prologue that gave *Paterson* the momentum to continue on through five books.

> To make a start,
> out of particulars
> and make them general, rolling
> up the sum, by defective means—

He intends the reader's mind to leap to the concept of particles and particle physics. Williams was adept at applying principles of science to art; he was an avatar of method. He treated formal questions in art with the zeal of a scientist who is in the process of bringing forth a new concept, like the unconscious, or relativity. For Williams, to whom "a new world is only a new mind and the mind and the poem are one," the truth could no longer be expressed through fixed forms that carried within them the ethos of the worldview prevalent at the time they were conceived. Many terms circulate through Williams and his correspondents, like Kenneth Burke, Robert Creeley, Denise Levertov, and Charles Olson: free verse, breadth, a variable foot, pauses (whose function is identical to that of a caesura). Robert Creeley's remark that Charles Olson tried to bend into a poetic credo in his essay "On Projective Verse" (to which Williams devotes a chapter of his autobiography)—"FORM IS NEVER MORE THAN AN EXTENSION OF CONTENT" (Olson's caps)—is utterly inadequate to its purposes. This laid the ground for the poetics to be embraced by some excellent Black Mountain poets, like Paul Blackburn, Denise Levertov, and Gary Snyder. Snyder's immersion in Eastern thought, along with redwood tubs (which he celebrates in the later work), helped in his knowing when and how to apply these dicta, which are as blatant as directions from the mouth of a megaphone. After hiking, when it was still light, Snyder sat cross-legged in his tent and studied Pound's *Cantos.* No one grasps better than Gary Snyder the curious link between variables and verse: the "variable foot," variable turns of phrase, and the variable washed out roads and rickety bridges imbue *Mountains and Rivers Without End* with a flexibility and rhythm to negotiate the variables the poet encounters on his way. Verse doesn't mean following prior forms and filling them by writing to the same beat or stanza pattern; it refers to a turning, the very twist that Williams calls "imaginative suspense." And when Olson reaches for a quotation to back up his inspired rant, who or what does he look to if not these lines by the man himself: but he achieves a subtle unstated effect by letting Shakespeare's lines cross over into the lowercase.

And instead of quoting any of a dozen or so poets, including Bunting and MacDiarmid, to illustrate how one perception leads without pause to another perception, he's back with a Duke by the name of Orsino "whose greatest comfort," like W. H. Auden's, "is music":

> If music be the food of love, play on;
> give me excess of it, that, surfeiting,
> the appetite may sicken, and so die.
> That strain again! it had a dying fall.

Maybe we should temper all references to Shakespeare by taking his characters and their speech patterns as more than just expedient. Without all these different characters, whose deepest nature is revealed in the way they use words, no man, not even Francis Bacon or Christopher Marlowe, could have come up with a gallery that extends through all reaches of life, death, and sexuality. By having men play women's parts, Shakespeare employs a language of double meanings, since everything the "woman" says means something other than the words themselves, "untimely ripped" from their context. Williams picked up the ball and ran with it for forty years before his readers/poets/critics let it sink in that Carlos was from the start an other, "un autre." He hands over all the evidence in *Kora in Hell: Improvisations,* but his readers were distracted by their own fascination with an underworld.

This is another instance where Williams's refusal to withhold information misleads the many brilliant minds who, having absorbed and "explicated" much of the great poetry in English—with dashes of Dante added to the broth—refused to admit being a bit stumped by the most immediately accessible of all radically original American poets. But Wittgenstein—I can imagine a class where he tries to get his students to hear "so much depends," "so much depends," as both an intriguing and a true fragment. And what's important is not any of the objects, but the remaining traces of rainwater; water that will sustain what's on earth enough to fill a wheelbarrow and at the same time sink into the underworld to enrich the earth and the men and women who walk up and down upon it.

The things we take for granted in prose we are often blind to in poetry. Let's pretend that Balzac had written the following prose specimen and that we were sharing a characteristic moment with his well-intended, ill-fated antihero, Lucien de Rubempré, in the one novel, *Lost Illusions* (which the poet and Blake scholar Kathleen Raine took upon herself to translate), that is rarely assigned to students in creative writing "programs," lest they become mistrustful of these institutions. And Lucien is also blinded to what the mirrors see outside of his immediate framework, which is a world geared to profit, not art. And his denial or constant bewildered amazement at the double-dealing he sees others practice every time he leaves his room, costs him the one thing which no one can afford to lose: his life. Denial. This gave Freud the urgency to push forward, despite resistances encountered everywhere. And Freud's patients shared one characteristic with Balzac's character(s): illusions. Illusions which caused many Jews to ignore the rise of the Third Reich, until they were curfewed, then corralled, then . . .—but that's history. And no wonder Simone Weil fixed our attention on attention itself.

> Checking himself in front of the foyer mirror before he joined the others, Lucien thought he not only looked like the others, but more like what the others would like to look like. He had discussed it with his tailor—whom he'd sought out on the advice of a man whose income was thrice his own and which reduced his savings to money for transportation and prayed that

the next gathering would offer a buffet. And the tailor chimed in: "They spend and they spend as if the paying out would improve the imperfections that are holding them back from getting what they want. What can you do? You can't buy taste. Or good tact. But without it there is only waste." But when the tailor handed him the bill Lucien had to force a smile to disguise his inward panic—which he realized later was hunger.

Here's part of a late Williams poem typed from memory as prose.

Sitting here in the country on an old farm we eat our breakfasts under an elm. The shrubs below us are neglected. And there, hemmed in, or he would eat the garden, lives a pet goose, a very quiet old fellow.

And here's how it appears in "To Daphne and Virginia."

Staying here in the country
　　　on an old farm
　　　　　we eat our breakfast
on a balcony under an elm.
　　　The shrubs below us
　　　　　are neglected. And
there, *penned* in,
　　　or he would eat the garden,
　　　　　lives a pet goose *who*
tilts his head
　　sidewise
　　　　and looks up at us,
a very quiet old fellow
　　who writes no poems.

The juxtaposition of Balzac and Williams was intended to illustrate the point I'm coming to; it inadvertently pointed to some of memory's distortions: but what I left out in my memory flash of these lines from "To Daphne and Virginia" are precisely those lines at the poetic heart and core of the passage. It's embarrassing, given that the very words at which my memory balked are those which transform an outwardly flat passage to one that is charming, magical, enchanting, and memorable. The difficulties are in our preconceptions, like the worm in the brain that Williams says wants to disrupt our thought and throw it "to *the newspapers or anywhere.*" "News," slyly sliding in the vowels in "anywhere" so that the throat opens and the ear recalls that he set it up in the previous line with "throw," "and throw it to the newspapers or anywhere." The words mesh, through a kind of cross-stitching, as we begin to hear why Lowell spoke of *The Desert Music* as indispensable as any poetry written by an American. When we went from one (Spender and Leishman) translation of *The Duino Elegies* to a hundred in no time flat once the fifty-year copyright ran out and Rilke's greatest single work was now in the public domain, David Young borrowed this triadic foot to accomplish the—impossible—task. Williams took up the triadic foot in the aftermath of a stroke, which slowed him down and caused him to weigh the value of individual words in a way he hadn't before. You can see it in the way Ginsberg read poems, not only his own, that to STRESS the stresses also gave the caesuras a chance to yawn. And I think that Bob Dylan was ATTUNED to the WAY a POET he could RElate to, like Ginsberg, MANaged to make words on a page come alive through the delivery. Dylan sings a lot of songs straight, the best he can. And there are others when the word asks to be extended; out of pain and as a premonition of shipwreck—whichever one is the order of the day.

Although he loved method, Carlos Williams is anything but methodical. But by, in Pound's footsteps, breaking the convention—pentameter—Williams evolves the paradigm, wherein every poem is subject to its own laws. Each poem has a different shape. Shape and sound, rise and fall and sigh.

The singular outcome of the task the young doctor set himself would allow him to relish, enjoy poetic composition in a way that spills over, foams, as Longinus puts it, into the sublime. He liked being humbled by the polyglot nature of English. And what Marianne Moore chastised him for calling the "American" language. In a televised interview with the talk show host Mike Wallace in 1957, the interviewer puts the interviewee up against the wall, and the latter does not quail.

> Q: . . . here's a part of a poem you yourself have written: . . .
> "2 partridges / 2 mallard ducks / a Dungeness crab / 24 hours out /
> of the Pacific / and 2 live-frozen / trout / from Denmark . . ."
> Now, that sounds just like a fashionable grocery list!

> A: It is a fashionable grocery list.

> Q: Well—is it poetry?

A: We poets have to talk in a language which is not English. It is the American idiom. Rhythmically it's organized as a sample of the American idiom. It has as much originality as jazz. If you say "2 partridges / 2 mallard ducks / a Dungeness crab"—if you treat that rhythmically, ignoring the practical sense, it forms a jagged pattern. It is, to my mind, poetry.

The weight of words, the intonation, the hesitations which are equivalent to the way Balzac liked to ponder physiognomy and furniture: outward appearance and surroundings. Williams uses facts but, through fusion, gives the most outwardly ordinary events the kind of power that would lead René Char—a poet to whom Williams pays significant homage in several ways—to phrase it in his Heraclitean manner: "Nothing had heralded so strong an existence."

The particulars are the earthly representation of the particles. Williams reveled in conveying a sense of there-ness, and thrived on the resistance of the real to his will. The inevitable friction allows the reader to feel as if he were living in Williams's own moment of perception. Stevens might allude to chaos, but there would be no chaos or ruffling of the language of the poem itself. Williams's great subject is risk. He not only risks failure, he does fail—often. The New Critics found Williams's freedom of composition, his willingness to improvise, threatening to their fantasy of order. By putting the burden on the reader to make a judgment call about something that is necessarily unfamiliar, he sets up a divide. The affinities Williams had with Einstein, Wittgenstein, and later, Jackson Pollock's drip paintings, reveal not only a discontent with outworn forms, but a willingness— much as he portrays Daniel Boone in *In the American Grain*—to continue along unmarked paths. As late in life as 1958, which would've made him seventy-five, while composing the fifth and final book of *Paterson,* he was both in tune with and felt vindicated by "the world / of the imagination [that] most endures":

> Pollock's blobs of paint squeezed out
> with design!
> pure from the tube. Nothing else
> is real . . .

I just read Williams's poem "The Trees" (*Poems,* 1930) for the first time, and felt elated, broken, and whole in the same instant. And to begin to take it in, I had to abandon any habits I had picked up along the way. . . . It reads like an action painting fifteen years before Pollock began to work movement and improvisation onto his immense canvases. And it's no accident that Pollock's revelation derived from the vast rocky spaces that were his landscape in Cody, Wyoming.

> The trees—being trees
> thrash and scream
> guffaw and curse—
> wholly abandoned
> damning the race of men—
>
> Christ, the bastards
> haven't even sense enough
> to stay out in the rain—
>
> Wha ha ha ha
>
> Wheeeeee
> clacka tacka tacka
> tacka tacka
> wha ha ha ha ha
> ha ha ha
>
> knocking knees, buds
> bursting from each pore
> even the trunk's self
> putting out leafheads—
>
> Loose desire!
> we naked cry to you—
> "Do what you please."
>
> You cannot!
>
> —ghosts
> sapped of strength
>
> wailing at the gate
> heartbreak at the bridgehead—
> desire
> dead in the heart
>
> haw haw haw haw
> —and memory broken

wheeeeee

There were never satyrs
never maenads
never eagle-headed gods—
These were men
from whose hands sprung
love
bursting the wood—

Trees their companions
—a cold wind winterlong
in the hollows of our flesh
icy with pleasure—

no part of us untouched

Read the poem aloud. Don't think about it, listen to it. Williams exhausts his subject early on, and the ensuing loss of control gives "The Trees" what the poem demanded: listening. This is the same street where Pasternak finds that "the poplars stand surprised." How far removed is this outburst from passages in Shakespeare, as when Lear is assaulted by the elements. First foray. In one poem Williams reveals the inherent absurdity of the pathetic fallacy as more than a corrective. It's only in America that hyperbole has a strong negative connotation. But to see it as written by a Spaniard addressing Lorca and Alberti and Vallejo is like having a cataract removed. The dance! *Duende!* And this recognition of uncertainty and the necessity of invention allows Williams to create poems that don't resemble poems that came before them—and in the process risk losing the reader. Holding volume 1 of the *Collected Poems* in my hands at this instant, it almost seems impossible that the poem on the facing page could clarify the thrashings in "The Trees."

The forms
of the emotions are crystalline,
geometric-faceted. *So we recognize*
only in the white heat of
understanding, when a flame
runs through the gap made
by learning

("APRIL," ITALICS MINE)

The Book of Samuel

What accounts for Williams's turbulence and intensity in this particular poem, presenting potential negatives in a positive light? His words have an equivalent of a physical presence, and that presence is: imagination. If I glance to the left, I see that Williams has set out to write something that does have strict form, rules, boundaries—but like many of Wittgenstein's propositions, they're inscrutable. The amazement we often feel reading Williams derives from the paradox that his poems are both on the surface and bottomless. And the "inexpressible crystalline world" that Wittgenstein reveals is uncannily close to the poetic truths that Williams exploded in *Spring and All* as the season burst forth with a violence that demonstrated that nature was neither alienated nor removed from the social, political, and scientific upheavals that had given birth to the book. Williams, like Wittgenstein, favors propositions, albeit ones that are slightly skewed; broken; missing whatever would pin the meaning down. ("And do not," Eliot warned us, "call it fixity.") And the common interpretation of both men's work often diabolically reversed its intention. And the philosopher and the poet are in uncanny concord when it comes to a definition like this: "A proposition states something only insofar as it is a picture." For Williams, poetry is a matter of becoming "reconciled with your world." He found a multitude of ways to define the poet's task through the way he sees it manifested by others, as in "Fine Work with Pitch and Copper":

> Now they are resting
> in the fleckless light
> separately in unison

How much more can any poet synthesize in three lines of from five to seven syllables? Knowing the ways he's touched on these matters in other poems with phrases like "isolate flecks" and "unison," the way "Pitch" is used here to pun on his many musical analogies and scenes, and the role copper plays as a conductor and conduit, the poem grows in richness and complexity.

Williams's laboratory was unbounded; it accompanied him everywhere: especially in his car, which allowed him to move through space with nothing in his mind "but the right of way" and the knowledge that he will not proceed for long without impediment: danger. And this is what he needed for his practice.

for I went spinning on the

four wheels of my car
along the wet road until

I saw a girl with one leg
over the rail of a balcony

(*SPRING AND ALL*)

The hybridity of *Spring and All*'s mixture of poetry and prose, of image and reflection, allows him to connect his imagination and analysis. He never tires of reiterating the impasse that set him on the road to poetry. The moment after he presents us with this provocative image, he accounts for its potency.

> When in the condition of imaginative suspense only will writing have reality, as explained partially in what precedes. . . . To perfect the ability to record at the moment when the consciousness is enlarged by the sympathies and the unity of understanding which the imagination gives, to practice skill in recording the force moving, then to know it, in the largeness of its proportions.

Spring and All was published in the auspicious moment in the early 1920s that also saw the release of *The Waste Land, Ulysses,* and works whose break with inherited forms, received ideas, was even more radical: César Vallejo's *Trilce,* Boris Pasternak's *My Sister—Life,* as well as Wittgenstein's *Tractatus Logico-Philosophicus.*

Williams addresses "St. Francis Einstein of the Daffodils" to Einstein, "bringing April in his head" in case the scientist missed it. Fifteen years later, after composing "Adam" and another poem called "Eve," he writes an abbreviated sequel to his first paean to the man whose work with relativity and atomic physics was somehow equivalent to the Imagination who conceived Eve and the women—the women!—who make life possible and allow him to sing the body electric until his vocal chords go hoarse and he stands—hopeless and erect. "They enter the new world naked, / cold, uncertain of all / save that they enter" ("By the Road to the Contagious Hospital"). The reader, tense, suspended, is desperate for resolution; resolution, not closure, and he gets it with the next vivid and unforgiving line from the first untitled poem in *Spring and All:*

They enter the new world naked

Naked! Finally—relief. The possibility that the reader will be awakened by art that stresses the reality of the imagination rather than the illusion of comfort that is a destructive form of magical thinking. Certainly some eighty years later people were eager to hear what Joan Didion had to say on that subject. And what does she stress? Awareness, attention. Williams consciously cultivated awareness and attention to detail. And every assertion as *Spring and All* begins is instantaneously reversed, the hospital contagious, death and rebirth conjoined.

> By the road to the contagious hospital
> under the surge of the blue
> mottled clouds driven from the
> northeast—a cold wind. Beyond, the
> waste of broad, muddy fields
> brown with dried weeds, standing and fallen

Williams moves so quickly the reader is in a perpetual state of catching up. I wonder if part of what has kept Williams exciting—"And after all, only Whitman and Crane and Williams, of the American poets," Frank O'Hara writes in his "Personism" manifesto "are better than the movies"—is that his mental slips and slips on icy roads, reaffirm the treachery of existence. But it's treachery inseparable from the language as well as the landscape. Incredibly, the key to people's resistance to Williams's work is that it's fun. And that this gaiety and wry humor enters in the face of life's vicissitudes both goes against the grain of modernism and enters the company of independent spirits like Villon ("I die of thirst beside a fountain"), Diderot, Apollinaire—even Tolstoy. But while everyone is pretty much willing to overlook Tolstoy's lecturing in *War and Peace,* problematical attitudes towards women and marriage in *The Kreutzer Sonata,* and the veiled tirade *What Is Art?* where for starters he wipes the slate clean of fifty volumes of Goethe and dismisses Shakespeare, especially *King Lear,* on moral grounds, people were looking for an excuse to dismiss Williams at every opportunity. They balked at the sheer bulk and unevenness of Williams's poetry—whose eternal freshness rouses wariness, hostility, and sometimes hysterical dismissiveness—which was demeaned by a surly quip: Williams wrote too much. And yet even the poems that are scarcely more than interesting notes scribbled down with his left hand on the driving wheel and his right hand on a notepad have a certain life and spark.

➤

As my fantasies began to run toward finishing this essay due to the growing rest-lessness of some poems in an open notebook on my bed, I was interrupted by "other cares, other phantoms," which Beckett—another writer who blended high seriousness and playfulness—claims appear the instant the prior crisis is resolved. My best friend's father died. I couldn't block out the dreams and thoughts that were roused by this death. Then a letter a week later, announcing that my father's best friend had died, brought me to a full stop and put me back in contact with his wife and son and daughter. This family was my real family—since there were no other candidates!—in the periods when I flew east. The happiness I felt in their presence—deserves an incomplete sentence. But on the bus to Teaneck, New Jersey—there had been mayhem in Paterson the night before—I noticed that it also brought me in closer proximity to Williams, as did the architecture with its odd mixture of futuristic and plain old plain old. As did the trees, whose presence announced themselves powerfully, and in silence, except for the sound of the light wind ruffling their branches, which caused me to look up and see—the sky! And underfoot, the earth, the root clusters that insisted I pay attention—watch out where I'm going. I imagined all Williams might take in while doing house calls: the weather's chaos which, in approximating his internal life, his moods, his muse, also kept him focused on the eternal within the ephemeral, the universal within everyday occasions. He had figured out, before Simone Weil said it epigrammatically, that absolutely unmixed attention is what counts, a sentence that can be raised from the local to the universal if we substitute, or just add in thought, "awareness" for "attention." I pictured Williams reading his anti-elegy "Tract" in front of the mourners, whom I pictured as if out of Courbet's panoramic ensemble format *The Burial at Ornans*. "I will teach you my townspeople / how to perform a funeral—." His agitation is palpable. "Is it for the dead / to look out or for us to see / the flowers or the lack of them—or what?" There's nothing like feigned sincerity at a ceremony like this to rouse the ire of this poet who believes that remaining true to who you are is a redeeming force.

No wreathes please—

Better, it is incumbent upon Williams to instruct them to bring "some common memento," old clothes, books, and—still struggling to turn this burial into a proper funeral:

> For heaven's sake though see to the driver!
> Take off the silk hat! In fact

there's no place at all for him—
up there unceremoniously
dragging our friend out to his own dignity.

damn him—
the undertaker's understrapper!

Now that the superfluous stranger has been put in his place, Williams addresses the people who showed up mostly so that others would note they'd been there. I would wager that he hit upon this complex internal dialogue through the unbearable emotional pressure that both Keats and Eliot claimed brought them to this place, the poem, where the burden of the mystery is lifted. And unbeknownst to me, it must inform the choice to include "Tract" in this essay. I hear an echo of Hamlet's directions to the players and his rejoinder to Laertes, whose actions purport that his grief over Ophelia's death is greater than Hamlet's: "to outface me with leaping in this grave."

Then briefly as to yourselves:
Walk behind—as they do in France,
seventh class, or if you ride
Hell take curtains! *Go with some show*
of inconvenience; sit openly—

Question: Does the stress here fall on "some" or "show"?

SOME show

Or

some SHOW

I think Williams would stress SHOW, as would Hamlet, while Polonius, for whom advice is always mere repetition, would stress SOME—and look what havoc the different emphases wreak on the stability of the passage. In poetry, as in music, sung and unsung, tone and phrasing are everything: it's not what you say but how you say it. "Is there a sound addressed," Williams asks in "The Orchestra," "not wholly to the ear" when "the purpose of an orchestra / is to organize those sounds / and hold them / to an assembled order / in spite of the / 'wrong note.'" Is this so different from what Hamlet might have said to a group of traveling musicians and his retinue had he lived to reach seventy? It's the direct opposite, a systematic deconstruction of what his appearance, dressed in black, means to the suspect witnesses: "these indeed seem, for they are actions that a man might play."

In the context of "Tract" a little acting is a good thing because going through the motions erases the purpose of the funeral being held in public.

> show
> of inconvenience; sit openly—
> *to the weather as to grief.*
> *Or do you think you can shut grief in?*
> *What—from us? We who have perhaps*

And doesn't that in most instances throwaway word "perhaps" cause the reader to pause, consider, and take in the painful yet inexorable truths in these utterances? It is these deft, delicate touches that led Robert Lowell to figure out that you could get anything into a poem "if you could place it properly." And the idea is consonant with everything occurring in "Tract." For it to be a proper funeral, the group must open itself to the weather before it can experience grief, mourning. Perhaps Williams is often this emphatic because he wants to break through the puritanical streak that binds his friends and patients—Americans everywhere—to a grim resistance to reality they imagine will protect them from harm, when that approach will always produce the opposite result. The reality they imagine is a construct, a fantasy, a screen, which allows them to act out a certain scenario from which imagination is banned. Americans' mistrust of imagination has been well documented. Empirical proof is what Americans want, not the truth of the imagination. The latter is painful, and requires all of our resources. (*Resources* is another word that automatically leads to energy sources, food, anything but the inner resources, sustaining vision, when "survival is all that matters." But once again, the priorities are reversed because the latter is nothing without the former, beyond staying alive. Emerson talked about this—but who goes to Emerson and not the Wikipedia entry on the box of Honey Nut Cheerios?)

> perhaps
> *nothing to lose?* Share with us
> share with us—it will be money
> in your pockets.
>   Go now
> I think you are ready.

Share the loss of control which he brings across by dropping the punctuation he's been using. Go. "Go a little before." Williams is worked up, like Hamlet when he is about to witness thousands of men, for the sake of appearances, go

The Book of Samuel

to their graves like beds and all for a worthless plot of ground that hasn't even enough room to "hide the slain."

➡

Williams's interaction with people at every level of society gives rise to tensions that move him to draw sustenance from Shakespeare.

> The crowd at the ball game
> is moved uniformly
>
> by a spirit of uselessness
> which delights them—
>
> all the exciting detail
> of the chase
>
> and the escape, the error
> the flash of genius—
>
> all to no end save beauty
> the eternal—
>
> (SPRING AND ALL)

Simple language, hard ideas. It's a double-edged crowd. "Alive, venomous." And there is no contradiction between the philosopher and the poet, and the crowd, which Williams regards as an instance of communality; a oneness against the isolation that is the constant undercurrent of his despair and sense of being an alien surrounded by a family which will never quite feel at home here, the strains are so mixed. And in the conclusion, in a few broken lines, he sets himself apart from the people of privilege. With regard to the latter, Bob Dylan would concur, in a stanza from "Desolation Row," with the third line of the stanza characterizing Williams's ancestors: "And Ezra Pound and T. S. Eliot / Fighting in the captain's tower / While calypso singers laugh at them. . . ."

While back at the game "the crowd is laughing . . . without thought." Without thought! These lines from *Spring and All* are the embodiment of poetry—like the throwing of a spear in the midst of a melee in the *Iliad* or *Henry V*. The poem I've been quoting has no title. None of Williams's poems in *Spring and All* or *The Descent of Winter* have titles (with the exception of "A Morning Imagination of Russia"), and attributing titles like "The Red Wheelbarrow" to a poem that doesn't even begin with that line has been particularly ruinous, in that it has added to his reputation as a poet of the snapshot. These titles haven't cut Williams down to size; they've sawed him in half, so that most people are uninformed about what I choose to call—and he would, too—the Shakespearean reach of much of his writing. Shakespeare is in large part the subject of *Spring and All* and *The Descent of Winter*.

> The expense of spirit in a waste of shame
> is lust in action
>
> The petty fury that disrupts my life
> at the striking of a wrong key
>
> (WILLIAMS, "THE DRUNK AND THE SAILOR")

The only other section that has a title in either book is called "11 / 13 SHAKE-SPEARE."

> (Shakespeare) a man stirred alive, all round *not* minus the intelligence but
> the intelligence subjugated—by misfortune in this case maybe—subjugated
> to the instinctive whole as it must be, but not minus it as in almost
> everything—not by cupidity that blights an island literature—but round,
> round, a round world *E pur si muove*. *That* has never sunk into literature as it
> has into geography, cosmology.
>
> (*THE DESCENT OF WINTER*)

I have found no critical consensus with regard to Williams's poetry. Donald Davie and Charles Tomlinson made a strong case for him in England, but he was never taken up by the mainstream, and he is similarly dismissed in America too. Hugh Kenner observed that while English poetry derives from Shakespeare and the stage, American poetry owes its origins to sermons and declarations. It is no *simple* twist of fate that Williams should, as a matter of course, get roped in with the poets who tend toward the monotonic, while Williams is dialogic. Yet for Williams, the operative phrase is: "All the world's a stage and all the men and women merely players." Williams's locale performs a remarkably similar function to the stage, lending both context and absence to his poems. So much of what he writes takes place at a certain moment, in a certain place, under a certain pressure, and in which weather and environment add an element of drama. His doctor's rounds increase the likelihood of "imaginative suspense." "To drive the streets at all seasons is also my delight, alone in my car, though it is only to return home at the end of an hour." An hour. Like a one-act play. He continues. The third sentence could have been from Lorca:

> It is not unexciting, either. It is a formal game. It is also moderately dangerous. The duels with the other guy—or woman—who takes a wide swing into the right of way are a test of skill. Any moment's heedlessness is a potential accident. I pride myself on my escapes.

(THE AUTOBIOGRAPHY OF WILLIAM CARLOS WILLIAMS)

Williams, like Shakespeare, knew that it was arbitrary to apply any qualitative standard to poetry and prose. Shakespeare achieves suppleness in his prose passages that are unthinkable in blank verse. But their being written in prose doesn't mean they don't approach the highest poetry. Falstaff and the Fool are not the only great poets in Shakespeare's work who speak in prose.

Pretend for a moment that Williams was a mixture of Hamlet and Prince Hal and Hotspur. Just as Hal is ensconced with every layer of society and Hamlet is "loved by the distracted multitude," Williams's job puts him in a parallel situation. His patients are so often the poor, and his poetry is claiming the high ground. The imaginative suspense that Williams points to is very close to what Shakespeare accomplishes in act 1.4 when "a flourish of trumpets" leads Hamlet to such a moment as when he, looking with contempt at Claudius, says

> The King doth wake tonight and takes his rouse,
> Keeps wassail, and the swagg'ring upspring reels,
> And as he drains his draughts of Rhenish down
> The kettle-drum and trumpet thus bray out
> The triumph of his pledge.

Hamlet is observing a moment in time, but as his anger and disgust at what he sees grows, the language thickens, and he follows the thought through to

> This heavy-headed revel east and west
> Makes us traduced and taxed of other nations.
> They clepe us drunkards

The first two lines are replete with alliteration, and "this heavy-headed revel . . . traduced and taxed" picks up the pace in the name of momentum, while "east and west" and "taxed of other nations" reverse the momentum, as if the guilty party were already being tried in a courtroom. The phrase that follows is the clincher: it makes our blood boil, just as the "draughts of Rhenish" dull the wits of the usurper. I hear a period after "drunkards," but there's none in the text. The starkness of Shakespeare's end-stopped pause is immeasurably more effective than a full stop that would pull us back into a more rigid arena than Hamlet inhabits. And just as Hamlet questions the accepted worldview, and reflects that in his discourse, Williams works against expectation, against the grain, received ideas, and grasps for definitions, which never quite match the changed world that he reflects in his poems. And that word—"clepe" (the verb as befits a man of the future like Hamlet), or "clept" (the past participle as befits a man who's chosen to close off his future)—is transmogrified by a character who puts himself above the men he hires to do his killing for him, a murderer who reviles murderers: "In the catalogue ye go for men, / As hounds and grey-hounds, mongrels, spaniels, curs, / Shoughs, water-rugs, and demi-wolves are clept / All by the names of dogs" (*Macbeth*, 3.1). Speech patterns are revelatory. Williams has a lot of passages that approach this torment, clarity, jarring word choices and uncertainty. Because Williams's pattern is indeterminate his adjectives, sparingly used, can signal a powerful agitation that underlies Williams's vision. If you keep on poking around, as Dr. Williams is wont to do, trouble will find you. One moment you're three thousand miles and an ocean away from the bombing going on in Europe, the next moment you're at the source.

> The red brick monastery in
> the suburbs over against the dust-
> hung acreage of the unfinished
> and all but subterranean
>
> munitions plant
>
> . . .
>
> But ranks
> of brilliant car-tops row on row
> give back in all his glory the
>
> late November sun and hushed
> attend, before that tumbled
> ground, those sightless walls
> and shoveled entrances
>
> ("THE SEMBLABLES")

His language grows more combustible because the poem juxtaposes a façade of religion with the munitions plant. And he doesn't linger. And as he traces the sources of weaponry as a destructive force from Samuel Colt's factory in Paterson to the developments at Los Alamos, he gives his writing a boundary that is similar to the locale—the stage set of the suburbs. And he rants—like Hotspur—beside himself with impatience and the desire for action. He also shares with Hotspur, whose wife speaks no English, and he no Welsh, a language problem in the household.

A good many of Williams's shorter poems are singular instances of dramatic speech. The speaker is in a situation with almost as much context as in a play. And if Lowell emphasized Williams's racy colloquial free verse with its seamless blending of high and low diction as the example that led to his breakthrough in *Life Studies* and beyond, it was almost implicit that Williams's poems took place in contexts that added an incalculable dimension. If there is one poem by Williams that combines all these elements, it is "The Desert Music." The reader knows where Williams is, what he's doing, what he's thinking; and when and why he's being discreet. It's worth repeating that several of the finest minds that have existed on American shores were all in step with Williams's beat. Some of the flaws they had the good sense to see as growing pains. But why is it that Marianne Moore and Wallace Stevens could see his wild originality, his genius, which knew what it wanted and went after it—"O brave new world that has such people in't"—while today's poets and critics whose exemplars are Moore and Stevens have no use at all for Williams? If Helen Vendler leaves Williams out of an anthology of twentieth-century American poetry (Oppen and Zukofsky too, but that follows as the night the day), I can only think of one response: blow it off. We can't disallow people their blind spots and compulsion to adopt a position for or against, and there is no longer a consensus with regard to who the real poets are. Anything but.

The most important indicator of an artist's effectiveness is how he or she is regarded by other artists apart from the welter of critical response, which almost always lags a quarter century behind what their peers recognized. One form of this is homage. A revealing tribute of this kind occurs in Malcolm Lowry's novella *Through the Panama,* which derives an entire intertextual substructure from *Paterson.* Lowry positions a prose narrative in the columns that refers both to "The Rime of the Ancient·Mariner" and Williams's use of prose for grounding and contrapuntal effect in *Paterson*. If this sounds like guesswork on my part, I can assure you that it isn't because Lowry's alter ego Sigbjorn Wilderness composes an absurd "poem" consisting of safety instructions and signs it "Wilderness Carlos Wilderness." Lowry constructs a mischievous narrative of William Paterson—but *not* the William Paterson who founded Paterson, New Jersey. This incites a dizziness in the reader that is similar to the experience of reading some of the stories and letters that Williams intersperses throughout the prose sections of *Paterson*. Both William Patersons look back at a time when individuals took larger-than-life risks, America was still a frontier, and the English were still in their big colonial phase, such as the Darian expedition in 1698 in which William Paterson participated. One reason I'm drawn to this juxtaposition of Lowry and Williams is how remote the two men were in their approaches to the problem of living. Williams's poem and Lowry's novella, read in conjunction, teach you how to read each of them better than a critical exegesis. Both writers, equipped with humor, intensity, and a mastery of many registers of diction, used the local (Paterson), the finite (Lowry's ship)—the bound—in such a way that it becomes cosmological. The rubbing together of the two forms—the high and the low—creates a friction, which is what the reader finds so exhilarating and liberating. Williams is not normally associated with the idea of "fine writing" as was the inveterate reviser Lowry of *Under the Volcano,* and yet for Williams, it was a matter of deployment; he was always choosing how to wield his instrument. "Rigor of beauty is the quest."

As always with Williams, there's an implied substance that can be transformed in several ways: "the American grain" can mean *ingrained* but also includes two other possible transmutations—bread and alcohol. Williams was ignited by D. H. Lawrence's *Studies in Classic American Literature*. He takes Lawrence's idiosyncratic approach and applies it to actual history and historical figures where Lawrence stayed with the literature. *In the American Grain* was his first book with a commercial publisher, and as he describes the experience, "as a book, it fell flat [. . . he sees] success go skittering out the window." He was reduced to buying remaindered copies wherever he could. Another bust. But what kind of success was Dr. Williams the poet imagining for himself? Well, imagination of this sort knows no bounds. I doubt that the failure of *In the American Grain* could have been as bitter to Williams as the failure of *Let Us Now Praise*

Famous Men, James Agee's more titanic, journalistic, yet immediate text, was to him. I find it significant that Williams makes no mention of an ecstatic review of *In the American Grain* in *The Nation* by D. H. Lawrence. Williams ought to have felt anointed by Lawrence's approbation, but you wouldn't know it from his account. I find it curious in another way that the terms Lawrence uses to evaluate "this record of truly American heroes" are congruent with those I've been developing.

> The author is seeking out not the ideal achievement of great men of the
> New World but the men themselves, in all the dynamic explosiveness of
> their energy. The peculiar dynamic energy, this strange yearning and passion
> and uncanny explosive quality in men derived from Europe, is American,
> the American element. Seek out *this* American element, O American!, is the
> poet's charge.

➡

When I pulled out the record—vinyl—of Steve Reich's composition, *The Desert Music,* hoping for inspiration in hearing Williams, I looked at the liner notes as the pulsations were beginning. I felt affirmed in the slant I've been taking, and even found Steve Reich using a quotation I had planned to include.

> I was fascinated by the symmetry of his name—William Carlos Williams. I
> have continued reading his work to the present. I find Dr. Williams' finest
> work to be his late poetry, written between 1954 and his death in 1963 at
> age 80. It is from this period that I have selected the texts for *The Desert
> Music*—a period after the bombs were dropped on Hiroshima and Nagasaki.
> Dr. Williams was acutely aware of the bomb, and his words about it, in a
> poem about music entitled *The Orchestra,* struck me as to the point: "Say to
> them: / Man has survived hitherto because he was too ignorant / to know
> how to realize his wishes. Now that he can realize / them, he must either
> change them or perish."

On one plane, Williams exhibits an absolute trust in imagination, which subsumes every category he dispenses, including his "things." On another plane, if I were to isolate a flaw in his work, beyond a fragmentation that resulted from his frantic daily rounds, it is a tendency to hector, buttonhole the reader to pay attention to his verse technique. This is even an issue in a great longer poem like "The Desert Music," which starts like a shot out of a cannon:

—the dance begins: to end about a form
propped motionless—on the bridge
between Juárez and El Paso—unrecognizable
in the semi-dark

    Wait!

The others waited while you inspected it,
on the very walk itself   .

    Is it alive?

          —neither a head,
legs nor arms!

    It isn't a sack of rags someone
has abandoned here   .   torpid against
the flange of the supporting girder   .   ?

    an inhuman shapelessness,
knees hugged tight up into the belly

    Egg-shaped!

        What a place to sleep!
on the International Boundary. Where else,
interjurisdictional, not to be disturbed?

How shall we get said what must be said?

Only the poem.

Only the counted poem, to an exact measure:
to imitate, not to copy nature, not
to copy nature

NOT, prostrate, to copy nature
        but a dance! to dance
two and two with him—
    sequestered there asleep,
        right end up!

Once again I am in concord with the composer,

> There is another desert that is central to *The Desert Music:* White Sands
> and Alamogordo in New Mexico, where weapons of the most intense and
> sophisticated sort are constantly being developed and tested. Hidden away
> from the eyes of the rest of the world are these infernal machines that could
> lead to the destruction of the planet.

In *The Descent of Winter* Williams sets out to make "a big, serious portrait of
my time." Now that's funny because he proceeds to do anything but that. But
he does do it, beginning twenty-five years later in *Paterson* and *The Desert Music*
and *Journey to Love.* I'd never thought there might be a future-tense aspect to
his claim, given the fragmented way it's all presented. It wasn't until age and
disability forced him to stop and take stock, and in the process find a way to
unite the discrete particulars. But it was a musical form he wanted; a poem like
a musical score—which Steve Reich intuited. I think it helps the reader, too,
to know that these books, and *In the American Grain,* and a hundred short poems
(many of which are hived in the eminently portable *Selected Poems,* superbly
edited by Robert Pinsky), are a treasure of immeasurable value, almost a kind of
invention. And New Directions has made the act of reading Williams especially
pleasurable in printing his collected poems in two beautifully set and substantial
volumes (minus *Kora in Hell*), neither of which is as heavy as the Manhattan
White Pages.

Writing, as Williams saw it, rescued him from "all sorts of conditions," whatever
had upset him. And from the time he was involved in medicine, he had birth
and death at the touch of his fingertips every day. Whitman flourished when
he tended the wounded during the Civil War; Williams tended the wounded
continually, for his entire life.

His American contemporaries, mostly, had only themselves to think about,
while Williams was carrying bedpans and working fourteen-hour shifts; he
was like the people he lived among; a man whose first priority was to support
his family, wife, two children, and extended family. No question: Williams's
poems are sometimes rushed; incomplete; something like negatives waiting
to be developed; but by the time he went back, his mind was on the present
and future: there was—the day: the one thing that had to be celebrated for
what it was every day. The day is new again every day. And then there were
unborn babies in danger of receiving hospital parking tickets unless the good

Dr. Williams arrived and pulled them into the world: "a world unsuspecting beckons to new places." (Louis Zukofsky would title a 1934 collection *Anew.*) The doctor from Rutherford/Paterson had given poetry a fresh start. What critics are eager to earmark as an awkwardness of style may be the sign of an inimitable originality. Hemingway says it best:

> I might say that what amateurs call a style is usually only the unavoidable awkwardness in first trying to make something that has not heretofore been made. *Almost no new classics resemble other previous classics.* At first people can see only the awkwardness. Then they are not so perceptible. When they show so very awkwardly people think these awkwardnesses are the style and many copy them. This is regrettable. [Italics mine.]

Nothing could dissuade Williams from his sense of the rightness of his direction, no matter how much resistance he encountered. He kept in mind that poetry begins with an "ah!," a sense of surprise or of being taken unaware. "The cello / raises his bass note / manfully in the treble din: Ah, ah and ah! / together, unattuned / seeking a common tone" ("The Orchestra"). He also knew how to deploy a preverbal utterance that kept him in touch with the origins of the poetic act—wonder, awe, and an American "aw shucks"—like "Oya!" as in "The Cold Night."

> In April I shall see again—In April!
> the round and perfect thighs
> of the Police Sergeant's wife
> perfect still after many babies.
> Oya!

Throughout his medical rounds, Williams maintained a state of erotic awareness that borders on the unthinkable insofar as it implies holding two opposing concepts in the mind at the same time, caretaker and lover. His exclamation points, erect, are visible proof of his conundrum. But no one should imagine for an instant that Williams is not aware that some of his stratagems might be seen as simplistic. He lights up at the sight of almost anything that catches his eye in a certain mood—"along / the gravel of the ravished park, torn by / the wild workers' children tearing up the grass, / kicking, screaming" (from *Paterson,* book 1, section 3)—and it's this lighting up, this internal energy, this imagination that are magnetic; not the so-called "objects." These three lines—"it is only in isolate flecks that / something / is given off"—connect the particles that lie embedded within to his "particulars." The scientific perspective that orders

Williams's worldview offers neither hope nor consolation. He seizes every chance he gets to revel in the visible manifestations of change that the average person has been trained to overlook and deny.

I am hesitant to draw neat comparisons between writers; nonetheless, the link between D. H. Lawrence and Williams is both unavoidable and fruitful to pursue. Think of it: Lawrence, the (impatient!) patient; Williams the doctor. The patient, Lawrence, has his own physical disposition toward praise, toward intensity, toward exclamation and exclamation points. Both men have an almost unearthly contact with the earth and the underworld. Williams's book *Kora in Hell: Improvisations* and Lawrence's poem "Persephone," in addition to numberless other, less explicit examples, bear witness to this identification. Just as the vessels in Williams's frequently anthologized poem "The Yachts" are "scintillant in mists," *Kora in Hell* is aswarm with fulgurations, and provides the template for the improvisatory tone Williams would cultivate. The sea imagery that Eliot and Stevens preferred addressed a totality in a way that recalls Emerson's sermons. The abundance of glorious oracular passages owes its eloquence to the absence of chaos and its irritants. Williams's small craft are subject to the caprices of the "ungoverned sea," followed by "lesser and greater craft which, sycophant, lumbering, / and flittering,"—three layered words which illustrate Williams's immersion in an ocean of language where the moody sea gives them a moment in the sun so that they appear "youthful, rare, as the light of a happy eye . . . of all that in the mind is fleckless, free and / naturally to be desired"—a reprise for that trio of isolate words. But that second's pause alerts the reader to this poem's intimate connection to Thomas Hardy's rendition of just what the elements can do with anything man made—the more hubristic the better: "And as the smart ship grew / In stature, grace, and hue / In shadowy silent distance grew the Iceberg too." If there's justice to be had, I once gave a graduate class called "Poetry Now and How it Got There" and students who embraced all the cool poets who worked in open forms absolutely hated Hardy; and what they hated were his rhymes which they thought "irrelevant"—a judgment arrived at conveniently without any idea of how the architecturally minded poet created the forms he needed for each new poem.

The wind dies and the sailors, no longer on full alert, become pawns of the elements as the water "effaces about them in agony, in despair / until the horror of the race dawns staggering the mind." The effect is underscored by the conscious absence of punctuation between dawns and staggering ("dawns, staggering" or "dawns—staggering!") or anything that might tone down: "the whole sea become an entanglement of watery bodies . . ." their reaching hands ignored, their hoarse, desolate cries unheard while "rising / in waves still"— still!—"as the skillful yachts pass over." The effect: a muffled echo. The figure this poem makes brings to mind the shades in the *Inferno* where a moist tear that falls on the lips of the two entangled shades, freezes, binds them together for what has to be one of the world's worst kisses, and in addition their mass of hair is entangled and they become indistinguishable.

How unusual a phrase Williams has constructed here as if drawing an enviable line between the two arts: poetry and prose. And the violation must be set down so that you and I can be present at the event. Dawn: new day, new world. Williams knows Homer, as he knew Darwin, in his blood and bones. Any human engaging the sea is signing a pact with something larger than the prior conceptions that live in his mind, impersonating facts which are deleted by the surf crashing against a jutting cliff: "left never alone by the waves from all the winds that blow, as they rise one place then another." The word "dawns" is forever changed through Williams's placement of it and anticipated pleasure. A generally positive phrase has now taken on a meaning that exceeds our regulated fear.

And Williams knew his Dante, and "The Yachts" clearly (in its packed tercets and deployment of so many things the English language can do with the exception of regular meter and terminal rhyme—as he does in all his true poems) is a nod to the master whose terza rima pressed Italian to the limits of the known world. "It is no small thing," Dante reminds us at the start of the thirty-second Canto, "to render the bottom / of the universe, not for our language / that still howls 'mama' and 'papa.'"

And I think that the common complaint about Williams having written too much can be resolved by taking this thought to the next plane. When he is *in* his poem in the way Pollock meant when he spoke of being "in [his] painting," Williams can improvise like a great jazz musician. But when the painter or the jazz player improvises, they've prepared themselves mentally beforehand. Those "poems" by Williams that are really notes toward poems come about when he writes without having taken thought—with nothing like a melodic line

The Book of Samuel

to stray from while delaying return to the ecstasy of the listener. In the italicized passages of *Kora and Hell,* Williams reflects on his work in progress.

> *Carelessness of heart is a virtue akin to the small lights of the stars. But it is sad to see virtues in those who have not the gift of the imagination to value them.*
>
> . . .
>
> *Remorse is a virtue in that it is a stirrer up of the emotions but it is a folly to accept it as a criticism of conduct. So to accept it is to attempt to fit the emotions of a certain state to a preceding state to which they are in no way related. Imagination though it cannot wipe out the sting of remorse can instruct the mind in its proper uses.*

The subterranean influence on the poetic development of Carlos Williams was both doctor and patient: John Keats. And *Kora in Hell* has the urgency of Keats in his letters. The result of this circuitry is manifold. Lowry writes to David Markson:

> On the tragic plane you have Keats' identification with Chatterton, leading, [Conrad] Aiken once suggested, to a kind of *conscious* death on Keats' part. However that may be, it is a force of *life.* But also it is an operation of the soul. As you have observed—in fact as you have proved yourself—it can be clairvoyant.

If Keats underwent a conscious death in relation to Thomas Chatterton, the same could hold true of Williams to Keats. Williams's identification with the young surgeon, John Keats, and his untimely death allows him to come to terms with mortality in an unusually decisive way. Surely, Williams's "shine alone" in "El Hombre" is an allusion to Keats's more companionable "Bright star, would I were steadfast as thou art——." Williams's work is saturated in sound, and infused with the very assonance and open vowels that Keats struggled to evolve in "Bright Star"—"Not in lone splendour hung aloft the night"—and worked out "deep in the shady sadness of a vale" in *Hyperion* as well as the odes. He also took from Keats and adapted from the stepped-up pace of the newsreel quality of twentieth-century life, a longer apprenticeship than medical school required: the careful, rigorous, study of sound—the use of open vowels especially while resisting metrical regularity—break the pentameter!—and deftly employed consonance, assonance, slant rhymes. "Wood-winds / clarinet and violins / sound a prolonged Ah! / Ah!" And "The Orchestra" functions as both overture and entr'acte in his great late work *The Desert Music,* which consists of poems so memorable that Robert Lowell fired off a letter to the seventy-year-old, post–stroke victim Dr. Williams—after having read it aloud to his wife, Elizabeth Hardwick—that concluded with the highest praise: "They are poetry and *go beyond poetry.*"

The hybrid aspect of Williams's poetic gesture merges the impulses of both Keats's letters and poetry. Keats's letters helped Williams trust in rapid composition, which suited his temperament as well as his situation as a doctor on call. In his autobiography, one of the best written by an American, he has a charming evocation of how, the moment a patient left the room, he would elevate his typewriter and proceed where he left off until the next—inevitable—interruption. Williams is among those few modern poets who would *not* have consented to this catching line by Baudelaire: "Life is a hospital where each patient is obsessed by the desire to change beds." Williams knows that there is no escape, and he reiterates the friction that results from his coming to terms with reality in poem after poem. Part of the pleasure of reading through Williams's work is watching him develop and, miraculously, leap to even higher ground, "beyond poetry," after he has suffered a stroke. He doesn't want to change beds with another person or patient because his capacity for indwelling is so acute. He's in touch with the creatures of the sea and air. He's in concord with their natural process.

> The way he swipes his bill
>> across a plank
>
> to clean it,
>> is decisive.
>
> [. . .]
> an effigy of a sparrow,
>> a dried wafer only,
>>> left to say
> and it says it
>> without offense,
>>> beautifully;
> This was I,
>> a sparrow.
>>> I did my best;
> farewell.

("THE SPARROW")

His choice of a sparrow can't be accidental, and yet I don't imagine that he was thinking consciously of the following passage from Keats's letter at the moment that he wrote the poem.

> I scarcely remember counting upon any happiness—I look not for it if it be not in the present hour—nothing startles me beyond the moment. The Setting Sun will always set me to rights, or if a Sparrow come before my Window, I take part in its existence and pick about the gravel.

Even Williams's impulse to take a stroll—in the hope that the pendulum might swing back?—is bound up with the rocks he is forced to negotiate—as in the great "Walking—" section of *Paterson,* book 2. The sound in his poetry is suffused throughout, just in the way Keats said it should be, with no sign of any palpable design, and the hard and soft sounds often clash. Williams's walk is abrupt because he's on the move. And in the longer poems he's abrupt because he's on the move and never far from another rock, and the hard sounds register the resistance of reality; he is constantly forced to stay on full alert, change directions; and as he turns his eye will so often light on something magnetic, charged; a constant oblique reminder that those boulders and rocks—the ones underneath—are the source of the radium and uranium that will spur explosions of another order than has yet been divined. He would surely have been in concord with Osip Mandelstam that "a stone is an impressionistic diary of weather, accumulated by millions of years of disasters, but it is not only the past, it is also the future: there is periodicity in it. It is Aladdin's lamp penetrating into the geologic murk of future times" ("Conversations About Dante"). And Williams's lifelong apprenticeship allows for a running dialogue with Pound and his sculptural notions of poetry and *The Rock-Drill Cantos,* which looks ahead to Donald Davie's terrific and convincing *The Poet as Sculptor.* Williams is both Dante and Virgil (Malcolm Lowry calls him "Dr. Vigil") rolled into one. "The patient," Shakespeare reminds us, "must minister to himself." American poetry might have taken a different turn had Mandelstam's rousing and profound essay been available in English (I'm not sure it was even available in Russian then) in the years when Charles Olson's "Projective Verse"—to which Williams devotes a chapter in his autobiography— became the poetic credo for poets desperate to have their developing methods dignified by something authoritative to counter the consummate brilliance of the New Critics. Their acumen is fascinating and instructive, but almost constrictive, closure-crazed, hostile to the new; both offended and threatened by the young poets who appeared to have taken flight from Pound's line that "the first heave" was to "break the pentameter." I think that Coleridge, in "Christabel," and Dickinson in Dickinson and Whitman in Whitman had already done that. The American poem cannot replicate the monotonic, if wise, tradition of the sermon. My own interest in Robert Lowell entered a new phase when I took a closer look at what he'd done with the preacher's prose in "Jonathan Edwards and the Spider." The result sculptural, but also bruising. Lowell destroyed monumentality. His own breakdowns were a record of that havoc.

Williams's outrageousness is so affecting, bringing attention to things that go unnoticed in daily life and certainly in poetry until he appeared on the scene. And he never tires of reiteration. "It is a principle of music / to repeat the theme. / Repeat / and repeat again / as the pace mounts." There is no getting used to a world that is atomized in quite this way. Williams's predilection is also in step with philosophical movements of his time, with Husserl's phenomenology and Merleau-Ponty's revelation of the marriage between seeing and being—that emotions are not invisible, they are apparent on a face, in a gesture. Williams's writing partakes of these sorts of insights, and the reading draws pleasure from his programmatically unsystematic approach as his mind leapfrogs from rock to rock, "wires and stars" (*Spring and All*). The strength that his imagination derives from breaking the particular down into the particle, releasing its explosive potential in the mind, eventually must have its limitations as well. He moves at such a speed whether on foot or in his car that we can sense a man also escaping from his inner life.

Williams's early internalizing of his sense of difference enabled him to combine clarity and lyricism, as he reports from the underworld from which he derives his power. Even his negations are affirmative. He shares the sense of nothingness and alienation for which so many twentieth-century authors are reputed—with Kafka, Beckett, and Celan at the top of the list—but he adopts the other point of view. Instead of isolation, he chooses participation. The elegance and simplicity of the following lines from "The Descent" reveal just how unusual an attitude Williams assumes.

> The descent
>   made up of despairs
>   and without accomplishment
> realizes a new awakening:

The Book of Samuel

which is a reversal

of despair.

He participates to such an extent that by the time he conceives *Paterson,* he will come to create a veritable environment. Paterson: a city, a man, and "Pater-son," Hugh Kenner says, "the molecule of generative succession." The microcosm he creates or re-creates in *Paterson* alludes to the Passaic Great Falls as an energy source for hydroelectric power as well as the imagination of the poet doctor. He is capable of reducing the "source" to the particular just as the scientists in Los Alamos had isolated the atom. The fission of an atom of uranium produces ten million times the energy produced by the combustion of an atom of carbon from coal.

Think of it: Dr. Keats, Dr. Johnson, Dr. Williams, Dr. Zhivago. It must have been in Boris Pasternak's subconscious for thirty years since he had first come across a poem by this "Dr. Williams," a man who, like Pasternak, had an overwhelming fondness for the curious, individual, and inexplicable aspects of nature—the nature you encounter upon leaving your dacha, or under an oak tree in summer while a revolution turns the human world inside and out and the players—or actors—are replaced by men whose faith in their conviction of their own right-ness fills the void inside. His principles are uncannily close to those of Williams, whose poetry with its sense of location and immediacy recapitulates Pasternak's definition of art. "The clearest most memorable feature of art is how it arises, and in the telling of the most varied things, the finest works in the world in fact tell us of their own birth." In the act of naming, the poet brings out the inner nature of the nouns, who mix, separate, and mix with the other words. and sounds. If you can't break through the fog to get to the things themselves, then turn the words into the things, make the poem dynamic, let it follow its internal laws. And then the poem can get over its fear of being unfamiliar and, simultaneously, demand closer attention. All of yesterday is in the language of the poem now. It becomes exotic if you listen to it long enough. The rhythm of rivers served as a subliminal murmuring surge for Williams and other poets who could transform the pulse into momentum—Edmund Spenser, of course, Basil Bunting, who launches *Briggflats* with "Brag, sweet tenor bull, / descant on Rawthey's madrigal," the role of the Liffey in *Finnegans Wake,* Eliot's echoes of Spenser in *The Waste Land* and "The river is a strong brown god" in "Dry Salvages," Hart Crane's "Repose of Rivers," Elizabeth Bishop's "The Riverman,"

James Tate's "River Story," Stanley Kunitz's "River Road," the ceaseless stream of versions of Joni Mitchell's song "River." . . .

The image of Williams as a country doctor is true to life and comforting, but it distracts from how penetrating his eye can be into the nature of things. Many passages indicate that his overarching interest is not in the immediate remedy for a problem, even one such as hunger.

> We are not chickadees
> > on a bare limb
> > > with a worm in the mouth.
> The worm is in our brains
> > and concerns them
> > > and not food for our
> offspring
>
> ("TO DAPHNE AND VIRGINIA")

In the same poem, he says with an authority that only he, as far as I know, can manage:

> The mind is the cause of distresses
> > but of it we can build anew.
> > > Oh something more than
> it flies off to:
> > a woman's world,
> > > of crossed sticks, stopping
> thought. A new world
> > is only a new mind.
> > > And the mind and the poem
> are all apiece.

Williams's way of breaking things down, of atomizing the particular, has an explosive quality if we are open to it. It is with an admission of "defective means" that he allows himself the imperfection that will let him make the mistakes out of which he will compose his epic: *Paterson.*

> A dissonance
> in the valence of Uranium
> led to the discovery

Dissonance
(if you are interested)
leads to discovery

—to dissect away
the block and leave
a separate metal:

hydrogen
the flame, helium the
pregnant ash

If we think of his strategy as that of a scientist, then his words have an altered potency. He regards his discoveries in verse technique as part of an evolutionary process. He is nothing if not, to cadge the phrase Matthew Arnold used to define Homer, "rapid." No wonder he's captivated by the rapids! His method misleads some to see his words writ small. He diffuses his own process as he tries to keep a step ahead of a chain reaction.

The rhythm of the human gait is the beginning of prosody and, as Mandelstam asserted, "standing still is a variety of accumulated motion." And during this legendary walk in the third book of *Paterson,* Williams also reaches an impasse, which he incorporates into the open structure he's devised.

Blocked.
(Make a song out of that: concretely)

If Williams could be blocked, perhaps I can be allowed to backtrack and not be guilty of overlooking the obvious, that *Paterson* also evolves out of the falls. He uses this massive but local energy source as a vehicle through which to probe the creative and the destructive aspects of power and its sources. If there is a villain in this tale, it is none other than Alexander Hamilton. Williams never veers from two concerns: the fate of Native Americans—and women.

The first move toward harnessing the energy of the Passaic Great Falls was set into action by Alexander Hamilton in 1791, to create a Society for Establishing Useful Manufacturing. "Useful" would prove a profitable qualifier, since a mere forty years later Samuel Colt was able to open a factory where he could manufacture his patented Colt 45 revolver—featuring mother-of-pearl handles—and other "repeating weapons essential in securing the American frontier." This may be why Williams was so ignited by Lawrence's insight into a pervasive American guilt over the genocide of the Indians. In *In the American Grain* he locates Hamilton's desire

> to harness the whole, young, aspiring genius to a treadmill? Paterson he wished to make capital of the country because there was waterpower there which to his time and mind seemed colossal. And so he organized a company to hold the land thereabouts, with dams and sluices, the origin today of the vilest swillhole in Christendom, the Passaic River; impossible to recover the nuisance so tight had he, Hamilton, sewed up his privileges unto kingdomcome, through his holding company, in the State legislature. *His* company. *His* United States: Hamiltovnia—the land of the company.
>
> You violate your own concept of what history should be when you speak so violently.
>
> The pendulum must swing. Is it not time that it swung back?

Now we come to women. In addition to access to women's bodies without limit, he's also voyeuristic and girl crazy; but mostly he celebrates women, and studies their separate reality: "All women are fated similarly facing men." Having said this, I now encounter a passage in the unjustifiably maligned book 5 of *Paterson,* and I feel like he's read my mind. It's now said that his womanizing had more to do with intimacy than sex. It's extraordinary how the seventy-year-old poet regards a woman he espies on the street. How the focus shifts to her potential. And he knows that he's alone in the perception, just as she's alone walking the street where there is no one else to "witness."

> There is a woman in our town
> walks rapidly, flat bellied
>
> in worn slacks upon the street
> where I saw her.
>
>   Neither short
> nor tall, nor old nor young
> her
>   face would attract no
>
> adolescent.

The Book of Samuel

Now that caused me to pause, and then.

> Gray eyes looked
>   straight before her.

Without making too much of her gray eyes and Pallas Athene, he is enamored
of her independence, and the way he describes her is imbued with longing; hers
and his. He sees this stranger is his ideal reader. She's in male attire—a sign of
disdain for the norm, "as much as to say to hell // with you. Her / expression
was / serious, her / feet were small. // And she was gone!" Muse and mystery.
But it's not a game. He's sought her "daily without success," and if he sees her
again he'll speak to her, "too late!" And then:

> What are you doing on the
>
> streets of Paterson? A
> thousand questions:
> Are you married. Have you any
>
> children?

Hardly the tone a womanizer would take.

> And, most important,
>   your NAME! which
>   of course she may not
>
>   give me—though
>   I cannot conceive it
>   in such a lonely and
>
>   intelligent woman

Those are a lot of suppositions. Could he have meant "lovely" instead of "lonely,"
especially this man so cued into visual over internal traits? Meanwhile, he'd been
writing the great poem to his daughters-in-law, Daphne and Virginia, "who
live in a world apart." His acknowledgment of otherness, difference, inscruta-
bility—all of it—shows that his doctoring, his attending to the body, was only
half the story. "Lonely" is a bit of a supposition, but "intelligent," given the spare
amount of information—that's a fabulous leap. It's as though to be a woman like
this, fully herself, was a ticket to loneliness.

➤

A valuable book could be written on William Carlos Williams and frustration, and how he learned, while fulminating, to transform it, along with many of the poets with whom he became associated, like the Objectivists: Lorine Niedecker, George Oppen, Carl Rakosi, Charles Reznikoff, and Louis Zukofsky. The list itself is almost an emblem of the ways in which time can heal wounds, and proves that the race is not to the swift. In the 1970s and '80s, Oppen came to be accepted as a poet of unassailable lucidity and integrity whose work is now seen as on a par with that of any other modern American poet; now it is Louis Zukofsky's moment. At the time of this writing, Zukofsky has become the single most powerful stimulant, causing poets of different formal orientations to recast the way we think about poetry—even if not, sadly, from the ground up. The embrace of Zukofsky simultaneously vindicates Williams's quest for a new art form, although an emphasis on nonreferential language has impeded the link between language and environment that makes Williams and Oppen poets for the future. Williams would have resisted these current codifications. His restlessness and independence would have led him to assert, along with William Blake in *Jerusalem*, that ur-modern epic and prelude to *The Cantos*, *The Anathemata*, *Paterson*, *A*, "I must create a system, or be enslaved by another man's."

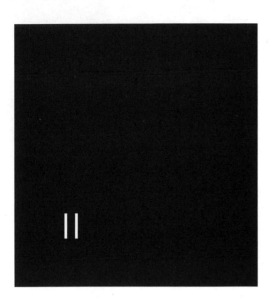

The Voyage That Never Ends: Hart Crane, Malcolm Lowry

As I was riding the bus to Mitla and gazing at the graded, layered mountain ranges, and the peasant plowing the field with two white oxen next to a disused tractor, I thought of how few works of art really stayed with me. And I remembered the injunction of Malcolm Lowry's contemporary Cyril Connolly, in *Enemies of Promise,* that an artist's sole responsibility was to create a masterpiece and that nothing else was worthwhile.

The way to go about writing a masterpiece is not necessarily by fixing the locus of the pressure on each line of a poem or each sentence of a novel. But Hart Crane and Malcolm Lowry consumed and tormented themselves daily with this task and considered themselves to be failures: not failures in comparison to their contemporaries, but in relation to the work which they had planned but could not execute. This would not be such a delicate and difficult matter had they not each produced masterpieces, works head and heels above those of their less ambitious, somewhat "saner," more tractable contemporaries, like Graham Greene and Archibald MacLeish. These works were masterpieces which they knew they could never exceed, only equal. (Yes, Crane might write a long poem that bettered *The Bridge,* but could he better, *on their own terms,* his best short and shorter poems, like "Legend," "Black Tambourine," "Repose of Rivers," "My Grandmother's Love Letters," "Praise for an Urn," and "O Carib Isle!"?) Perhaps it was this sense of failure they were trying to assuage which took the form of a thirst—a thirst alcohol only magnified.

➤

The conflicts of a life show up on the litmus of form. I pose the question: did the "problems" of Hart Crane and Malcolm Lowry result more from accumulated desperation or from a failure to find, in the long run, significant forms as artists? Or, to put it another way, did Crane and Lowry drink as they did because they were mysteriously tormented, battered inwardly by sexual confusions and unremitting longings for something more than "existence as *sold*" to them (Lowry's phrase, my emphasis), or because, as artists, or poets and novelists, they failed to find forms that allowed them *to go on* without extended blockage, hiatus?

Hart Crane went to Mexico in 1932 on a Guggenheim Fellowship, ostensibly to write a history of Mexico in verse: a spectacularly unrealistic project. He barely had time to get settled and write letters and a few poems before the year was out.

Malcolm Lowry (following in Crane's footsteps and aware of Ambrose Bierce's mysterious disappearance) wrote most of *Under the Volcano* in Mexico and conceived a trilogy (*The Voyage That Never Ends*) to rival Proust, Joyce, Mann, and Musil in its architectonic complexity.

What drew Lowry and Crane to Mexico? Certainly one reason was that it was possible to live more cheaply on a modest income there than in the United States or Europe: Crane could stretch his fellowship and Lowry his small allowance from his father.

Mexico offered "a collective desolate fecundity," which Lowry sought and Crane evoked in his last and perhaps greatest poem, "The Broken Tower."

Mexico was a kind of solution to the problem Henri Lefebvre sets forth in *Everyday Life in the Modern World:* "Our aim is to prove that a system of everyday life (in America and Europe) does not exist, notwithstanding all the endeavors to establish and settle it for good and all, and that there are only sub-systems separated by irreducible gaps, yet situated on one plane and related to it."

I have been walking for days in Oaxaca, the valley of the acacias. As you go higher, the town thins out and the air gets clearer. Each day I climb a little farther into the hills. I watch the clouds darken over the mountains. There's the sense of a city in flotation, of a place not fully of the world, a presence bordering on the magical, the marginal. The architecture is not so different from what it was five hundred years before. Steep streets sweep downward toward the zocalo and upward toward the mountains, mountains that hold the valley gently, mountains that build up the wall of the sky. There's mystery in the play of light-shadow over the landscape.

In the evening, we go to a Spanish restaurant whose balcony overlooks the zocalo. A demonstration which had been going on in the streets all day, on the avenues Juarez and Constitution, has moved to the center of town. They are demonstrating for more money for teachers and freedom of expression: ¡Viva La Libertad de Expresión! As we watch the demonstrators congregate, the sky turns black, lightning begins to flicker in the hills above the city, and thunder rumbles. It is as dark and ominous a sky as I have ever seen. It would have needed an El Greco or Albert Pinkham Ryder to do it justice. But the demonstrators seem oblivious to the symbolism of the weather, and in spite of the imminent deluge, continue to shout through megaphones.

Outside the bus depot of the Hotel Meson del Angel a dark-eyed child is bottle-feeding an infant. She looks up as if to say, do you think I was born to do this? The woman beside her on the street has set out half a dozen straw baskets brimful with dark roots and branches.

How advanced the Mayans and the Olmecs and the Zapotecs were. The mounds are still under excavation as we walk over them.

Each instant another minute layer is uncovered, as if these vast tumuli were metaphors for the process of knowing—always partially—our own minds.

The myriad maize and rain-gods seated like Buddhas; the mad, wild, expressive faces; the decorated skulls drilled all the way through.

Do the images on the stele arise from where the Indians settled? *In* the valley, *on* the mountain?

The beautiful place-names of the ruins: the ones with the soft x- sounds, like Uxmal; the ones with the drawn out ch- and tz- sounds, like Chichen Itza. Ruins are replete with steps that lead nowhere. Dusty side streets veer off into the blinding light; stretch through roofless houses and houses that are only roofs.

The poppy-red blossoms on the jacaranda trees.

Mexico is exotic; it's a culture that still has celebrations, outlets for the inner, darker self; it offers release from the fixity of worldly identity—the name attached to the face. Everyday life is at times a celebration, a festival, even a festival for the dead.

Travel in Mexico is like the fiesta: while it opens you up it also wounds.

Mexico provides a perverse twist on traditional values. When a plan to share a house with friends in Cuernavaca fell through in the spring of 1970, I decided to go to Mexico anyway.

I went with a woman I scarcely knew, but was fiercely attracted to. We were en route to Mexico City, from where we'd catch a bus to Cuernavaca, when I changed my mind in midair, changed the destination of our tickets when we stopped to change planes in Austin, and went on to Puerto Vallarta instead, to begin the summer in some proximity to the sea after the year in the city.

Why Puerto Vallarta? Once, returning from Mazatlan to Los Angeles with my father, we changed planes at a small airport with a single runway. I had no sooner walked a few steps past the "terminal" hut than I was in the jungle. Vines from the nearby trees choked the gutters under the eaves. A brash, arrogant film crew stomped through, en route to "Puerto Vallarta"—the place-name hung in the air like a song named after a town, "Córdoba," or "Laredo." I asked my father where it was, what it was like. "Now that *was* a paradise," he said, and I trusted his judgment though I knew he'd never been there, "but now it's ruined." He thought I was slow, and I was: I just couldn't grasp how a paradise could be ruined *overnight* because some movie had been shot there. The movie took it off the map for him, and the name of the town remained in the back of my mind as a place I would have to see for myself some day, just to see it.

In Puerto Vallarta the sea blazed. In one torrential summer rain, I huddled in a doorway and saw some children cutting the tail off an iguana. And one afternoon, while I was walking aimlessly on the sun-baked main street, two barely disguised plainclothes cops, dressed in Hawaiian shirts and light-colored polyester slacks with pockets bulging just below their shirttails, requested to see my passport, which I'd left back at the top-floor villa apartment we'd rented dirt cheap.

This gave the cops an excuse to inspect the apartment. One of them unearthed, in the top drawer of the dresser, unhidden, a wooden hash pipe in the shape of a turtle that a hippie social scientist had given me, from which he dislodged a few specks of tar. I decided on this story, which, as it turned out, was neither a good nor a bad tactic and which may or may not have been the full truth: "I had hoped to score some hash in Mexico, but once I discovered it was illegal, I decided not to."

His silent, reactive, mime-like partner came across a copy of the Bible, a new translation of the Old Testament my stepfather had given me and which I'd brought along to study Ezekiel—to help myself better understand Blake and Eliot.

They exchanged solemn, sincere glances. "Do you read this?" "Yes." They looked at me now with no uncertain respect. I could sense our fortunes were turning, but still feared incarceration in a Mexican jail. From the way the first cop squinched his features and grimaced, I thought they might take the pipe, issue me a warning, and split. But no, they decided to leave my fate up to the Captain.

It seemed wet as a cave inside the Captain's office in the jail, where I was seated in a straight-backed chair facing his desk. I sat up very straight. In his blues, the Captain at least looked like a cop. There was no excess flesh on his bones. Everything about him said: no nonsense.

"Des ees hash," he said, tapping out another tarred speck from the pipe. "It's just tar," I said, "and it's been there for a long time. Someone gave me that pipe in New York." "No. I say ees hash. I could throw you in jail right now."

He looked up at the first cop to corroborate his findings. The first cop leaned over and whispered something in the Captain's ear.

"My man tells me you read the Bible." "All the time, sir, all the time." "All right, since this is all we found . . . youcangothistime," he said, running the words together as he rose to shake my hand.

➤

It is always tempting to look at the crises of writers in light of their personal histories. The lives concern me here *only* as they intersect with the art. Crane and Lowry were both deeply estranged from their families, offspring of wealthy businessmen who were unreachable.

Crane was moving toward a reconciliation with his father, who died when Hart was in Mexico. This inventor and manufacturer of the Life Saver candy was no fool—he wrote Hart that "The River" was the best thing he had done. Hart's relationship with his mother, Grace, was an emotional catastrophe. Her demands increased as she became less focused to the point that Crane felt like he was in loco parentis for his own parent.

Lowry abandoned any hope of intimacy with his father as a teenager and, before consenting to go to Cambridge, shipped out as a deck hand on a tramp steamer. At nineteen he wrote and asked Conrad Aiken to serve in loco parentis. His first letter to his literary hero ("I know you are a great man in your own country") has the feel of "Après le Deluge" and shows what Lowry could do right from the start when he wasn't pressing:

> I have lived only nineteen years and all of them more or less badly. [He quotes from Aiken's "The House of Dust."] I sat opposite the Bureau-de-change. The great gray tea urn perspired. But as I read, I became conscious only of a blur of faces: I let the tea that had mysteriously appeared grow clammy and milk-starred, the half veal and ham pie remain in its crinkly paper; vaguely, as though she had been speaking upon another continent, I heard the girl opposite me order some more Dundee cake. My pipe went out.
>
> . . . The sunlight roared above me like a vast invisible sea. The crowd of faces wavered and broke and flowed. . . . Sometime when you come to London, Conrad Aiken, wilst hog it over the way somewhere with me? You will forgive my presumption, I think, in asking you this.

➤

The Book of Samuel

Disaster dogged Lowry's heels every step of the way. He lost the suitcase that contained the manuscript for his first novel, *Ultramarine,* and had to reconstitute the book from notes. To write *Lunar Caustic* he checked himself into Bellevue and then was "mistaken" (like the Pulitzer-hungry journalist in Samuel Fuller's *Shock Corridor*) for one of the mad. It was fifteen years before his second novel, *Under the Volcano,* appeared. His squatter's shack in Canada went up in flames, consuming his magnum opus in progress, *The Voyage That Never Ends.*

The contradictions, the inevitable failure of Crane's verse epic already lay in the tortured history of Mexico itself, in the heart of the very problem he intended to wrestle with: the Conquest. Unable to reconcile himself to his project, unable to ply contradiction as "a lever of transcendence" (Simone Weil), Crane leapt into the sea, into oneness.

> As silent as a mirror is believed
> Realities plunge in silence by . . .

Lowry's suicide was more ambiguous. He didn't exactly intend to kill himself, and his death was labeled Death by Misadventure. While on a walking tour of England (always dangerous inflammatory ground for him), he and his wife had a fight, and he swallowed booze and pills, perhaps not enough to kill him in themselves, but a bad enough combination to make him choke on his own vomit. This eruption seemed all the more cruel in that it followed the healing years in Canada with Marjorie, all the work he had done on himself toward a fresh start—for which no one had ever been more willing.

> One evening on the way back from the spring for some reason I suddenly thought of a break by Bix in Frankie Trumbauer's record of Singing the Blues that had always seemed to me to express a moment of the most pure spontaneous happiness. I could never hear this break without feeling happy myself and wanting to do something good. Could one translate this kind of happiness into one's life? Since this was only a moment of happiness I seemed involved with irreconcilable impulses. One could not make a moment permanent and perhaps the attempt to try was some form of evil. But was there not some means of suggesting at least the existence of such happiness, that was like what is really meant by freedom, which was like the spring, which was like our love, which was like the desire to be truly good.
>
> ("THE FOREST PATH TO THE SPRING")

Crane and Lowry were unwilling to make any concession to what Frost praised in Wordsworth—"necessary dullness." Everything had to be a monumental undertaking or it wasn't worth doing. (Monumental and coherent, like [theoretically] *Ulysses*.)

Though drawn to grandiose schemes with cosmic implications, they were both writers of consciousness, not of history. Crane's imagination was synthetic, not dialectical. Lowry said that any defect in *Under the Volcano* sprang from "something irremediable in the author's equipment" that was—he confessed with remarkable candor in his letter of appeal to his publisher, Jonathan Cape—

> subjective rather than objective, a better equipment, in short, for a certain
> kind of poet than a novelist.

Crane was the kind of man who would allow himself to become converted by a book, and more fierce in his defense of an idea that bloodied him than the author might have been. The most nervous moment in Crane's letters is when he undertakes to read Spengler.

Eliot may have written—exploded and secreted, actually—*The Waste Land* at different times because it was a poem he had to write, but Crane interpreted the act as another of Eliot's definitive demonstrations of how the individual talent should incorporate tradition: one had to mix the symbolic and the real, the modern and the ancient, in such and such a way. Crane is at his most Eliotic in "General Aims and Theories" when he writes of what he set out to do in "For the Marriage of Faustus and Helen":

> to embody in modern terms (words, symbols, metaphors) a contemporary
> approximation to an ancient human culture or mythology . . . build . . .
> a bridge between the so-called classic experience and many divergent
> realities of our seething, confused cosmos of today, which has no formulated
> mythology yet for classic poetic reference or for religious exploitation. . . .

Some passages in the poem accomplish this desired synthesis ("I found 'Helen' in a street car"):

The Book of Samuel

And yet, suppose some evening I forgot
The fare and transfer, yet got by that way
Without recall,—lost yet poised in traffic.
Then I might find your eyes across an aisle,
Still flickering with those prefigurations—
Prodigal, yet uncontested now,
Half-riant before the jerky window frame.

But later, in the midst of struggling with *The Bridge,* Crane would pay the price for having taken Eliot straight, and lost confidence in the twisting, uneven passages that astonish the reader when metrics and mischief transcend though the poem continues to lurch.

Crane and Lowry created the myths by which they are judged. Their great works are not failures: they are great works.

Crane and Lowry found apt objectifications in the bridge, the bell tower, and the two volcanoes, Popocatepetl and Ixtaccihuatl. But in their respective use of Brooklyn Bridge and the volcanoes they came dangerously close to placing the symbol OVER the real:

> O harp and altar, of the fury fused,
> (How could mere toil align thy choiring strings!)
> . . .
>
> Ixtaccihuatl and Popocatepetl, that image of the perfect marriage, lay now clear and beautiful on the horizon under an almost pure morning sky. Far above him a few white clouds were racing windily after a pale gibbous moon. Drink all morning, they said to him, drink all day. This is life!

What are the artistic consequences of employing an aesthetic that goes against the grain of one's gifts? Structure becomes external. Technique becomes an overriding concern. Joyce and Eliot and Kafka rarely mention adopting techniques (the latter had contempt for Apollinaire's "pyrotechnics" in "Zone"). But Crane and Lowry obsessed about structure and technique all the time. They were both eclectic, consciously cadging montage from John Dos Passos and William Carlos Williams. This from Crane's "The River":

Stick your patent name on a signboard
brother-all over-going west-young man
Tintex-Japalac-Certain-teed Overalls ads
and lands sakes! under the new playbill ripped
in the guaranteed corner-see Bert Williams what?

These passages from *Under the Volcano:*

DAILY GLOBE intelube londres presse collect following yesterdays
headcoming anti-Semitic campaign mexpress propetitionsee tee emmamexworkers
confederation proexpulsion exmexico quote small jewish textile manufacturers
unquote twas learned today per reliable source that german legation mexcity actively
behind. . . .

The dehydrated onion factory by the sidings awoke, then the coal
companies. *It's a black business but we can use you white: Daemon's Coal. . . .*
A delicious smell of onion soup in sidestreets of Vavin impregnated the
early morning.

Lowry found new uses for montage in a literary work, as when the poster for
the film *Las Manos de Orlac* (*The Hands of Orlac*), playing in Quahnahuac on the
day in which the novel takes place, reappears at strategic moments in the book,
and it becomes, by extension (as every such repeated image does in *Under the
Volcano*), a symbol of the book itself. *Orlac* symbolizes the Consul's misuse of his
powers; he becomes a kind of black magician, another double within the book's
plethora of doubles.

Yet what a complicated endless tale it seemed to tell, of tyranny and
sanctuary, that poster looming above him now, showing the murderer
Orlac! An artist with a murderer's hands; that was the ticket, the hiero-
glyphic of the times. For really it was Germany itself that, in the gruesome
degradation of a bad cartoon, stood over him.—Or was it, by some uncomfortable stretch of the imagination, M. Laruelle himself?

In *Las Manos de Orlac*, a pianist, whose hands are somehow (I have never seen it)
ruined by a train accident, has a murderer's hands sewn on by an evil Doctor
Gogol. And so the pianist, in good doppelganger fashion, becomes a murderer
against his conscious will. I think Lowry was drawn to this tale because he liked
the idea of an external agent being the cause.

For a more immediate sense of what *The Hands of Orlac* was really like, I must look to another of Lowry's doubles, Graham Greene, who reviewed *Orlac* (as *Mad Love*) during his sojourn as a film critic while he was writing *The Power and the Glory*.

> Guiltily I admit to liking Hands of Orlac because it did make me shudder a little when Dr. Gogol grafted the hands of a guillotined murderer onto the smashed stumps of Orlac, the great pianist whose hands had been destroyed in a railway accident, and because Herr Karl Freund's romantic direction did "put across" the agreeable little tale of how the dead murderer's fingers retained a life of their own, the gift of knifethrowing, an inclination to murder. . . .

Even sharper is his praise of Peter Lorre:

> Those marbly pupils in the pasty spherical face are like the eye-pieces of a microscope through which you can see laid flat on the slide the entangled mind of a man: love and lust, nobility and perversity, hatred of itself and despair jumping out at you from the jelly.

And Graham Greene is great when he is the least programmatic; I like the travel book that's referred to as the rehearsal for *The Power and the Glory* better than that overrated novel. It's painful to think of what Lowry might have accomplished if he could have accessed fallibility to the extent Greene does throughout his diverse and productive career.

➤

The Consul, a shell of a man, must become no-man, like Odysseus in the cave of the Cyclops, in order to become himself again, and see things shorn of an alcoholic haze and heightening. Wandering through a plaza with wooly nerves, the Consul is drawn toward a Ferris wheel, a "little Popocatepetl":

> ¡BRAVA ATRACCIÓN!
> 10 C MÁQUINA INFERNAL

Again Lowry is throwing a little wink toward his own life. He asked his French translator, Mlle. Oarisse Francillon, if she could smuggle a copy of her translation to

> Jean Cocteau, and tell him I have never forgotten his kindness in giving me a seat for La Machine Infernale at the Champs Elysees in May, 1934. . . .

And so you see his infernal machine comes back to torment the Consul in Chapter VII.

His worldly identity is wrested away from him as he is flung about and then hangs upside down in the grip of this "infernal machine," the sensation of falling "unlike anything, beyond experience."

> Everything was falling out of his pockets, was being wrested from him, torn away, a fresh article at each whirling, sickening, plunging, retreating, unspeakable circuit, his notecase, pipe, keys, his dark glasses he had taken off, his small change he did not have time to imagine being pounced on by the children after all, he was being emptied out, returned empty, his stick, his passport—had that been his passport?

Lowry was a Cambridge-educated Englishman living unmoored in the Third World. (He could not, like Graham Greene, change locales with each book.)

The Liverpool cotton market "fluctuated nervously on the day Clarence Malcolm Lowry was born in 1909," the son of a successful and teetotaling cotton merchant (crowned England's Best-Developed Man of 1904). His mother, remote and unaffectionate, was roused to interest by her son's eventual success, but not enough to read any of his work. Lowry had his share of handicaps at a young age: an apparently minuscule penis and sight-endangering eye-ulcers. But the latter did not stop him from becoming a good enough golfer by the age of fifteen to win a two boys' championship at Holyoke. At seventeen, inspired by the sea stories of Joseph Conrad and Eugene O'Neill, he shipped out on the SS *Pyrrhus* on a voyage to the Far East. (Against his protestations, he was chauffeured to the docks in the family's Minerva, and relentlessly ragged for it throughout the voyage.) This disappointing journey, which taught him another form of the very snobbery he was trying to escape—it was rampant aboard ship, infecting everyone from cook to boatswain to carpenter—supplied the material for his brilliant but derivative first novel, *Ultramarine*. Apart from this stint as a deck hand, the Leys- and Cambridge-educated Lowry never had a job; he survived on a monthly allowance until he was almost forty.

Both Crane and Lowry felt orphaned before they arrived in Mexico with its cult of orphans, "orphanos."

I remember walking, in the summer of 1970, across the courtyard of the orphanage in Guadalajara where José Clemente Orozco's great mural is housed. Walking from the silence of that space into the maniacally kinetic howl of his work. (Better for it to be housed in an orphanage than in a church.) No one has rendered force more viscerally than Orozco, who harnessed the erotic shapes of surrealism and merged them with a cubist rigor. And fragmentation here provides its own quota of torque. My footsteps echoed. Where were the orphans?

Orozco shows not only the horrors of war, but the historical process through which the use of force becomes preeminent. Force permeates the living: the fuselage in the horse's belly makes him reel with agony. Orozco knew in his bones that the attempt to force Mexico into a European mold left a howl at the center, the cry of the orphaned, those who, as Lowry has Dr. Vigil (Virgil) say, "have nobody them with."

I was not prepared for what I had seen and longed to rest in the shadows under the colonnades.

The Third World/the desert—these are like a chemical mixture that magnifies and highlights the core of certain frustrations.

Nowhere is this anguish more apparent than in Antonioni's *The Passenger* when Jack Nicholson's character "Locke" falls to his knees in the sand beside his broken-down Land Rover—it is a moment of ultimate, pure frustration, which mirrors his spiritual crisis. The desert, with its codes that the reporter (Locke) cannot understand, cannot *process,* becomes a source of terror in which the mind can only break itself. The values of Western civilization are thrown into question by this world of silence, of eternal waiting. A man passes on a camel in a kind of final comment. Locke realizes that what he thought was true is only a partial truth, that what he took for reality is only part of reality, i.e., a man in a Land Rover is essentially superior to a man on a camel. But in the desert this is not so.

Crane and Lowry were spiritually exiled from a literary community that had put aside the verbal rhetoric, the richness, and the grandeur they sought. They resented the limitations and constraints imposed upon them by the ethos of the time.

> Though tragedy was in the process of becoming unreal and meaningless it seemed one was still permitted to remember the days when an individual life held some value and was not a mere misprint in a communiqué.
>
> (*UNDER THE VOLCANO*)

Most modernists were able to take for granted a vast storehouse of meaning and symbol which allowed them to stray, digress, and play without evident strain. Their work is playful and confident and almost serene in spite of its "dark" themes.

Lowry and Crane tried to do with premeditation what Joyce and Eliot did with irony, panache, and nerve, and neither trusted the spontaneity, the pulsing electric responsiveness which William Carlos Williams and D. H. Lawrence employed—that submission to the process of working itself.

Here's the catch. It could be argued that neither Williams nor Lawrence ever wrote a single poem or novel as great, as *finished,* as any of a dozen poems by Crane or *Under the Volcano,* but nor were they "finished" by the writing of a work. One work cleared the ground for the next work.

Even Proust "had not gone in search of the two uneven paving-stones upon which [he] stumbled." It was the "fortuitous and inevitable fashion" in which this occurred that showed him the truth of the past, and how lost time could be retrieved, brought back to life. His discovery has the force of a revelation which owes everything to chance. "What we have not had to decipher," he writes, "to elucidate by our own efforts, what was clear before we looked at it [plans, stratagems, symbols] is not ours."

Robert Lowell, whose work represents a bizarre fusion of elements in Crane and William Carlos Williams, called Crane "the Shelley of our age." To enter the realm of pure possibility for a moment, it seems to me that Shelley has a poem, "Julian and Maddalo: A Conversation," that might have served as a model for Crane's Mexican project. Formal discoveries are contextual as well as metrical, and the graceful movement of Shelley's poem has as much to do with the situation he creates for his "characters" to engage in dialogue in their movement through physical space as it does with his deft heroic couplets: a conversation between Julian and Maddalo is conducted—in an almost electrical sense—as they ride along the Venetian shores at dusk.

> So, as we rode, we talked; and the swift thought,
> Winging itself with laughter, lingered not,
> But flew from brain to brain—such glee was ours,
> Charged with light memories of remembered hours,
> None slow enough for sadness: till we came
> Homeward, which always makes the spirit tame.

The movement through imagined space draws our attention away from the closure of rhyme. "Julian and Maddalo" is as provisional as it is unwilled; it feels as if it wrote itself; it has the ballast—the gravity—most of Shelley's poems lack. But nothing has been lost in terms of aspiration—he has his eye on a moving object—from the "hillocks, heaped from ever-shifting sand" in the

> waste
> And solitary places; where we taste
> The pleasure of believing what we see
> Is boundless, as we wish our souls to be:

to the endearing moment when Maddalo's child "after her first shyness was worn out" can be seen "rolling billiard balls about." And I like to fantasize that just as Shelley projects his affectionate "quarrel" with Byron onto Maddalo, Crane might have dramatized his own conflicts and fashioned a Cortez out of his more severe arguments with Tate, Winters, and others. And had a good time doing it.

The bias in American modernism, in Pound, Williams, Moore, even Eliot, was toward a hard, sinewy, antipoetic (non-Romantic/Victorian) style. It was an attempt to purge themselves of the afflatus of the late nineteenth century and make it possible for poetry to renew itself by taking on some of the materials and textures of prose.

Crane and Lowry wouldn't settle for a flattened idiom. They wanted to pull out all the stops, and didn't see why their language shouldn't be as rich and supple as that of the Elizabethans. They wouldn't accede to the implicit guidelines as to what writing at that time should be: Pound's "direct treatment of the thing"; Hemingway's "iceberg," with nine-tenths underwater.

Lowry's gesture is closer to that of Wolfe and Faulkner than to his countrymen born at the same time as he—Waugh, Orwell, Auden, Spender, Day Lewis. He comments wryly on his remoteness from the world of letters in "Through the Panama."

> I am capable of conceiving of a writer today, even intrinsically a first-rate writer, who simply cannot understand, and never has been able to understand, what his fellow writers are driving at, and have been driving at, and who has always been too shy to ask. This writer feels this deficiency in himself to the point of anguish. Essentially a humble fellow, he has tried his hardest all his life to understand (though maybe still not hard enough) so that his room is full of *Partisan Reviews*, *Kenyon Reviews*, *Minotaurs*, *Poetry* mags, *Horizons*, even old *Dials*, of whose contents he is able to make out precisely nothing, save where an occasional contribution of his own, years and years ago, rings a faint bell in his mind, a bell that is growing ever fainter, because to tell the truth he can no longer understand his own early work either.
>
> Despite this, he still heroically reads a few pages of William Empson's *Seven Types of Ambiguity* each night before going to sleep just to keep his hand in, as it were, and to keep up with the times.

Lowry wrote to Jacques Barzun that he had never read all of *Ulysses*. But he knew how it worked: that every word in the novel referred to something else, that nothing had been left to chance. So Joyce's 7 Eccles Street becomes Lowry's magical cabalistic 7 in *Under the Volcano*.

"Here we come to seven," Lowry writes to Jonathan Cape,

> the fateful, the magical, the lucky good-bad number and the scene in the tower, where I write this letter. By a coincidence I moved to the tower on January 7. . . . My house burned down on June 7; when I returned to the burned site someone had branded, for some reason, the number 7 on a

burned tree; why was I not a philosopher? . . . Philosophy has been dying since the days of Duns Scotus, though it continues underground, if quacking slightly. Boehme would support me when I speak of the passion for order even in the smallest things in the universe: 7 too is the number on the horse that will kill Yvonne and 7 the hour when the Consul will die.

And since everything in the book is doubled, trebled, and quadrupled, the Consul, whose sexual shyness is telegraphed when he's caught fucking in a sand trap on a golf course by Jacques Laruelle in the flashback in chapter 1, is hurled into the ravine in chapter 12. Every page of *Under the Volcano* expresses this tension, like the real but also symbolic rider who always seems to be losing control, drunk, "sprawling all over his mount, his stirrups lost, a feat in itself considering their size, and barely managing to hold on by the reins, though not once did he grasp the pommel to steady himself." This tension finally explodes when Yvonne is trampled to death in a dark wood by a rearing horse, as the Pleiades wheel like a transmogrified white whale. The "sharp pistol-like report, from somewhere ahead, as of a backfiring car," which she hears, is from the bullet that kills the Consul; it spooks the "riderless horse," "with number seven branded on its rump," who runs off into the forest and causes her to meet a real death in a "forest of symbols."

There is a dryness which draws one to Mexico. (Heraclitus says, "A dry soul is wisest and best.") All this week I built up a great thirst—how blessed a Coke seems with its heady mixture of water and sugar and caffeine. And yet, seeking relief from the blinding light in Milta in a cavernous cantina which sells everything under the sun, I look at the bottles of mescal, where a slice of carrot has been inserted to replace the glorious horrific worm, with a kind of longing, a thirst that's been instilled by the very maguey plant, which looks like an octopus on its back, that mescal comes from.

My disappointment in mescal did not originally stem from its smelling like ether or the hideous taste—only that the high is merely alcoholic, not hallucinatory, like mescaline.

Lowry's thirst found its form in what he called Mexico's "churrigueresque"—florid—architecture which paralleled—and satirized—his book's "overloaded style." He was driven to anthropomorphize Mexico's "tall exotic plants . . . perishing on every hand of unnecessary thirst, staggering, it almost appeared, against one another, yet struggling like dying voluptuaries in a vision to maintain some final attitude of potency, or of a collective desolate fecundity."

In Mexico, Lowry found the landscape and culture mirrored his aesthetic concerns. His practice is congruent with this culture where everything stands for something elsewhere—the full moon *is* the lopped head of a goddess. Lowry interpreted events in his life as signs and portents and wanted them to assume symbolic significance in his work, like the shifting shapes of the volcanoes that reveal the mind's cliffs and falls.

> Popocatepetl loomed, pyramidal, to their right, one side beautifully curved as a woman's breast, the other precipitous, jagged, ferocious. Cloud drifts were massing again, high-piled, behind it. Ixtaccihautl appeared.

Even the serpentine ravine where the Consul is hurled to a "dingy" death was waiting for Lowry in the "real" Cuernavaca.

Spain did not transplant to Mexico. And Indian Mexico lies like a ruin under Spanish architecture.

Ruin as final form.

All that remains of the sacred is the silence.

The value of a ruin is inseparable from how much grandeur it has lost. How pure and fabulous the projections of lost magnificence! Loss is somehow at the heart of it, loss of what was never possessed except communally.

I take as germane to current aesthetic practice Godard's statement that his films have a beginning, a middle, and an end, *but not necessarily in that order.*

Strange as it may seem now, Lowry was always in danger of being compared to writers as different as Graham Greene (whose *The Power and the Glory* "takes place" in Mexico, and Greene's whisky priest is not so far removed from Lowry's drunken Consul) and Charles Jackson (whose *Lost Weekend* Lowry nicknamed *The Drunkard's Rigadoon*).

D. H. Lawrence had pointed to what energies could be stirred on a journey down what Graham Greene would call *The Lawless Roads,* the travel book, the record of a brutal trip through Chiapas, that was his rough sketch for *The Power and the Glory.* I think that these Englishmen, whose best work is equal to anything written in the language, were also drawn to Mexico because their concept of repression was also inextricable from the insularity of the England in which they were raised; each knew he would have to strip off mask after mask to tap into the throttled energies that brought with it the phobias through which Greene and Lowry have come to be known. To rebel against the externally unruffled nature of their backgrounds, Greene and Lowry, heeding a call from *daimon,* demanded to be in places where the external horrors exceeded their fears.

Neither man could drive or read a map. In *Journey Without Maps,* a second travel book by Greene that would supply him with a point of reference for *The Heart of the Matter,* he clues us in to his dilemma with this insight: "But in Africa one couldn't avoid them [rats, mice, moths, birds] any more than one could avoid the supernatural. The method of psychoanalysis is to bring the patient back to the idea which he is repressing: a long journey backwards without maps, a clue here and a clue there, as I caught the names of villages from this man and that, until one has to face the general idea, the pain or the memory."

Archibald MacLeish made a stab at a verse epic about the Conquest, but I can't see that his tepid *Conquistador* ("This is Cortes that took the famous .land") is anywhere within range of the tension Crane wanted to explore.

Once in Mexico, Crane knew he could not escape his demons. He'd ingested, metaphorically, the worm, internalized the other, the criticism of *The Bridge* by his onetime friends and supporters (by then young old men) Yvor Winters and Allen Tate, who took Crane to task for his Whitmanian optimism, his—in Tate's words—Romantic "rejection of a rational and qualitative will." Tate's "will" of intentions is a far cry from that wild conflux of energy and desire that altered the course of Western philosophy. Tate may have felt betrayed when Crane, the potential hero of the New Criticism, had blasted open the poem as self-contained object.

Crane was an optimist but not a shallow one: his optimism had nothing to do with an idealistic notion of history—it came from his ecstatic core. He sought an undivided wholeness. And drink helped him envision "new thresholds, new anatomies!" Ecstasy was the only solution he would entertain. He warred against the fallibility that might have been his own "lever of transcendence." He acted as if he owned his suffering and he refused to scrutinize it.

Paradoxically, Crane might have listened less to Whitman's vision and learned more from how Whitman expanded the self, his liberating and fictitious trope of the cosmic "I." Instead of plotting a grandiose epic, he might have paid attention to "the world dimensional," which he saw, in a Blakean sense, *through,* not merely *with,* his eyes.

Crane was never one to play his cards close to his chest. He once began a letter to Yvor Winters: "You need a good drubbing for all your talk about the whole man." He must have sensed the finality of his estrangement from Tate when he adopted a somewhat formal tone in a late letter to him: "The fact that you posit the Bridge at the end of a tradition of romanticism may prove to have been an accurate prophecy, but I don't yet feel that such a statement can be taken as a foregone conclusion. A great deal of romanticism may persist—of the sort that deserves serious consideration, I mean."

And now he recognized that his connection to God was broken, that his image of a continuous span of generations in resounding harmony was a fantasy, broken, like his sundered parentage, like the broken tower, like the tragic and abrupt breaking of Indian Mexico, when so many secrets were lost, or went underground.

The history of the Conquest is a history that cannot be healed.

To write his verse epic, he would have had to reconcile Mexican history and heal the quaking rift between the Spanish and the Aztec, the Catholic and the pagan, given his temperament and design. This could not be done. A broken tower is the perfect expression of this rift—as well as of themes indigenous to Crane. "The Broken Tower" is a more apt image of Crane's inner life than *The Bridge,* which Crane *willed* into triumphal completion.

The bells, I say, the bells break down their tower;
And swing I know not where. Their tongues engrave
Membrane through marrow, my long-scattered score
Of broken intervals . . . And I, their sexton slave!

In a sense, Crane's Mexican project was doomed because he planned it in advance. And so it was with immense sadness that I read of Crane's desire to write the history of the Conquest in verse, because the project put him at a remove from his own life, while his letters from Mexico are steeped in the spirit of the place. They show how intensely Crane, always the symbolist in his poems, was present in everyday life—and a creature of enthusiasms.

> I rushed from the bar where I was drinking tequila—up the dark corridors and stairways of the church and on to the roof, expecting to be thrown over when I got there, but still too excited to resist. . . . Can you imagine the strange, strange mixture, the musicians standing with their faces toward the high dark cliff surmounted by the temple of the old barbaric god that they were propitiating, and stopping every 15 minutes while the sextons rang out the call of the Cross over the same dark valley!

When the fit was not upon him Crane had a strangely amicable relationship to his environment. And the effect of his poetry is inseparable from its unforced exuberance, sweetness, and charm, as when, in "Repose of Rivers," "the singular nestings in the hills / Where beavers learn stitch and tooth."

"Be reconciled with your world," Williams urged his fellow poets: and, in many ways, Crane was—but he never found a way to consistently bridge his perceptions, to join the grand and the commonplace, aspiration and actuality, in a sort of mystical fusion. Crane's problem was how to recover from that moment of ecstasy, that moment of pure duration—how to get through the rest of the day or night without seeking to recapture that state whose precise nature it is not to be in time.

Crane is the man who rose before dawn to meet the bell ringer; who rode the wild bell ropes before writing "The Broken Tower":

> The bell-rope that gathers God at dawn
> Dispatches me as though I dropped down the knell
> Of a spent day—to wander the cathedral lawn
> From pit to crucifix, feet chill on steps from hell.

His metaphysical lines had a root in physical life, in the life of the body, which, Donne reminds us, "makes the minde." That is why when Crane failed to make the imaginative leap he needed, a leap which would have demanded Houdini-like mental resources, his next leap was from the prow of the *Orizaba* into the sea, which welcomed him, where he could be whole again. He'd already noted in "Voyages" that "the bottom of the sea is cruel." He'd already written his underwater epitaph in "At Melville's Tomb":

> The dice of drowned men's bones bequeath
> An embassy.

Crane set his acoustical register at the highest pitch, as in the layered sonics in the opening passage of "The Harbor Dawn":

> Insistently through sleep—a tide of voices—
> They meet you listening midway in your dream,
> The long, tired sounds, fog-insulated noises:
> Gongs in white surplices, beshrouded wails,
> Far strum of fog horns . . . signals dispersed in veils.
>
> And when a truck will lumber past the wharves
> As winch engines begin throbbing on some deck;
> Or a drunken stevedore's howl and thud below
> Comes echoing alley-upward through dim snow.

But where could Crane go from this exhausted gorgeousness, this plenitude of impressions? Crane idealized poetry. He resisted taking the next step into further impurity. He denied himself access to the errors that might have comprised the work. The highest note is not the only note (any more than we would like to listen to an opera in which only a coloratura soprano sings), and Crane had the heart and mind to expand, to harden and see the world through a crueler eye, without sacrificing the rising swell of the ecstasy he strove to recapture as in "Voyages":

> —And yet this great wink of eternity,
> Of rimless floods, unfettered leewardings,
> Samite sheeted and processioned where
> Her undinal vast belly moonward bends,
> Laughing the wrapt inflections of our love;
>
> . . .
>
> Bind us in time, O Seasons clear, and awe.

O minstrel galleons of Carib fire,
Bequeath us to no earthly shore until
Is answered in the vortex of our grave
The seal's wide spindrift gaze toward paradise.

▶

Lowry was a novelist in search of a new form, and he saw man—as in his letters he frequently embraced Ortega y Gasset's idea that man was like a novelist, making up his life as he goes along, trying to find his vocation.

Lowry, in adopting the Flaubertian ideal of language, applied it to the writing of essentially Romantic works. But Lowry had a special problem. He was a novelist who, as he admitted, could not create characters apart from himself, one who had no access to the idea of other people. His was an inward gaze.

His fatal defect as a novelist was that he was only interested, *finally,* in himself. Everyone in *Under the Volcano* is another facet of the Consul's personality. By creating a character with whom he didn't share any external occupational hazards, Lowry adapted the formal principles of the "objective" novel and then put himself, in the guise of the Romantic figure of the Consul (or later, Sigbjorn Wilderness), at the center of the novel.

(It is as though Flaubert had tried to write a bildungsroman in which the author would "identify" with a "positive hero": the artist in him would have been at war with the lyricism of his work in progress.)

▶

But writing *Under the Volcano* closed the door to Lowry for future work that had the possibility within itself to be completed within a finite stretch of time. In the ten years in which he lived after the publication of *Under the Volcano,* he wrote voluminously and finished (much less published) almost nothing. This sense of failure was not appeased by having created a masterpiece, because the essential project wasn't working. (Lowry's "blocks" took the form of logorrhea.) "Do I contradict myself?" I hope so. Because this is dangerous ground. It verges on arrogance to say that in writing *Under the Volcano* in the way he did, as evidenced in his letters, Lowry cut himself off from his future.

▶

Lowry might have taken the success of his marvelous novella, "Through the Panama," with its judicious merger of journal and journey—its carefully delineated voyage—as a sign that he was onto something; he might have found a form that would have allowed him to write the books he had to write, which would be without some of the strain and forced quality of his unfinished epic attempts. He was even partially sympathetic with an argument in which *Portrait of the Artist as a Young Man* was flawed because there was not enough differentiation between Joyce and Daedalus.

In certain passages of Crane's poetry and many of his letters, and in Lowry's prose, especially "Through the Panama," you sense an opening, a manner of expression that seems native, if not natural, to the writer. It is in this brilliant novella that Lowry, after twenty years, discovers that "Frère Jacques," a children's song, is as close as he can come to the onomatopoeia for a ship's engine. By paying acute attention to the audible, Lowery adds another dimension to the term *cinematic novel:* surround sound. Yet the writing I'm referring to has little to do really with the aesthetic and the drive behind the modernist masterpieces with which Crane and Lowry were competing—the works that set the standard for contemporary practice. Both men wrote elaborate descriptions and defenses of their work ("At Melville's Tomb," *The Bridge, Under the Volcano*) that stand among the great literary letters of all time. In fact, the descriptions in these letters are almost too schematic to be entirely believable: they almost go so far as to say *no one can tell me anything about my work which I haven't put in there.* I am aware of the contexts in which they wrote these letters: they were trying to convince patrons and publishers of the unassailable rightness of their works. These letters indicate that the process of writing these works left little to chance. And if you abolish chance you abolish possibility, and the next work, still percolating in the unconscious, becomes an endangered species.

"I shall . . . give my brush rein," says Kenko, a fourteenth-century Japanese poet and essayist who worked in a form called *zuihitsu* (which means "follow your brush"). I like to imagine Crane and Lowry taking nourishment and courage from his example, as, say, Philip Guston could from Fra Angelico. "Leaving something incomplete makes it interesting, and gives one the feeling that there is room for growth."

The writer must create the form anew in order to work in it.

"One reaches certain truths," Natalie Sarraute says,

> but truths that are already known. At a level that's already known. One can
> describe the Soviet reality in Tolstoy's manner, but one will never manage
> to penetrate it further than Tolstoy did with the aristocratic society that he
> described. It will remain at the same level of the psyche as Anna Karenina or
> Prince Bolkonsky if you use the form that Tolstoy used. If you employ the
> form of Dostoyevsky, you will arrive at another level, which will always be
> Dostoyevsky's level, whatever the society you describe. That's my idea. If you
> want to penetrate further, you must abandon both of them and go look for
> something else. Form and content are the same thing. If you take a certain
> form, you attain a certain content with that form, not any other. . . . Each
> time has to find its form. *It's the sensation that impels the form.* [Italics mine.]

Because of its relative wholeness, Teotihuacan is the least ruined and least interesting of the ruins I have seen in Mexico. I had no burning desire to go back to it
after twenty years, but my wife wanted to go and I had nothing better to do, and
a restless curiosity impelled me. Besides, it would be nice to see it unescorted
by a guide and without time constrictions. Years before, I had made the mistake
of taking a guide, an impatient man dressed in a black suit as if for a funeral,
who insisted that we visit the gift shop at the god-awful shrine of the Virgin of
Guadalupe, wasting valuable time we could have spent at the pyramids. I saw
women crawling on bloody knees toward the shrine; at least they wore scarves
in their hair to keep off the sun. And the sun in Mexico is direct and ubiquitous.
Everything, even the canary yellow walls of cemeteries, reflects the ferocity of
the sun.

Mexico encourages ecstatic negation. I had the sense, once, at Chichen Itza, that
when you reached the top steps of the pyramid you were meant to hurtle into
space, into the nowhere—that endless space was the next date on the Aztec
calendar. In the Mexican "universe of time" (Paz) there is no duration. The only
time is eternal time.

I don't need my son's erect painted reptile, the upsweep of his tail, to remember Mexico, or where we bought it—on a high hill in Oaxaca as the sun still swept across the valley in broad, swift strokes; and the police eyed us as we fondled serapes and beheld well-wrought pottery, and that pinkish glow—Oaxacan— was on the stones: everything was imprisoned in light. I stood looking down the steep street toward the zocalo and up into the hills—past the market's vats of fly-infested pulque, past the barrels of fried pork rind, past the wicker baskets brimful with dark, gnarled roots and branches, past tatters of the word "Olmec" on crumbling walls, past ragged gates and scorched, disfigured streets drenched in the smell of garlic and cayenne, past the ordered and chaotic light in the late Rufino Tamayo's small, pristine museum where torrents pour down through the open roof and soak the courtyard. The light, curved space—yet there was something sinister and menacing about it too, this lost light, lashing the streets, articulating shadows and creases, as another day was coming to an end in Oaxaca.

I tried to imagine what the body of Lowry's work might have been, and it is at that moment I am most aware of the lack of a social matrix. His character(s) are always adrift and far from their native land. Lowry, a novelist of the self and of consciousness, would have needed to thicken the broth of *The Voyage That Never Ends* by attempting to explore his own childhood. His friends talk about how his face clouded over whenever the subject of his family arose. Childhood may have been too painful for him to reenter, but could it have been any worse than what he afterward endured, and the repercussions of his romance with the bottle?

It is difficult to sustain an orotund note, an elevated, hieratic tone, "in the bleak time," when, as Ammons puts it in his nonchalant way in "Doubling the Nerve," you can

> look for no cooperation
> from the birds: crows show up, black blatant
> clarions in the gawky branches, to dominate
> the rain's dark

Lowry and Crane both felt artistically bankrupt, bereft when they died. Crane wrote one of his greatest shorter poems in Mexico, but it wasn't what he set out to do. Lowry's Consul, like Casaubon, is unable to complete his secret work: his definitive tome becomes his tomb. Lowry quotes—intentionally misquotes—Marlowe's *Faustus* when Jacques Laruelle, remembering the Consul as he looks into a book of Elizabethan plays, reads:

> "Then will I headlong fly into the earth:
> Earth, gape! it will not harbour me!

. . . Only Faustus had not said quite that. He looked more closely at the passage. Faustus had said: 'Then will I headlong run into the earth,' and 'O, no, it will not—.' That was not so bad. Under the circumstances to run was not so bad as to fly." Lowry hacks a few consoling syllables—signifying delay—out of Marlowe's mighty line, and makes the pain more acute than:

> Then will I headlong run into the earth:
> Earth, gape! O no, it will not harbour me!

Mexico supplied Crane and Lowry with the symbols they needed, but it did not leave them with a way out. Lowry, in moving from Cuernavaca to Dollartan, Canada, imagined he could substitute a heaven for a hell, cutting himself off, with strange psychic deliberation, from the purgatory of his past. Where Beckett chose the inevitability of "failure" as the condition of the artist in mid-century and used it (plying contradiction!) as a goad and challenge to "go on," both Crane and Lowry were condemned to chronicle a Dantean upward movement of the soul "toward paradise."

I knew that Crane and Lowry were troubled men, but when I first read them, when still in my teens, I had no sense that their crises might have had anything to do with their lives as artists—I couldn't see through the rosy tints of my esteem for what they *had* done.

The same is true of my idealization of a couple whom I saw play a variety of classic roles in repertory at the same time I had first discovered *Under the Volcano* and *The Bridge*.

Back in Manhattan, looking up from my table at a sidewalk cafe on Broadway, I notice the actor walk by. When I first saw him in the lead role of *'Tis Pity She's a Whore,* he was almost too pretty for the part of Giovanni, his then sandy hair parted Prince Valiant–style down the middle, but he was very good, and

I remember now the scene where he cuts out his sister Annabella's heart and holds it out to the audience—a bloody gory pulpy heart—very *real*.

GIO: The glory of my deed
    Darkened the mid-day sun, made noon as night.
    You came to feast, my lords, with dainty fair:
    I came to feast too; but I digged for food
    In a much richer mine than gold or stone
    Of any value balanced; *'tis a heart,*
    A heart, my lords, in which mine is entombed:

The actor has since perfected degenerate roles, white trash killers, sinister businessmen, etc. And at this moment I think of him holding out the heart with an Aztec innocence—it is already set within the context of a *feast*.

ANN: Be not deceived, my brother;
    This banquet is an harbinger of death
    To you and me; resolve yourself it is,
    And be prepared to welcome it.

In other words, in his preconquest, "Aztec," phase he played Ford and Shakespeare and Chekhov and Pirandello, and when he "grew up," that is, metaphorically speaking, after the conquest, he played villains in mediocre movies and made a lot of money.

It is as if the actor's lines predicted his life. Once he cut out his sister's heart, *his* heart, "entombed" in it, no longer retained its purity of ambition. His act, *in the play,* put him in the role of Mexico after the Conquest. Before that Giovanni heartily and willfully violates the incest taboo.

In the mid-1970s, when I lived in Greenwich Village, I used to see the actor's wife, herself a well-known stage actress, pushing a baby carriage on West Fourth Street or in Abington Square Park on Hudson Street from where you could glimpse the river, or having tea, with her baby in tow, at Arnold's Turtle.

She seemed absolutely at home on stage. Her gentle and quiet and understated demeanor placed her at the center of the audience's attention, like the eye of a hurricane.

The play I saw the couple in that year had such a deep effect on my life that I had to speak to her. One day I overtook her and the stroller and told her the theater had never had such magic for me before or since as when I saw her and her husband in '*Tis Pity She's a Whore*.

"But I hated it," she said. "It was a terrible year, the worst year of my life, I'd never do repertory again. The conditions were terrible, the pay was terrible, we'd no sooner mastered one thing and we were off onto another."

➤

The conversation caused a rupture in reality for me. I had misjudged everything, I had projected my then eighteen- or nineteen-year-old consciousness and innocence and experience onto her twenty-eight- or twenty-nine-year-old consciousness. It had never occurred to me that the circumstances could matter, that the pay (give or take a few hundred a month) could matter when you were performing Shakespeare and Ford and Chekhov and Pirandello to rapt audiences. I could never have predicted that the actor would switch physically from being an Adonis to a Magwitch in so short a time, from a perhaps too ethereal presence to an ugly, brutal, distorted one, the quintessential evil scum like those portrayed by Strother Martin in Westerns like *The Wild Bunch*.

The actress stuck to her guns, performing mainly great classical roles, and remained known to few outside that sphere. She did not utter her words in anger. She was a gentle, serene presence, even as she quietly excoriated her repertory year. I realize now that she was probably in a fury at having been abandoned by her husband. So it was in essence *her* heart the actor gouged out of her chest in a play written only some seventy years after Cortez arrived in Tenochtitlan.

The actor, Artaud says, is an athlete of the heart.

The actor crosses over the boundary between the living and the dead.

> CRUELTY. Without an element of cruelty at the foundation of every spectacle, the theater is not possible. In the state of degeneracy, in which we live, it is through the skin that metaphysics will be made to reenter our minds.

➤

From Ford's *The Broken Heart:*

ARMOSTES: Quiet
  These vain unruly passions, which will render ye
  Into a madness.

ORGILUS: Griefs will have their vent.

➤

The cutting-out of human hearts was also a Provençal practice. Pound deftly adapted the story of Guilhem de Cabestan in *Canto IV.*

  "It is Cabestan's heart in the dish."
  "It is Cabestan's heart in the dish."
  "No other taste shall change this."

Then the Spanish came and put a stop to Aztec sacrifices. Yet it is this direct, savage reality of the Aztecs and Jacobeans that drew Crane and Lowry to Mexico. But they had it in their minds to become something better.

Both Crane and Lowry tried for Elizabethan grandeur within a decadent Jacobean frame. That is one reason for the strain you feel in their work, a strain that seems to say: *if the world were different the work would be different.* The "fallen world" would not accept the burden of their praise—beyond a certain point.

  Wer immer strebend sich bemuht, den können wir erlösen.
  Whoever unceasingly strives upward . . . him we can save.

  (GOETHE, *FAUST*)

The irony of Lowry's epigraph is that he and Crane, in the verticality of their striving, lost sight of the advantages of being where they were in reality— "in the last bloody ditch where," as Beckett once put it, "there is no choice but to sing."

The Book of Samuel

The Milosz File, and
Choruses of Ghosts (II)

So, I don't know, maybe it's childish, a childish attitude. I've done extensive reading in philosophy and
so on. But the poetry comes only from pain, only
from personal experience. Not because I wanted
to create any philosophical theory. The philosophy
simply grew out of the pain.

—CONVERSATIONS WITH CZESLAW MILOSZ

We cease to recognize reality. It manifests itself in
some new category. And this category appears to be
its own inherent condition and not our own. Apart
from this condition everything in the world has a
name. Only it is new and is not yet named. We try
to name it—and the result is art.

—BORIS PASTERNAK

Prologue

Czeslaw Milosz received the Nobel Prize in the fall of 1980 some weeks after I
was invited to write an essay on him for one of editor Michael Cuddihy's special
issues of *Ironwood*. At the time, there were few works by Milosz available in
English. It was easier to make an educated guess about the quality of his prose
than his poetry: the poems available in *Selected Poems* left the latter an open
question. I remember the thrill I felt a year later upon opening *Ironwood* 18 to
encounter his early poem "The World," in the vivid Hass and Pinsky translation,
and significant sections of his important later work from *The Separate Notebooks*
and *The Land of Ulro*. It was also disconcerting to encounter central texts that
would have affected what I had written, especially on the issues of Milosz and
childhood, his faith, his use of form (particularly rhyme), and his sensuality.

At this point I want to make clear that in addition to my own analysis, I intend to show Milosz through his critics, interlocutors, and readers, because for all his extraordinary stature and the high visibility of his works, he remains a mysterious figure, especially in the United States and England. I would feel limited in expression if I had to use any other language but English, which every day grows more branches and assimilates words into itself at an increasingly rapid pace. And yet, for reasons I haven't begun to consider until this instant, I wonder why the infinite pliability of the language hasn't led to greater flexibility of mind in the people who speak it. I associate this flexibility of mind with the far more limited Slavic languages and, in a slightly different way, the Spanish language in the hands of its literary practitioners.

1

Donald Davie, a fascinating, vastly complicated, almost tragically mistaken literary figure, many of whose most original and invaluable contributions are sort of "under the radar," took me and others to task in a pioneering book *Czeslaw Milosz and the Insufficiency of Lyric.* We are so used to thinking of Davie as a kind of conservative figure, here to inform us of the wrong-headedness of our loves, that I skipped a beat to connect the title of the book with the man who wrote it. I wouldn't have predicted that Davie would be sympathetic with a gesture such as that of Milosz. Davie's titles pack a bite. His translation, and even more importantly, his commentary on *Doctor Zhivago* and the poems Pasternak wrote under that aegis—Pasternak wasn't capable of persona—is a classic. Best read in conjunction with *Pale Fire.* And within reach of a reproduction of Delacroix's painting, *Liberty Leading the People (La Liberté Guidant le peuple),* which I often imagined I had entered, and spun, whirled in the course of events, exhilarating, defiant, honest, carried in by the chaos emerging through the actual contents of the books I've just named, all blood pause and crisscross, maneuver, under the Soviet spectre. First and foremost Pasternak survived, and Milosz survived.

And Milosz's response to Pasternak is tortured and ambivalent until the resounding note he sounds at the end of his essay "On Pasternak Soberly." But everyone begrudged Pasternak the elusiveness that led him to escape familiarity; he was consumed by anxiety, but no one could get him to unravel; he was his convictions. But he spoke through landscapes and objects to embody the fullness of life in actions that take place in front of our eyes. Here is Pasternak on art:

> Contemporary trends imagined that art is like a fountain, whereas it is really a sponge. They decided that it should gush forth, whereas it should dry up and become saturated. They figured out that it should be assigned to the means of its figurative nature, whereas it is composed of the organs of understanding. It must always be present in the observers and see most purely, receptively, and truly, but in our days it got to know make-up and dressing-room and it lets itself be shown from the screen.

But he expressed his convictions, in his prose and ordinary speech, as well as in his poetry, unconstrainedly—which in retrospect turned out to be the right move. Everyone in Russia had embraced or pretended to embrace a platform, and to take sides. Whose side is Zhivago on? Nothing ambiguous there: the side of life. And to look at his poem "The Steppe" in light of Chekhov's novella "The Steppe" is to glimpse, albeit in the fog that surrounds his tent on "all four sides," one way Pasternak perceived reality. It's palpable, vague, mysterious, mundane, expansive, cramped, allusive. Its subtitle could have been: VOYEURS NOT WELCOME. "The steppe wide and quiet, as a bay," is how I chose to translate it, but in the original Pasternak says "marina," mingling a foreign word with a Russian one, and signaling his inspiration for the poem: Marina Tsvetaeva. It's fantastic, ineradicably grounded. In the metrics. In the soft undercurrents of speech. Like the buzzing sound in the Russian word for life, *zhizn,* which takes on many layers of meaning throughout *My Sister—Life.* In the tenderness engendered by being surrounded on all four sides by the fog, "like a tent." The poems are embedded; he could have set down the words with a paintbrush, with a variety of oils borrowed from his father's studio, which he became curious about after he glimpsed Rilke departing, wrapped in a black cloak.

> Midnight stands darkly on the road,
> And burdened by stars, tumbles down.
> You can't step beyond your fence
> Without trampling the universe.
>
> ("THE STEPPE," MY TRANSLATION)

His mother was Jewish. His father, Leonid, who painted Rilke and Tolstoy, was not. He tried to be Christian. Nothing ever quite fit for Pasternak. He spoke in complete candor—through images and the adventures they sweated through:

"the gutted whistle gasps / clogged by agonizing dust" ("Policeman's Whistles"). If he'd written Chekhov's "The Steppe" he would have devoted half of it to the reactions of the stones and pebbles on the road, and what the grass witnessed, and the stunned blinks of the birch trees, voiceless, worn down, dejected, after days of being sprayed without mercy by dust, even the stellar stuff Pasternak imported from the Milky Way, and no water. Water: he heard the word form as it whooshed through the trees. Tilt of the driver's cap: he's thirsty too and doesn't know it. Earth, dust, thirst. The lash of drivers' whips. Flash to the serfs. The undertrodden. Like a stepson.

It irritates Milosz that when he wants to communicate with Pasternak soberly he is confronted with his sacred dance. Milosz really doesn't like it when the parts don't come together. He's lucid in his objections; too monolithic when it comes to instructions—although I nearly reeled when I discovered that several poets he had problems with were ones about whom I think the same thing, but have found little or no company. I agree with Milosz that as far as Larkin is concerned, it's just too much. This is his response to Larkin's first book, *The Less Deceived;* he's distressed that Larkin's mentality is so insular "that he doesn't realize that elegant, genial skepticism is an abomination in poetry, which is possible only as a game to which one bets everything one has." I don't know if Czeslaw could steel himself to think hard about Larkin, but I have. It's not about skill, or "verse." Poetry is the internal workings of verse. But versifiers think verse is poetry. We can't separate what Larkin says from how he said it; at bottom it's insular, conservative, gloriously impervious to the dimension of space and time where people like Czeslaw Milosz are forced to be preter-naturally aware, in order to move deftly within the rapidly shifting currents of change. And this pertained to some of the century's best poets who did not live under a totalitarian regime as such, like César Vallejo (fled from Lima to Paris), Saint-John Perse (diplomat), Edmond Jabès (fled from Egypt to Paris), Muriel Rukeyser (went on behalf of Loyalists to Spain), and George Oppen (twenty-five years in Mexico "between poems"). But I force myself to look at Larkin again, and wonder who among the poets I know would agree. And glancing at the bookshelf the hall light has fallen upon late this January afternoon, they illuminate Thom Gunn's space. And there are two books of prose. I open . . . and voilà: he finds it incredible that more people would want to read Larkin than Robert Duncan or Basil Bunting.

Bunting seems to me the most interesting poet in Britain since the death of Yeats. . . . The trouble is the English are hung up on Larkin. Larkin was a poet of minute ambitions who carried them out exquisitely. But he really isn't a very important poet and exercises a terrible influence on English poetry because if you admire somebody like that so much it means you're not going to be aiming very high. His distrust of rhetoric was also a distrust of feeling, a distrust of daring.

And you can learn from Bunting how to take the melody further, timing the rhythm to the human action or meditation, just as Dante found the form for his *Comedy* wandering the goat paths of Italy.

"There is an immense distance between the necessary and the good," Milosz quotes Simone Weil as saying in his introduction to his translation of her into Polish. The distance between life and death the night of the Warsaw bombing is something less than immense, like a fractured fraction, busted up, but not irretrievable. Milosz took on whatever had to be done. Camus, whom he knew quite well and who accepted his novel *State of Siege* in his role as an editor at Gallimard, had been severely depressed for years before he died; he saw no escape from the burden of appearing to be who he wasn't in his role as a public figure, post–Nobel Prize; and his energies, which ran deep, Algerian-style, froze. Czeslaw had room in his life for everything he wanted to do and every-thing he had to get done. So there is a Pasternakian (Zhivagoan) miracle in the destiny of Czeslaw Milosz; the man we needed was the man we got. He didn't get uptight. He composed books most poets would consider chores: *A History of Polish Literature*. I'll say it another way: he did what was called for; but there was no division between the inner and outer call.

Davie is especially emphatic about Milosz's departure from lyric, a point which in my essay I tried to make in another way. Responding to work that appeared in the Milosz issue of *Ironwood* Davie comments in *Insufficiency*:

> To Marisha Chamberlain it seemed clear that "he [Milosz] possessed that characteristic that Keats called 'negative capability,' which distinguishes the great artist: the ability to stand in doubt for a long time, to proceed from failed attempt to failed attempt, keeping alive the appetite for the problem itself." To Mark Rudman on the other hand, it seemed that "maybe the best way to put it is that Milosz has rejected a concept that formed the basis of romantic poetry, 'negative capability,' to which poets who might

not agree on anything else often cleave." So far as Rudman was concerned, this was an unavoidable implication, seeing that "Milosz writes in the first person a poetry of statement and, with some irony, is willing to address us all, a generalized or ideal-typical other, abjuring metaphors and riddles— anything that can be construed as poetic device, and demands of himself a lucidity so that he can't be mistaken." Rudman is surely wrong in detail; for, as we saw from Milosz's comments on his own poem "No More," there is in poetry no way to abjure "anything that can be construed as poetic device." Still, as will be gathered from the tenor of my argument so far, I am sure that by and large Mark Rudman is right on this large issue, and Marisha Chamberlain is wrong: Milosz is not a Keatsian poet, is not prepared to be.

Even though Davie agrees with the gist of my risky remark about Milosz's rejection of "negative capability," I regret having overstated my case with the outrageous claim that Milosz abjures all poetic devices. How grateful I am to him for not skewering me for a phrase that was both hyperbolic and inaccurate.

In 1994 I was asked to introduce Milosz at the Miller Theater at Columbia. I balked, but figured that I could cannibalize my 1980–81 *Ironwood* piece, "No Longer in Continuous Time," and address some of the aspects and concerns of his work that I had come to appreciate over the years. While we waited in the green room (whose gray linoleum couldn't have demanded too much maintenance) I unburdened myself to Czeslaw, whom I had come to know, by confessing I had often thought of writing a sequel to my essay because I knew my emphasis would have been different if I had known. . . . But before I could complete my confession he interrupted and said, "But you have already written a fine essay on my work, Mark, it is not necessary . . .," and his wife, Carol, nodded as if to reaffirm his approval of the earlier document. "Well, I try to do a little more in this introduction."

Most of the introductions I've been asked to give, while not overlong, have been flawed by the desire to go to the essence of a poet's work without, of course, filling in the blanks, and in retrospect I wonder if the audience in Miller Theater could have followed this one except for a handful of Milosz aficionados and the author, for whom it was ultimately (perhaps inappropriately) written. I'll let you be the judge.

Czeslaw Milosz: An Introduction, 1994

The complexity and massiveness of Czeslaw Milosz's contribution to literature is worthy of three or four Czeslaw Miloszs. He has written blank verse, free verse, the rhymed quatrains in "The World," and revived the dithyrambic, cadenced long line of Greek choral meters. His prose is no less passionate and detailed than his poetry. Also too important to pass over is his advocacy of the Polish poets whom he brought to our attention in English translation, and of Simone Weil, whose work he translated into Polish, and of his cousin Oscar Milosz, whose poetry with its "passionate pursuit of the real" he translated *into* English.

In some ways it's distracting to have Milosz written of so often as a witness in a historical/political sense to the Nazi assault on Warsaw. He did see machine-gun fire make the cobblestones stand up like porcupine quills. He did see throats cut and fingers sinking into flesh, but the precision of that witnessing is an extension of his subjectivity, his fervent dialectic between mind and the sensual world, between ontology and sensation—how the sun feels on the back of your neck. Casting the net of his imagination into the past, he retrieves details of startling immediacy.

Milosz does not neglect first principles. Nor does he place poetic devices above their spiritual source. The myriad details in his work are neither interchangeable notation nor symbols: underneath phenomena and action from the pinprick stars in August on a peak in the high Sierras to the rustling satin underskirts and black lace panties of chanteuses, to the tossed-back scarecrows of the trees, he turns our attentions to attention itself, to the viable and useful discipline of Weil's great aphorism (though arguably filched from Malebranche): "Absolutely unmixed attention is prayer."

And yet, in addition to moral seriousness and intensity, Czeslaw Milosz's poetry is immensely playful, as you can see from "And Yet," his homage to Issa's haiku whose final qualifying line "and yet" reverses what came before and opens up infinite possibilities. I remember every detail surrounding reading Milosz's *Provinces* on a bench at Ragdale on a late morning in early May.

> And yet we were so like one another
> With all our misery of penises and vaginas,
> With the heart beating quickly in fear and ecstasy,
> And a hope, a hope, a hope.

And yet we were so like one another
That lazy dragons stretching themselves in the air
Must have considered us brothers and sisters
Playing together in a sunny garden,
Only we did not know that,
Enclosed in our skins, each separately,
Not in a garden, on the bitter earth.

And yet we were so like one another
Even though every leaf of grass had its fate
Just as a sparrow on the roof, a field mouse,
And an infant that would be named John or Teresa
Was born for long happiness or shame and suffering
Once only, till the end of the world.

He is also outspoken about his attraction to childhood and to children,
"avid, gluttonous, minds not yet caught by the will of the species . . . though
led . . . by an Eros . . . who is still free and dances, knowing nothing of
goals and service. And the gift of the artist or philosopher likewise has its
secret in a hidden hostility toward the earth of the adults." He resolves to
reach no other resolution to the conflicts that engage him beyond the surety
that there is no resolution to any of them, except an acceptance of the
persistence of change.

It makes sense that a poet who asks us to consider a concept as tantalizing
and potentially hopeful as *apokatastasis*—the idea that every occurrence is
"stored somewhere"—would, in the last section of his long autobiographical
poem "From the Rising of the Sun," speak of a "consciousness that is
unwilling to forgive," not because he or it is vindictive, but because it's
beyond subjectivity, out of his hands; he can't undo an instant that has been
stored away.

For me, therefore, everything has a double existence.
Both in time and when time shall be no more.

2

There is something about the man himself, despite his copious works and confessions, that remains elusive, slips out of our grasp every time, like a trout you try to catch with your hands in a river. Be reconciled: Milosz must remain somewhat unassimilable for the Anglo-American reader. The English-speaking world still has a long way to go in understanding Milosz. A lot of the criticism of Milosz, especially that which appears in journals with circulation beyond the merely literary, approaches him as a political writer or as a witness. This may have moral value, but it is the least interesting thing about him as a writer.

I turn to his contemporary, Witold Gombrowicz, for whom Milosz's elusiveness had nothing to do with his origins and culture. He was thinking hard about Milosz twenty-five years before anyone thought about him in America. But it's our great fortune that Gombrowicz, who was fascinated by Milosz and who fascinates Milosz, devoted a fascinating and incisive section of his *Diary* to the analysis of Milosz's character and contributions.

Milosz: *La prise du pouvoir.*

A very strong book. Milosz is an experience for me. He is the only émigré writer who was really drenched by that tempest. Others, no. They were out in the rain but they all carried umbrellas. Milosz was soaked to the skin and at the end the hurricane even tore the clothes off his back. He returned naked. Be happy that decency has been preserved! At least one of you is naked! You, the remainder, are indecent: dressed in your pantaloons, various style jackets, your ties and handkerchiefs. What shame!

There is no lack of talent among us . . . but neither of them [two other contemporaries] is sufficiently initiated. Milosz knows. Milosz looked and experienced: in the flashing tempest something appeared to him . . . the Medusa of our times. Milosz fell, ravaged by her gaze.

Ravaged? Perhaps too much so. Initiated? Perhaps excessively or perhaps the initiation was too passive? To listen to one's time? Yes. But not to submit to it. It is difficult to talk about this on the basis of his works in prose up to now, *The Captive Mind, Seizure of Power,* and his one volume of poetry, *Daylight,* because their theme is special: a recapitulation of a certain period and also a testimony and warning. Yet I sense that Milosz has allowed History to impose not only a theme but also a certain attitude that I would call the attitude of a man who has been overthrown.

But isn't Milosz fighting? Yes, he is fighting, but only with means his opponent allows; it looks as if he had actually believed in Communism, that he is a devastated intellectual and that he has risen to participate in the last heroic battle as a devastated intellectual. This beggar, enamored of his own Job-like nakedness, this bankrupt engrossed in his bankruptcy, has probably voluntarily limited his chances for effective resistance. Milosz's mistake—this is how I see it and it is a mistake that is quite prevalent—consists of his reducing himself to the level of the poverty that he describes. Afraid of rhetoric and denying his right to luxury, he, Milosz, is loyal and true to his brothers in misfortune and wants to be poor like them. Yet such an intention in an artist is incompatible with the essence of his actions, for art is a luxury, freedom, play, dream, and power. Art arises not from poverty, but from riches. It is born not when one is under the wagon but when one is on it. Art has something triumphant in it even when it is wringing its hands. Hegel? Hegel doesn't have much in common with us because we are dance. The man who does not allow himself to be impoverished will respond to the creativity of Marxism with a different creativity, with the astounding, new, and unforeseen riches of life. Has Milosz made a sufficient effort to extricate himself from the dialectics that have shackled him?

If not, I know that it is not due to lack of strength, but to an excess of loyalty.

Gombrowicz's *Diary,* translated by Lillian Vallee, who also translated *Bells in Winter,* has an afterword by Jan Kott, who refers to it not as ancillary to his novels and plays, but as "great literature." I agree. But a diary that goes by that name is less likely to be taken as a serious—and structured—literary work than writing called poetry or fiction or the bridge between reality and imagination: nonfiction. Jan Kott's writing, like Milosz's *The Captive Mind,* was as engrossing as anything I read in those (still continuing) formative years. And this sense that the difference between literary genres can't be delineated without references to specific works is one reason I felt pressed to invent a form for the *Rider Quintet* that would not disallow any form per se—but I could never have set out to include all these forms in different forms. The last thing I wanted was a response more geared toward Italo Calvino's *If on a Winter's Night a Traveler*—a tour de force, a work distinguished by retro-pyrotechnics that Joyce and Faulkner did with immeasurably more power. Especially in translation, I find that book of "finish the sentence each time in a different style" saturated with a cleverness beneath the marvelous Calvino's standard of excellence. When I was considering pursuing a doctorate in English at Columbia (after receiving an M.F.A.), I sat in on a few seminars and mentioned Mr. Kott's name with regard to his insight about the changing of kings being a "grand mechanism." I was quickly informed that "that kind of thing may be interesting, but it doesn't really have anything to do with Shakespeare." The slightly bemused expression I'd attempted had been replaced by a rebellious feeling I could not squash. Not only had Peter Brook based his production of *King Lear* on Kott's incisive essay "*King Lear* or Endgame," but Kott's breakdown of what he called "the Grand Mechanism"—in light of what he'd experienced when the Germans invaded Poland and could just as well have been experiencing in today's war zones—is the kind of insight that restores an order, a pattern, onto history, when a psychotic chaos (lest "chaos" as the source of creation be mistaken for its debased use in everyday speech) is the only order of the day. "Rashly, and praised be rashness for it, let us know our indiscretion sometimes serves us well when our deep plots do pall."

3

If *apokatastasis* did not lie at the core of Milosz's vision of life, I doubt he would have placed it at the climactic moment of his most definitive poem, his response to *The Prelude* and *Four Quartets,* "From the Rising of the Sun."

> Yet I belong to those who believe in *apokatastasis.*
> That word promises reverse movement,
> Not the one that was set in *katastasis,*
> And appears in the Acts 3, 21.
>
> It means: restoration. So believed: St. Gregory of Nyssa,
> Johannes Scotus Erigena, Ruysbroeck, and William Blake.
>
> For me, therefore, everything has a double existence,
> Both in time and when time shall be no more.

After I hunted down various definitions of the term *apokatastasis,* there remained a profound anti-obscurantist obscurity. Anything having to do with the afterlife is hell for Jews. Thanks to *Conversations with Milosz* we are granted an intimacy with the author that might not have otherwise been possible. He preferred to hear confessions, such as Aleksander Wat's, than confide.

Apokatastasis is a concept that first appeared in the Epistles. It was developed extensively by Origen, who is not considered a totally authoritative Church Father because he held very heretical views, but let's not go into that here. In any case, he was very much a believer in apokatastasis. *In Greek it means more or less the same as "reinstatement," the restoration of the state before original sin, a repetition of history in a purified form. It's a risky concept, very heretical. I'm not saying I'm a great believer in apokatastasis since the word can have a variety of meanings.* In any case in this poem, apokatastasis tends to mean that no detail is ever lost, no moment vanishes entirely. They are all stored somewhere and it's possible to show that film again, to re-create a reality with all those elements restored.

When it comes to teleology, Milosz both commits himself to a vision and makes sure no reader will be tempted to take his statements at face value. His work has the type of ambiguity that does not come from perplexing the language, as does that of poets like Pasternak and Hart Crane. Milosz doesn't court mystery; he introduces mysteries. My willingness to let Milosz speak for himself—take him at his word—is only possible because his self-estimation seems both accurate and commensurate with his own experience and achievement. (Since the "death of the author" and the current fad of dismissing whatever instructions authors offer in terms of how to read their work, readers who buy into those views amputate their chances of attaining a full perspective of these capacious imaginations. And I refer you to the prefaces of George Bernard Shaw and Henry James, and Marcel Proust's too-often-disregarded insistence that he and the narrator "Marcel" were not to be conflated.)

"From the Rising of the Sun" ends on this resounding note. (The year in question is that of William Blake's birth.)

> And if the city, there below, was consumed by fire
> Together with the cities of all the continents,
> I would not say with my mouth of ashes that it was unjust.
> For we lived under the Judgment, unaware.

> Which Judgment began in the year one thousand seven hundred
>   fifty-seven.

> Though not for certain, perhaps in some other year,
> It shall come to completion in the sixth millennium, or next Tuesday.
> The demiurge's workshop will suddenly be stilled. Unimaginable silence.

The Book of Samuel

> And the form of every single grain will be restored in glory.
>
> I was judged for my despair because I was unable to understand this.

No one can answer. Everyone can conjecture. And maybe the mind's capacity to conceive of such an eternity suggests there is such a phenomenon. Otherwise, keeping evolution loosely in mind, why, out of all the creatures on the earth, would *Homo sapiens* be alone in being condemned to futile consideration of that Time Out of Time which does not exist; or worse, which has no chance of existing? Or are we entering the realm of Vladimir Nabokov's Charles Kinbote, who was absolutely positive that an alternative kingdom exists? And didn't Nabokov himself hold somewhat similar beliefs that the real thing was happening elsewhere?

4

Milosz has spent his life trying to make others aware of what he cares most deeply about, driven by the knowledge that if he doesn't do it, no one else will "drive the car." Why else would he have written *The History of Polish Literature*? I feel obliged to emphasize to the reader / writer / rider that Milosz has spent more years than I've been alive struggling to get an audience for other writers, most of whom, but by no means all, are Polish. Obviously in a self-enclosed master-work, like Thomas Mann's *The Magic Mountain,* which was an important book for Milosz—who must have been drawn to the emphasis on classification—the microcosm is complete, the artist's work is done. But with poetry, it's never like that, or else why would T. S. Eliot or Marianne Moore have written about ten pages of prose for every page of poetry? Why isn't more demanded of American poets in this way?

Milosz's anthology of *Postwar Polish Poetry,* with its converse influence on American poets with minimalist applications, such as W. S. Merwin, Charles Simic, or Mark Strand, piqued interest in Zbigniew Herbert and Tadeusz Rosewicz, but not in Milosz himself, nor in fellow Nobel laureate Wislawa Szymborska, nor in Aleksander Wat, a book of whose Milosz would later translate.

At the moment that I am composing this sentence, I open the November 28, 1996, issue of the *New York Review of Books:* the lead essay, "Man in the Otter Collar," is a review by Neal Ascherson of a new book about the Polish poet

Aleksander Wat by the Lithuanian poet Tomas Venclova, and who should emerge as a key figure in Wat's reputation being rescued from oblivion— Czeslaw Milosz!

The only one of the three works translated into English is Aleksander Wat's memoir, *My Century,* published in the United States in 1988. This is one of the great classics of prison experience; it can take its place beside Silvio Pellico's *My Prisons* or Dostoevsky's *The House of the Dead.* Properly speaking, it is not a memoir but a series of taped conversations with Czeslaw Milosz at Berkeley and then in Paris, in 1964 and 1965. Aleksander Wat was ill and in too much pain to write, and Milosz decided to tape his recollections. What developed from these meetings was not so much a series of conversations as what Milosz called "seances" in which he had the "honor to serve as a medium"; and it is one of Milosz's own great achievements as well as Wat's testament. Coming from the same background, Milosz well understood what his fellow poet was saying, and what he found difficult to say. In the foreword to the book, Milosz wrote:

> *I quickly realized that something unique was transpiring between us. There was not a single other person on the face of the earth who had experienced the century as Wat had and who had the same sense of it as he. This has nothing to do with the cruelty of fate or history, for an enormous number of people were more grievously afflicted by it than he was. No, what matters here is a cast of mind, a culture . . . specifically, the culture of the Polish intelligentsia.*

My first acquaintance with Aleksander Wat was in Milosz's anthology *Postwar Polish Poetry,* and the poem was "If the Word 'Exists.'"

How good it is to return to old rejected concepts!
(N.B. The meaning of that "let us return" is common. So,
for example, Odysseus returned to Penelope, to
her who knew the secret:
that one must weave and unweave. And again weave and
unweave.)

Not long after, Wat's *Mediterranean Poems* in Milosz's translation appeared along with two other books in a translation series Ardis Press had just begun. One of them, *Square of Angels: The Selected Poems of Bohdan Antonych,* I had translated in collaboration with Bohdan Boychuk and Paul Nemser.

By 1980, I couldn't have been the only one who was becoming inured to a generic quality in the flood of eastern European poets appearing in translation. If another Milosz convert passed through New York and said, "I have to read you Milosz's '*Ars Poetica?*'" I would have had to devise a Rube Goldbergian contraption through which either I could escape or they could be, à la Bond's "Q," ejected. It wasn't that I disagreed with Milosz or didn't myself aspire "to a more spacious form / that would be free from the claims of poetry or prose," but at the time I had a positive allergy to that Horatian tone. If there was anything I didn't care for in poetry at the time, it was advice. And if there is a problem with Milosz's poetry, it's that often he just says what he wants to say, artfully, but not always intriguingly.

But I have loved Zbigniew Herbert's "Study of the Object" from the first time I read it in Milosz's anthology *Postwar Polish Poetry,* which doesn't mean that I find its tone persuasive.

> The most perfect object
> is that which does not exist.

Milosz, who admits to being a realist, is also far less tolerant of Herbert's thinking here, yet he still gives it a prominent place (and space) in his anthology. Milosz's personal philosophy is at times as childlike or elemental as "The World." Reality exists: relativity belongs to physics and perception and motion; not objects. In *Conversations with Czeslaw Milosz* Milosz defines his contradictions, and how hesitant and trepidatious that "By conviction . . ." really is:

> By conviction, I'm actually a realist. That means that I struggle to seize hold
> of fragments of reality. . . . Anything really concrete is beyond our reach.
> One of my old poems comes to mind as an example here: "Encounter,"
> written in Wilno in 1937:
>
>> We were riding through frozen fields in a wagon at dawn.
>> A red wing rose in the darkness.
>>
>> And suddenly a hare ran across the road.
>> One of us pointed to it with his hand.
>
> That's a moment. A hare really did run across the road. The point there was
> to catch something that had actually happened. At one moment, one second.
> Odd that I should feel the need.

Milosz has a wide range—he ranges. This in itself doesn't warrant interest. Apprised of Milosz's range, some critics thought Zbigniew Herbert the better poet because he struck a purer note. Which leads me to ask, why must relative equals be ranked in just this manner, as long as they have created works of comparable excellence? Sylvia Plath, in the harrowed weeks before her death, struck a pure note of crystalline intensity, poems whose brilliance Robert Lowell compared to Sir Walter Raleigh's as he faced the hangman. Zbigniew Herbert may strike a comparably pure note, but the source of his intensity transcends the personal. In his own journal, *A Year of the Hunter,* Milosz expresses his distaste for a generation of American poets who sought out desperate straits in order to achieve poetic intensity. And he has always fiercely opposed the modern equation of the artist's ability with madness or sheer self-destructive capacity.

> Whenever Robert Lowell landed in a clinic I couldn't help thinking that if someone would only give him fifteen lashes with a belt on his bare behind, he'd recover immediately. I admit, that was envy speaking through me. If I cannot indulge myself, why should he be free to indulge himself?

If this is a bit harsh to Lowell personally, whose clinical condition probably would have resisted "fifteen lashes" as much as it did electroshock treatments, I empathize with the sentiments of the émigré writer best known in his adopted country for a book of political prose, ablaze with a relentless scrutiny, and reluctance to draw the equal signs when it comes to the results of how the minds of his four "examples" become "captive."

> When I found myself an émigré and wrote *The Captive Mind,* my poetry was completely unknown; no one knew that I was a poet, but I became known to many readers as the author of *The Captive Mind.* Then the fact that not all my poems can be translated—for example, those that use meter and rhyme are practically untranslatable—also distorts my image.

It took me a while to absolve Milosz of what I first thought was his cerebral side, as it was manifested in his poetry. Around this time I encountered Harold Bloom at a party after a panel on Oscar Wilde, "the divine Oscar," at the Ninety-second Street Y. I was pleased that he seemed familiar with my work—given that at the time it had only appeared, though with some frequency, in journals. When I leaked out that I'd accepted an invitation to write a book about Robert Lowell, he seemed shocked: "I would have thought that you, Mr. Rudman, would be more . . . Stevens." Another deadlock. I thought I knew what he meant. For

Stevens, the foreground of the poem is imagination, and the stress is on invention. For Lowell, it was Lowell and metrics, Lowell and history, his and ours. I tried to set out that Lowell's attempt to render thingness in words that didn't really attempt to hit their mark, or connect—just look at the dissolution of the nouns as they're surrounded by adjectives and adverbs!—gave his apparent "accounts," studies from life, an opacity, an abstract quality. Lowell's thingness was his attempt to convince himself, day by day, throughout the trial of onsets of madness, that there was something outside himself that could be relied on. "Oh," Bloom said, "well if you come at it from THAT point of view. . . ." I saw Lowell's poetry as abstract. He had no doubts about the reality of realism; he had major doubts about his own connectedness to anything close to a stable reality. And one way he had of touching base was to translate Russian poetry, especially Pasternak's. For Milosz, objects exist outside the poem and within the flow of the poem, which is a complete utterance. His parallel for his belief in realism is Dutch painting. One telltale sign is his predilection for nouns.

5

Initial antipathies signal that an eventual appreciation has at least been arrived at, rather than passively accepted. I warned Michael Cuddihy of the problems I had had with Milosz ("remote . . . science fiction quality . . .") on an admittedly superficial reading of this and that, and he said in his craggy voice that "a lot of people like the things that . . . get in their way." Now there was a provocative statement.

And as it turned out, it was Milosz's astounding prose work *The Captive Mind* that helped me become more receptive to his poetry. It was as if he could really see through other people, and expose them like photographic negatives. As a young American growing up absurd in a post- or pseudo-Freudian age, I had been surrounded by psychologically oriented people who were always reluctant to risk judgments about other people's lives, being desperately afraid of appearing to appear superior. Milosz, contra this kind of timidity, appeared to hold nothing back. The thinly disguised portraits of contemporaries in *The Captive Mind* were like devastating Proustian miniatures with a bomb that exploded at the end—due to the political context. And his autobiography *Native Realm* was nothing less than astonishing in its range and detail.

Looking back, reading Milosz with an eye for writing an essay helped sustain me through one of the most bizarre and difficult years of my life. It was late at night, and my wife, laying naked on the white sheets, flew into the fiercest of her periodic fits about money. Nothing could be more severe than her just wrath, so I wrote a letter and sent it to every local college asking for work and called equally desperate friends, one of whom, the poet Phillis Levin, said "there might be some openings at Queens." Queens College, that is. I wrote, they called back with the usual "of course I know your poetry, and your CV is" blah-blah, "but all we have left is two courses that begin at eight in the morning and demand you come out here three days." To a preternaturally late riser, the thought of having to RISE at 5 A.M. to make it to QUEENS COLLEGE by 8 (A.M.) wasn't exactly . . . thrilling . . . but I rose to the CHALLENGE and said I'd do it if they promised me a two-day schedule the next semester. "I think we can do that." Looking back, I should have called my essay on Milosz, "No Longer in Continuous Time, Reading Milosz at Six A.M. on the Subway." When I complained about my arduous schedule and slave wages, the Ukrainian poet Bohdan Boychuk said "it is good for a man to be drained," and he was right, but I vowed never to get into such a position again for those wages. I got off the subway three days a week and, running on adrenaline and will, headed straight for the gym where Harold Brodkey, fresh from his day's labors on his magnum opus, would ask my opinions about various poets, and then offer correctives. I liked Harold personally, but he didn't seem to hear me when I explained that I had been talking all morning and couldn't say more. . . . But I had one consolation: C.M. C.M., that is, without "The World" or *The Separate Notebooks,* the first sections of which appeared in *Ironwood* the following fall. Once again we owe these succinct, direct, and helpful sentences to his interviews and conversations with Ewa Czarnecka, Aleksander Fiut, Renata Gorczynski, and Richard Lourie. Should the interview be admitted into the domain of art, if it's good enough? Or is Boswell's precedent sufficient?

MILOSZ: . . . My feeling is that my own poetry is a poetry of incantation. . . .

FIUT: What do you mean by incantation?

MILOSZ: A sensitivity to the rhythmic structure of a line even if I'm writing prose.

The Book of Samuel

It's hard to explain, but probably much time spent with Blake's "The Marriage of Heaven and Hell," with its "spacious form / . . . free from the claims of poetry or prose," contributed to my endorphin rush when I opened *Ironwood* and encountered "The Wormwood Star" from *The Separate Notebooks.*

The Wormwood Star

Now there is nothing to lose, my cautious, my cunning, my hyper-selfish cat.

Now we can make confession, without fear that it will be used against mighty enemies.

We are an echo that runs, skittering, through a train of rooms.

Seasons flare and fade, but as in a garden we do not enter anymore.

And that's a relief, for we do not need to catch up with the others, in the sprints and the high jump.

The Earth has not been to Your Majesty's liking.

The night a child is conceived, an obscure pact is concluded.

And the innocent receives a sentence, but he won't be able to unravel its meaning.

Even if he consults ashes, stars, and flights of birds.

A hideous pact, an entanglement in blood, an anabasis of vengeful genes arriving from swampy millennia.

From the half-witted and the crippled, from crazed wenches and syphilitic kings.

At mutton's leg and barley and the slurping of soup.

Baptized with oil and water when the Wormwood Star was rising.

I played in a meadow by the tents of the Red Cross.

That was the time assigned to me, as if a personal fate were not enough.

In a small archaic town ("The bell on the City Hall clock chimed midnight, as a student N . . ." and so on).

How to speak? How to tear apart the skin of words?
What I have written seems to me now not that.
And what I have lived seems to me now not that.

When Thomas brought the news that the house I was born in no longer
    exists,

Neither the lane nor the park sloping to the river, nothing,

I had a dream of return. Multicolored. Joyous. I was able to fly.

And the trees were even higher than in childhood, because they had been
    growing during all the years since they had been cut down.

The loss of a native province, of a homeland,

Wandering one's whole life among foreign tribes

Even this

Is only romantic, i.e., bearable.

Besides, that's how my prayer of a high school student was answered,
of a boy who read the bards and asked for greatness which means exile.

The Earth has not been to Your Majesty's liking,

For a reason having nothing to do with the Planetary State.

Nonetheless I am amazed to have reached a venerable age.

And certainly I have experienced miraculous narrow escapes for which I
    vowed to God my gratitude,

So the horror of those days visited me as well.

Formally Milosz's dithyrambic lines that he unleashed in *The Separate Notebooks*
derive more from Greek choral odes and the Psalms (which he translated
into Polish) than from Blake's more end-stopped eloquent sentences in "The
Marriage of Heaven and Hell." I remain as dazzled by Milosz's kinetic way around
an aphorism as I am by the leaps from line to line that, without losing fluidity,
eventually come full circle, form a whole, in spite of the word "notebook" in
the title of the book-length poem *The Separate Notebooks*. A poem inside a larger
poem; even another kind of poem: an evolutionary step in the art of poetry. I
find *The Separate Notebooks* to be the least dubious—the freshest and the most

spontaneous of Milosz's other long poems. ("The World" is of a different order, but then the "magical" aspect of the child's garden is a familiar conceit and the same form—rhymed and metered quatrains.) Many of his most anthologized poems, usually about specific events, run toward the sententious. I see Milosz walking the Berkeley coastline in the morning fog and humming to himself the sounds that would become the poems we most deeply want to hear—which are strange, which are not logical. Could it be he'd taken a cue from Gombrowicz? I think the *Notebooks* are Milosz's most radical, free, and least conforming to prior notions of "poetry" poems—a more successful, impactful, internally cohesive, and subversively structured venture into the open-endedness of so many of the twentieth century's attempts at epic poetry. It is in what appear to be his more offhand compositions that he and Zbigniew Herbert meet on common ground, shorn of the concept that Milosz had range and Herbert music: both had both. I can hardly think of any poetry after Rimbaud that matches Milosz's rhapsodic verses in *The Separate Notebooks*. The few exceptions include Saint-John Perse, whom Milosz acknowledged as a source, and someone like David Jones.

It was only much later, when recovered from the ecstasy of being carried away, that I became curious about the subject. In the interim, after countless hours giving readings and lectures all over the world throughout the 1980s, Milosz must have noted that there was a pattern to the questions he was being asked. He empathized with his Western audience and consented to do a book of inter-views with Ewa Czarnecka and Aleksander Fiut to provide a kind of grid of his imagination. What has to appear obscure to the non-Slavic reader is just part of Slavic history and folklore. And perhaps the most noble function of the Nobel Prize is to enable authors of Milosz's stature to publish (or get back in print) not only their own works, but other necessary books that would have almost no chance in the marketplace, like *Conversations with Czeslaw Milosz* and even such marvelous personal works as *The Land of Ulro* and his recent *A Year of the Hunter*.

▶

Maybe there should be a posthumous Nobel Prize, a Nobel Prize for the Dead, with no cash but lots of hoopla around the reissuing of an author's out-of-print works. (And the Nobel Prize for the Dead should by no means overlook certain authors who received the prize but whose best works are still out of print, etc.) Once again, his *Conversations* are profound as well as illuminating:

MILOSZ: The subject of "The Wormwood Star" is apocalyptic, of course. The Wormwood Star also appears in Dostoevsky's work. In *The Idiot,* Lebedev predicts that railroads will be the end of the world. And he's right, too. Dostoevsky treats him somewhat humorously, but Lebedev explains what he means. It's not a question of the railroads themselves but of the technology they symbolize. And so, the Wormwood Star is the fulfillment of one phase of the Apocalypse by twentieth-century civilization.

CZARNECKA: You said that this is a random collection of poems. I had the impression that these were purposely fragmentary images that were often in contrast but had an internal unity. What at first seemed a loose blend of poetry and prose took on a structure. .

MILOSZ: Yes, but let's not forget that I have many slips of paper in my hat. I can always pull them out and arrange them so they have a sense of harmony and unity.

6

Catching "up with the others" through his Nobel Prize, which corresponded with Lech Walesa and Solidarity, the youthful seventy-year-old Milosz could luxuriate in what must have been an awesome pleasure for a long-exiled author: his past works reappearing in freshly minted editions; his poems, old and new, translated by "two of the better younger poets" (as Milosz referred to them publicly in the early 1980s), Robert Hass and Robert Pinsky. His earlier translators, such as Peter Dale Scott and Lillian Vallee, could convey his narratives and ideas, leaving the reader with an "idea" about what the poem might be in its original Polish. A lot of Milosz's poems went well into English even before Hass and Pinsky came on the scene, like "Throughout Our Lands," but while the oft-quoted (and often read by Milosz) first and third sections ("If I had to tell what the world is for me / I would take a hamster or a hedgehog or a mole / and place him in a theater seat") are charming and accessible, by the time he reaches the end of the poem, he's in another "land" entirely and brushing up against the limits of ordinary language, and resorting, like an Antonin Artaud or a Peter Brook, to a language of shrieks and groans. He wants to put forth a stable and consistent exterior in the homage to Whitman and even more contemporary populist poetry "Throughout Our Lands" but is undone by his Slavic access to all the mess the unconscious dredges up—and at the most awkward times!

> But afterward? Who am I, the lace of cuffs
> not mine, the table carved with lions not mine, Dona Clara's
> fan, the slipper from under her gown—hell, no.
> On all fours! On all fours!
> Smear our thighs with war paint.
> Lick the ground. Wha wha, huh huh.

Let me back up and try to underscore the complexity of the issue of the right translator in a more roundabout way.

A package arrived while I was contemplating how to broach the question of translation without getting embroiled: it was Joseph Brodsky's last book, *So Forth,* largely translated by Joseph Brodsky and several other translators, or ostensibly written in English by Joseph Brodsky. Any poet who presents his work to the public in the manner of a Brodsky or a Milosz has to take a leaf from Ringo's book and admit that "I get by with a little help from my friends." Joseph Brodsky, bless him, was clueless when it came to translation, and his own poems (of which only a few good English versions exist) suffer immensely as a result. I open *So Forth* immediately, and my eye lights upon the following couplet:

> Trekking in Asia, spending night in odd dwellings, in
> granaries, cabins, shacks—timber abodes whose thin

Now if Brodsky had found a first-rate poet to work with him, his collaborator would have explained that this enjambment opens the rhythm to a pushing off that longs for elision and not, in this case, the closure of rhyme. Brodsky and George Kline fail to break it down, to genuinely recast the poem in another tongue. (I find myself admonishing "An Admonition," wishing I could feel as sure as some of my friends that Brodsky was an awesome poet, that his tone wasn't a bit arch, that he was a man always reaching beyond his capacities so that the reader senses the strain.)

> Trekking in Asia, spending night in odd dwellings, in
> granaries, cabins, shacks—timber abodes whose thin
> squinted windowpanes harness the world—sleep dressed,
> wrapped in your sheepskin, and do your best

"Thin / squinted windowpane" is overloaded, like a line from Derek Walcott around that time, where "the first cigarette triggers the usual fusillade of coughs." This is more amusing in isolation than inside a verbose *Collected Poems*. It was sad, even in the early years, watching Brodsky try to get his translators to appropriate W. H. Auden's metrics. (Auden offered to translate Brodsky in 1968, but Brodsky understandably couldn't imagine his hero working for him.) Elizabeth Hardwick, beside herself with laughter, recounted how Brodsky and Lowell, having been at loggerheads all afternoon, emerged from their translation session red-faced with frustration. If you want a somewhat far-fetched but ultimately appropriate comparison between the fates of Brodsky and Milosz in translation, imagine these lines from "An Admonition" having been translated by Auden, Richard Wilbur, Gary Snyder, or Anthony Hecht, whose version of "Cape Cod Lullaby" is still the high point of Brodsky in English. Rhythm and phrasing count for infinitely more in poetry than the cultural significance of proper nouns of which Brodsky's poems are chock-full. Milosz never sent his translators jumping through hoops, and the result of his restraint is successful.

Hass and Pinsky, formal virtuosos who to their credit resist pyrotechnics in favor of mastery in their own poems, created lively and catching equivalents to Milosz's rhymed and metered poems (or sections of poems), as in the Yeatsian fifth and seventh sections of "City Without a Name," which add to the splendor and variety of *The Separate Notebooks*. Without these radical juxtapositions, how can a poem satisfy like one of Bach's extended projects, which won't let you move and which reward this sternness when the ending leaves you ecstatic, transformed, and unable to recognize yourself, which is the first essential step toward recognition? To "you" stripped of all the roles you've had to play, now under the rubric of "multitasking," so that you've begun to doubt what you really feel, who you really are, ultimately. To give you a sense of how Milosz rhymes the original, I'll begin with the first two stanzas in Polish, each of which covers a broad spectrum. The many syllables of "zrozumiebie" don't make it sound Latinate or grand, and the rhyme of "slawa" and "brawa" brings in the language of the cradle.

> Litose I zrozumienie
> w wysokiej mamy cenie,
> no bo co?
>
> Pycha ciala I slawa,
> pocalunki I brawa,
> komu to?

Understanding and pity,
We value them highly.
What else?

Beauty and kisses,
Fame and its prizes,
Who cares?

Doctors and lawyers,
Well-turned-out majors,
Six feet of earth.

Rings, furs and lashes,
Glances at the Masses,
Rest in peace.

Sweet twin breasts, good night.
Sleep through to the light,
Without spiders.

Section 7 threw the translators back on their resources once again, and Milosz, more concerned with formal integrity than rigid rules about meaning, was receptive to Pinsky's innovative solution, and allowed him to add a line—with a Yiddish feel to it that wasn't in the original Polish—to keep the rhyme: "So what else is new?" Slavic languages allow for an immense number of unforced ways to rhyme, as a glance at Milosz's first two rhymed stanzas indicates.

From nails, mucous membrane,
Lungs, liver, bowels, and spleen
Whose home is made? Mine.

So what else is new?
I am not my own friend.
Time cuts me in two.

Milosz insisted on a few changes between *The Separate Notebooks* and *The Collected Poems,* particularly the translation of "The World." Pinsky and Hass altered a few lines, and Milosz chose to replace their artfully rhymed versions with his own more literal one for his *Collected Poems.* I was disappointed until I saw what the poets had altered, left out, or added to make the poems in "The World" sing. The models they used were William Blake's songs and Roethke's crisp, staccato poems that delve into childhood. Here are both translations of one section of the poem.

Parable of the Poppyseed

On a seed of poppy is a house.
Inside it are people, a cat and a mouse.
Outside in the yard, a dog barks at the moon.
Then, in his one world, he sleeps until noon.

The earth is a seed, and nothing more.
And that seed's a planet, and that seed's a star.
And even if there were a hundred thousand
Each seed would contain a house and a garden.

All in a poppyhead. They grow taller than hay.
The children run through, and the poppy plants sway.
And in the evening, when the moon is aloft,
You hear the dogs barking, first loudly then soft.

A Parable of the Poppy

On a poppy seed is a tiny house,
Dogs bark at the poppy-seed moon,
And never, never do those poppy-seed dogs
Imagine that somewhere there is a world much larger.

The Earth is a seed and really no more,
While other seeds are planets and stars.
And even if there were a hundred thousand,
Each might have a house and a garden.

All in a poppy head. The poppy grows tall,
The children run by and the poppy sways.
And in the evening, under the rising moon,
Dogs bark somewhere, now loudly, now softly.

Why did Milosz choose not to use Hass's version in his *Collected Poems*?

Write your answer here: "The distance between the meaning of the original and Hass's translation are too large," Hugh says, but _____

_____

_____

If you need more space, feel free to use a separate page.

I can't help believing that it is pitch and tone that are crucial; that the "words" will be subsumed by the music, which gives the reader a shot at transformation, being changed by the poem. I think Milosz was wary of pitch and tone. And so he overstressed "reality" as time went on. He might even have been suspicious of art. And while I remain charmed and warmed by Hass's familiar image and Roethkean music, it does lose sight of the philosophical argument, which for Milosz is the point.

I can see Milosz's objections, beginning with "Inside it are people, a cat and a [nonexistent] mouse" and continuing throughout the first stanza, but it's a pity to resign Hass's version to the archives. What would *you* have done: ask your translators to revise their errant lines, or, risking tone deafness, abandon the hard-won primer-like *Child's Garden of Verses* tone that Hass and Pinsky worked hard with a deadline to preserve? Pinsky, though far from impartial on this subject, is on target in his wager.

> RP: So I can identify with Czeslaw in saying, well, this thing that has slouched and slanted its way into our committee [Hass, Pinsky, and Milosz] is living and breathing in some kind of half-assed way; the sense is pretty literal, but there is also this smell of an alien, English-speaking animal, and *I* [Milosz] *don't want to listen to it inhaling and exhaling and grunting around in its cage, I want something more like a telephone or a conduit.*

That is a multidimensional cage. The cage of metrics decided upon in advance. The tightness required by the metrical decision. And how, charm aside, the translators may have reversed the poet's intention for a far simpler rendition of a poem in a language which has something like three times the possibilities for rhyme as does English, just as Italian has three times the possibilities for rhyme as does Russian. Italian, where as Osip Mandelstam noted, "everything rhymes" and opens the door to "slawa" and "brawa," "an infantile phonetics," where lines are tied together by words a child could utter like "abbo" and "gabbo." And rhyming, in the Slavic languages, isn't a strain. It's possible that the emphasis compensates for the absence of verbs.

7

And around the time modernism was spoken of in the past tense, Milosz chose to write a poem in the vein of Blake's *Songs of Innocence and Experience* and Stevenson's *A Child's Garden of Verses*. "The World" is delightful and it is deep. It was as he wanted it to be: different from other poetry.

> CZARNECKA: Besides, in *The Land of Ulro* you say that reading Blake's poetry, which you found in an anthology in occupied Warsaw, returned you to your childlike sense of enchantment, of experience, the child's sensual feeling for things.

> MILOSZ: Yes, but to write a work of that sort under those circumstances was a way of going against the grain. It turns out that all my work had gone against the grain. In a certain sense, I was sticking out my tongue at the world, sometimes consciously, sometimes less so. But I wasn't thumbing my nose, not jeering. "The World: A Naive Poem" is similar to *The Issa Valley:* unfashionable writing.

Hass, who would eventually become Milosz's unofficial official translator, felt connected to Milosz formally through their mutual admiration of Robinson Jeffers's long line, and his intuitive grasp of how to make the sensual detail come alive through accurate, deft, impactful phrasing, which gives a choral sound to modest, but moving in their accuracy, passages such as this:

> Northern sunset, beyond the lake a song of harvest wheat
> They move about, tiny, binding the last sheaves . . .

> You, my young hunter, had better just ease your canoe from the shore
> And pick up the killed mallard before it gets dark.

> (*THE SEPARATE NOTEBOOKS*)

The last two lines struggle to bring out open vowels, and then hard sounds at the end, and picking up the killed mallard seems a joyless act. Phrasing and attention to detail, a vital combination, make even the prose paragraphs in *The Separate Notebooks* capable of being memorized because the mind, mesmerized, returns and returns to vivid and arresting passages such as this one, which carries within it untapped—possibly inexhaustible—openings for writing in the future.

> In a night train, completely empty, clattering through fields and woods, a young man, my ancient self, incomprehensibly identical with me, tucks up his legs on a hard bench—it is cold in the wagon—and in his slumber hears the clap of level crossings, echo of bridges, thrum of spans, the whistle of the locomotive . . . one blood-red star is glowing.

But why shouldn't Milosz's work possess this quality? Approaching time and eternity from an entirely different perspective than his list of cohorts who also believe in *apokatastasis,* Milosz, like Gottfried Wilhelm von Leibniz, would say that whatever has come to be is somehow indestructible, not because we remember, but because the will can't alter what has been.

Notes

Ironwood 18 remains a great source, containing excellent essays by Robert Hass, Patricia Hampl, John Peck, Leonard Nathan, myself, and others, in addition to the new works by Milosz which are cited in this essay. Michael Cuddihy commissioned the essays for this issue before Milosz won the Nobel Prize. If I hadn't written an essay on Milosz which recorded my discovery of his work, and my reading everything he'd written that was available at that time, I would not have adopted the more intimate, decentralized tone of "The Milosz File." In the intervening years Milosz has become an institution, revered beyond measure, with his poetry rendered into English by one of the half-dozen best poets writing in English, who treated it, I hope, as an extension of his own work, and the best example of which is his re-creation of the medieval style in the prose section of Milosz's "From the Rising of the Sun." The poems I read in *Ironwood* at that time had the same effect on me that reading Beckett's story "Ill Seen, Ill Said" had on some of the language poets. They led me out of the "cage"—the familiar entrapments of English-language poetry that vacillated between two untenable poles—the familiar and the experimental, the too "comprehensible," and therefore "commensurate with paraphrase," road of the formalists, and, to choose Milosz's own phrase, "incomprehensible poetry." I have a different view of realism in relation to reality than the one offered by Milosz when he cites Dutch painting for confirmation.

But in essence I agree with Milosz's up-front rebuttal of poetry in his sequence of essays "Against Incomprehensible Poetry," whose tension is diminished by its settling on that side of the river where language is king, and the body and the environment are ancillary to the word. And where specious analogies between writing and the visual arts, considering that words like *reality* and *representation* mean something very different for the latter, only serve to widen the gap between language and reality.

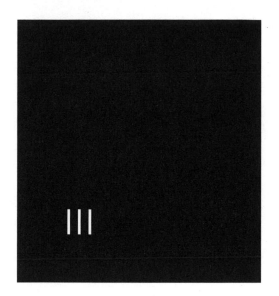

Reading T. S. Eliot on My Cousin's Farm in the Gatineau

1

We were staying with my wife's French-Canadian cousin and his lady friend Ros at their farm in the Gatineau Valley.

It was the end of August. I walked dry dusty roads bordered by milkweed pods. Something would have to burst, soon.

My left arm began to hurt as August wore on. Something minuscule and hard had begun to form. Something that didn't want to be dislodged. These were lazy days. I chose to read Armand's books in the shade on the porch while he and our future wives were beekeeping. Both Armand and my girlfriend are among the world's great "Tom Sawyers," masters at getting others to join them in doing innately uninteresting chores, like rehabilitating the chicken coop. But I would not take the bait. Many of Armand's books were both familiar and unfamiliar. Unfamiliar because they were different editions than ones I had known, both from Quebec and England, where he had gone to public school as a boy. My editions of T. S. Eliot's essays such as *The Sacred Wood* hadn't included gems on Baudelaire and Pascal.

The consensus of the group was that I should let this thing burning into my left triceps be exposed to the sun. That made it harder, that made it burn. That made it painful. There's nothing like a group of zany nonmedically oriented people (that is, not Jewish) oohing and aahing and poking at your body. Reluctantly prying myself away from these days of meditation at the end of summer, I forced myself to study this nameless inhabitant in the tarnished mirror they had purchased, like everything else, at a yard sale: it formed—of all things—a target! And it continued to grow. And it had a hardness I found hard to imagine on my skin, but it wasn't *on* my skin; it had rooted in, from within or without. I had reached my limit. It was time for a visit to the local doctor, whom Armand said wryly had a fine reputation, along with his brothers.

"Is it near?" I asked.

"Oh yes. Only twenty miles or so"—over dirt roads to where the Geggis had set out their shingle.

The carpeting was thick, the smell rank. (The Geggis, according to Armand, had been known to treat animals in a pinch.)

No white coat here—a short-sleeved print shirt. Dr. Geggi was around fifty, medium build with abundant coarse black hair that wasn't limited to his head.

"I see you're from New York City. How can I help you?"

"I have something on my arm."

"That's it? So you're from New York City, huh?"

"Yes."

"The doctors really soak you there, don't they?"

"They sure do."

"A few hundred bucks for a visit, right?"

"Yup."

"Those fancy doctors must sure know a lot. Let's have a look at your arm."

I laughed at Geggi's crustiness.

"Do you like the country?" he asked.

"Yes."

"It doesn't like you."

"Do you know what I've got?"

"Oh sure. Took me a second to identify that."

Is he going to wait until I've asked him what he's seen?

"You've got ringworm."

The Book of Samuel

"Ringworm! Can you remove it?"

"There are no instant cures. The last thing you'd want is for me to cut into it."

"What is the cure?"

"Well," leaning back in his swivel chair and gazing out the window at the distances, unbroken except for dilapidated fences on the weedy fields, "if you'd gone to one of those fancy Park Avenue doctors they'd have charged you a fortune for the visit and prescribe some heavy antibiotics that would cost you another hundred bucks and weaken your system, but all I want you to do is to apply iodine twice a day."

"Only twice?"

"You are in a hurry. More than twice and you'd burn the skin around it. And I want you to keep it out of the sun. If it doesn't begin to improve in ten days, come back and see me again."

I couldn't believe the recalcitrance of this hard target. Days passed; infinitesimal improvement.

This was life.

2

I think it was an encounter with Eliot that made me want to write poetry. His lines infiltrated my cadences and dreams. Here is the passage from "Ash Wednesday" that I couldn't shake:

> Lady, three white leopards sat under a juniper-tree
> In the cool of the day, having fed to satiety
> On my legs my heart my liver and that which had been contained
> In the hollow round of my skull. And God said
> Shall these bones live? shall these
> Bones live? And that which had been contained
> In the bones (which were already dry) said chirping:
> Because of the goodness of this Lady
> And because of her loveliness, and because
> She honours the Virgin in meditation,
> We shine with brightness.

And then I had a dream that I took as the sign to change my life—to separate from a girl (who rode every morning at dawn) and come to New York
to finally get to know my elusive and enigmatic father. I was riding a horse at
a canter through a dark eerie landscape and uncertain black earth riven with
ditches when we approached a high corral. There was no hitch in movement,
no anxiety as such. On the other side of the corral there was a leopard curled
into a ball, asleep, dreaming, and his unconscious emanations floated above his
head: "go on, go." So we jumped the corral.

> And I who am here dissembled
> Proffer my deeds to oblivion, and my love
> To the posterity of the desert and the fruit of the gourd.
> It is this which recovers
> My guts the strings of my eyes and the indigestible portions
> Which the leopards reject. The Lady is withdrawn
> In a white gown, to contemplation, in a white gown.
> Let the whiteness of bones atone to forgetfulness.
> There is no life in them.
>
> ("ASH WEDNESDAY")

I had—and still have—what I considered Eliot dreams. While "Ash Wednesday"
touched me in a way that no other poem had, I found relief from my idealization
of Eliot in Vladimir Nabokov's ludicrous parody of the poem in *Lolita*. (In *Ada*,
Nabokov's irreverence allowed him to conflate Auden and Lowell into a poet
named "Lowden.")

> Because you took advantage of a sinner
> because you took advantage
> because you took
> because you took advantage of my disadvantage . . .
>
> . . . when I stood Adam-naked
> before a federal law and all its stinging stars

The early Eliot is so hypnotic it sinks right into the unconscious. It is as immediately seductive as poetry gets. One of the tasks of contemporary poetry is to
get beyond hypnosis and memorability per se and replace them with a trace of
something different but equally indelible. The antidote to the hypnosis in this
passage, in which Eliot snaps us out of our trance with a shocking formal tone, is

The Book of Samuel

in the phrase "and that which had been contained." There may be more apparent Eliot effects—spry rhythmical mixture of repetition and biblical allusion—in a song by Nick Cave like "The Mercy Seat" than in a fine contemporary poem. "An eye for an eye and a tooth for a tooth / but anyway I know the truth / And I'm not afraid to die." The consummation of Eliot's appeal was the longest-running musical in history, *Cats.* And Eliot is so hugely communicative, so dry and funny, he doesn't have to say much. We don't feel he's trying to impress us. What appears to be pyrotechnics is part of a tonal register to which one would not have thought that an objection was possible.

I should mention, in case anyone should think that Eliot was so canonized as to be unassailable, that there are poets and critics, poet-critics actually, who reject the later Eliot. Two who stand out with laudable passion are Donald Davie and Geoffrey Hill. It would take a separate essay to state "The Case Against (the Later) Eliot" in its bizarre combination of complexity, rigidity, and severity. Briefly, Davie's objection (and Denis Donoghue recounts in *Words Alone* that he backed it up in heated conversations) has a lot to do with his notion that in *Four Quartets* Eliot abandoned the world of objects for an art that approached the detested Paterian condition that art aspires to the condition of music.

In an essay called "Dividing Legacies," Geoffrey Hill is adamant that Eliot went soft, Parnassian, and that *Four Quartets* are too cozy and comforting, too obliging rather than challenging to the reader. Some of Hill's quotations of a slackening, a loss of sensuous interest, in Eliot's critical prose are well taken. And he craftily selects one of the weakest passages in "Little Gidding" to cement his indictment. There is something peculiarly rigid in these criticisms, as if these men were reproaching Eliot for attempting what he attempted even if he did not, in their view, accomplish his goal.

I think Hill's diatribe shows a kind of tone deafness. On another note, I have always been more partial to his poetry than his criticism. God bless Geoffrey Hill for writing these lines in *Mercian Hymns:*

> Brooding on the eightieth letter of Fors Clavigera,
> I speak this in memory of my grandmother, whose
> childhood and prime womanhood were spent in the
> nailer's darg.

"Lady, three white leopards sat under a juniper-tree / In the cool of the day, having fed to satiety." I never tire of the word "satiety," and I will never tire of Eliot's use in *Four Quartets* of the phrase "haruspicate or scry." The first thing I remarked on as I branched out in my reading of contemporary poetry was that I could instantly detect the operation of the will, of artful construction. Exceptions were certain poems by Robert Duncan and W. S. Merwin, like "My Mother Would Be a Falconress," "Lemuel's Blessing," and "The Last Ones," and their books with titles suggesting a fresh start like *The Opening of the Field* and *The Moving Target*. Theodore Roethke's "The Lost Son" came closest to what I wanted from poetry, yet I found his veritable palimpsest of *Four Quartets* in *The Far Field,* while tremendous, still a bit desperate, as if it were a competition.

Eliot mastered the dark art of misdirecting others.

John Coltrane takes "My Favorite Things" out of the realm of objects. Eliot's emphasis on an "objective correlative" has fallen too much on the literal. Otherwise, how to explain how he inaugurated the surfeit of "objects" and "things" in Anglo-American criticism and poetics for close to a hundred years? This is not the Kantian thing of Rilke's *New Poems* or Pasternak's early work. Even a term like *objectivism* lends itself to misinterpretation. It's not exactly the kind of intoxicating credo that would send an inspired youth on the mad path of poetry. There is some parallel to Eliot in the way George Oppen evolved from the thingness of materials (and *The Materials*) in his middle period to the visionary in-seeing of *Seascape: Needle's Eye.*

> in the multiple world of the fly's
> multiple eye the songs they go to hear on
> this occasion are no one's own

> ("SOME SAN FRANCISCO POEMS, I,"
> SEASCAPE: NEEDLE'S EYE)

I would guess that Oppen's *Seascape: Needle's Eye* is in part a response to the vivid sailing imagery in *Four Quartets* that is in part Eliot's response to Melville.

I visited Oppen once. I was invited cautiously for an hour on Sunday afternoon and stayed until dark and would have stayed for dinner if I hadn't already abused the generosity of a friend who'd given me a ride and was now waiting patiently

The Book of Samuel

in his car while George and Mary concocted a scenario in which my wife and I would move to California, and she would teach mathematics at Cal Tech. . . . There were only two books visible on the wooden table in the starkly furnished living room: a library edition of the *Selected Writings of Martin Heidegger* and the *Collected Poems of T. S. Eliot*.

Eliot's forte was identifying lines that stirred emotion. He is by all rights a "wounded surgeon who plies the steel." I have just come across a bizarre corollary to these lines in a poem by a Dutch poet named Hans Faverey whose work appeared in book form in English for the first time this month, March 2004. He is a poetic descendant of Paul Celan, not Eliot, but his obsession with wounds and thresholds is Eliotic.

> Towards the end the cut withstands
> the wound itself. Many of these worms
> hope for recognition. The yielding
>
> holds out a little longer.
>
> A velvety tissue grows over
>
> unjoyment, once most has been
> seen through and wiped out. And so
> it finally takes shape: a flake of
> darkness, reborn through
> insight into denying
> this insight.

(FROM *THRESHOLDS*, IN *AGAINST THE*
FORGETTING: SELECTED POEMS)

In *The Waste Land* Eliot set 433 lines together with Ezra Pound's assistance who had stripped them of context or placed them in a setting that would allow us to see them as if for the first time. Every line of Eliot's repeats the previous line: that's why, as in dreams, there is no time. In *The Waste Land* the quotations Eliot used were more for tonal effect than didactic purposes. But in the twenty years separating *The Waste Land* and *Four Quartets*, he became dependent on quotations—many of them wisdom sayings—to convey his meaning, as in this one from Heraclitus.

> And the way up is the way down, the way forward is the way back.

("THE DRY SALVAGES," III)

3

I was restless in Canada for the simplest of reasons. I couldn't write. I was too close to my personal ring of fire that was living, rent-free, in my triceps, and pleased with itself, like the alien in *Alien,* for having remained undetected long enough to cause pain in a so-called superior species. It was an impressive target, but I could hardly throw darts at my own arm.

As the war in Iraq began, I became nauseous in the mornings whenever I glanced reluctantly—and against resolution—at the front page of the *New York Times.* I lost my concentration and yet I was consumed with the desire to respond, to leave my mark, as I eventually did with certain passages in poems written after 9-11—not that certain of my poems written prior to 9-11 weren't imbued with, if not prophetic of, that terror. I purchased my edition of *Four Quartets* in Bologna a month before 9-11.

The tone of the poems I was to write after 9-11 would owe something to Eliot's direct insinuations. I had to become another in order to begin again (Rimbaud is useful and true at fifty as well as fifteen). From the time of the Gore-Bush recount, the world became unfamiliar. I was raided by interminable viruses—beginning in November and lasting through the winter—vertigo, and fear of the reoccurrence.

It may seem disingenuous to hang a date on the beginning of my own deliquescence, and I'm not saying that the dire election was the only reason for what happened, but my crisis did begin at that precise moment in time, in the monsoon weather of that afternoon. If I tried to work or exhausted myself mentally in other ways, such as having a draining conversation with another person whose feelings I may have been trying to protect, strange goings-on

The Book of Samuel

would happen in my head. I reeled, laid waste. If I walked a half a mile in the cold I might break into a sweat. I began to feel panicky about going where I would normally go in case the symptoms would occur, sweats and a pounding heart. I had lost my resilience, my bounce, to cadge a phrase from a film to which I accompanied my son and his girlfriend. And I wasn't used to it. I knew people with strict boundaries around their lives, often indisposed; I hadn't lived that way and didn't plan to. But for the time being I was flattened.

There was very little I could read and very little poetry, especially in English, that spoke to this devastation. And that is how I found my way back to *Four Quartets* (and of course, other poems of Eliot). It was as if Eliot had already been there, or that these horrors that had finally come true were always implicit in his work, as they were explicit in the work of postwar European poets whose work I read in translation. For some reason, these poets, several of whom I consider among the great poets of all time as well as of the twentieth century, names that have by now become familiar and who I'd been reading for my entire writing life, weren't giving me what I needed at this moment of crisis.

It was May when I discussed what I was going through with a poet friend. She asked me a curious question. Had I seen the movie *Gladiator*? That was what happened to the Russell Crowe character, she said; once his mistrust and disillusion were complete (the murder of his family being an extension of this), he became depressed and wanted to die. "That's what depression is like," she said. I watched the movie again and I realized I had been too distracted by the spectacle to be receptive to the deeper theme. She was right. What had happened to Maximus personally was a mirror of a state he could no longer abide. Surely a mistrust of our own institutions must take its toll on the psyche. She may have known more about depression in a clinical sense than I did, but I saw in the gladiator's disenfranchisement a reflection of my own, both in terms of things that had happened to me recently and my absolute disgust and nausea with regard to the public sphere—as if they could be divided. When I was in psychoanalysis at twenty my analyst was very brutal whenever I tried to pin my state of mind on something happening outside my own specific emotional sphere, my own realm of efficacy or inefficacy. He impressed upon me that people used world issues to escape themselves. I couldn't really argue with that, or let's say I didn't want to waste time on that particular battle. Truth is not the adjunct of bias and opinion.

There were only two lines of poetry that defined my condition during this time, whose duration I cannot quite remember; they were my mantras, my sole inconsolable consolation: Eliot's "between melting and freezing the soul's sap quivers," and Donne's "Those are my best days, when I shake with fear." I have never read anything having to do with self-improvement, but a friend gave me a book by Pema Chödrön (she's under Buddhism, not self-help) called *The Places That Scare You* where I found the kind of insights I needed to hear, such as what she calls "Rinpoche's cheerful reminder that there is no cure for hot and cold."

> A first step is to understand that a feeling of dread or psychological discomfort might just be a sign that old habits are getting liberated, that we are moving closer to the natural open state. . . . Awakening warriors would find themselves in a constant state of anxiety. . . . After a while I realized that since the shakiness wasn't going away, I might as well get to know it. When our attitude toward fear becomes more welcoming and inquisitive, there's a fundamental shift that occurs. Instead of spending our lives tensing up, as if we were in the dentist's chair, we learn that we can connect with the freshness of the moment and relax.

I would remind myself that whenever I broke into a torrential sweat, what I loved most was when someone would remark "My god Mark, look at how you're sweating, and it isn't even that hot in here. . . ."

4   *"Tradition and the Individual Talent"*

The other poet I found I could read intensely was Horace, who I now understood was one of the shrewdest, subtlest, most worldly and sophisticated people to have graced this planet. I found that modernism was implicit in Horace, with his sudden leaps, allusions, reversals, turnings, and complex use of form and sound based on Greek models, "lines imbued with a rhythm rooted in Greek choral meters / that lashed his Latin into a faster dance" ("Hidden Clauses in the Lottery You Can Enter for Free," after Horace, Ode 2.3). Horace's sudden leaps to another plane were prophetic of catastrophe theory.

I didn't know Horace's work well until I was in my forties. Over several years I adapted a half-dozen of his poems for which I felt I could find precise parallels in contemporary life. The concordances providing word-for-word breakdowns of Horace's Latin provided quite a challenge. Each word, each phrase, was imbued with allusions to Greek poetry. I tried to incorporate as much of Horace's world and method as I could without torturing English.

➤

When I was in my early teens in the early 1960s, *Cleopatra* was being filmed. It was way over budget—and fast becoming the most expensive movie ever made. Richard Burton and Elizabeth Taylor were cast in the roles of the doomed lovers, and then fell in love on the set. Fell like the characters whose roles they played.

American power was reaching its height. There was unprecedented tabloid coverage of this affair and the end of any hope for privacy among celebrities. My contempt for the paparazzi did not extend to the people who bought these papers on their way to their jobs. The public turned to the stormy liaison between Liz and Dick to satiate their hunger for whatever was lacking in their lives, which was not so much power and money as love. They could sense an authenticity in Burton and Taylor's love for one another, and it held them in its thrall.

The Burton/Taylor liaison and the Kennedy assassination are not unrelated. Once Burton starred in *Camelot,* the actor's notoriety would be forever linked to the politician's. Notoriety. Being in a public space. Worshipped and envied. Tracked and traced. Stalked. Hunted.

Horace's Ode 1.37 (known as the "Cleopatra Ode") was the source of my first palimpsest. Like most of Horace's poems, it resists translation per se and cries out for transposition. This poem was the source of Andrew Marvell's "An Horatian Ode," in which he waits until the end, as does Horace, to portray the death of the hero, Cromwell. In my Horatian palimpsests, I inject the Latin poet's structures and strategies with an American context. As the Burton/Taylor love affair began to mingle oddly in my imagination with the Kennedy assassination, I began "Role Play."

And yet the public loved to hear about the real
love that flared on the world's

stage between the long adored actress
(from the ingénue's "pre-erotic sentience")

and the upstart mercurial Welshman.

And yet the American poet is often deluded by the fantasy of not being weighed down with antiquity, of having an opportunity to encounter history anew without an overlay.

Here's section 5 of "Role Play":

Love isn't a bad way to go when the cells of
the body politic are still

stunned by a regicide in which the victim
had no time to display

Cleopatra's uncommon courage . . . and fix
one serene final gaze on the reeling globe.

In the foreground I placed the affair between Richard Burton and Elizabeth Taylor in parallel with Antony and Cleopatra. Ode 2.3, the "Dellius Ode," is remarkably prescient in the way it predicts the double, triple, and quadruple agents of Joseph Conrad, Graham Greene, and John Le Carré. In real life, Dellius brought Antony and Cleopatra together.

If everyday life pretzeled everyone
I doubt the species could have come this far.
            And you, Dellius, couldn't have lived
                so many lives—would-be

assassin, traitor, ambassador, double-agent, go-between,
pornographer, procurer—without keeping your head.
            Marc Antony might never have set
                eyes on Cleopatra had you—

circus-rider of civil war—not handled the reservations.
When others would have hidden, you rode where you had to ride.

("HIDDEN CLAUSES IN THE LOTTERY YOU CAN ENTER FOR FREE,"
AFTER HORACE, ODE 2.3, IN *THE COUPLE*)

5

Few contemporary American poets had devised a way to engage with the world at large.

How could such a severance between public and private occur?

The Waste Land is indebted to *Heart of Darkness* in the construction of a work in which something terrible is going to happen and be happening in other forms along the way. Something terrible, in an apocalyptic sense, that will lead to a deluge. A deluge not unlike Rimbaud's. Or the cleansing that Birkin called for in *Women in Love.*

I don't know that anyone has pointed out that *Four Quartets* shares many attributes with Conrad's later, slower-moving masterpiece of inaction, *Victory.* We are afraid for Axel Heyst from the start, long before he is stalked. We worry for him, as we do for other of Conrad's romantics, because they don't worry enough for themselves. The sense of menace and foreboding—and longing and transcendence and hope and love—are present in both works. The authorial voice has placed the world in such a fragile condition—"words slip, slide, crack under the tension." Both works contain implicit pleas to goodness and acknowledge how fragile, difficult, and dangerous it is to get other people to collaborate because they're so mired in habit; habit has replaced being. It occurs to me that two of the finest writers to have emerged since the Second World War—writers to whom Eliot was undoubtedly important—are a playwright and a poet, Harold Pinter and Frederick Seidel. Both wrote screenplays of *Victory.* Somewhat paradoxically, Seidel's was filmed, Pinter's wasn't. This is the menace that replaces the more palpable and immediate and concrete dangers of World War II, during which time Pinter and Seidel were young boys. Seidel has a sinister, cynical, creepy (and crawly) poem called "Victory" about his experience on location during the shooting of *Victory.*

> The Steadicam glides everywhere,
> Holding its head in the air like a King Cobra.
> The ecology
> Of the island is fragile, but the second airport will never be
>   built.
> This isn't Acapulco 1949 about to Big Bang.

You might step into a jungle and it's thick.
You step into the warm water and it's thin.
But nothing jiggles the Steadicam.
The poisonous viper is authorized to use deadly force
Only on the jungle path to the waterfall above the golf
      course.

Someone has seen a ten-foot lizard
Near the set. Someone was seen feeding a monkey
Bananas. The set itself is a subset of itself,
A jungle set in the jungle.
Islam is aerosolized into the atmosphere,
Coating the jungle scenes with time.

St. Agatha is the martyr whose breasts got hacked off,
But in the movie they don't.
The breasts that don't get removed
Anticipate the replenishing monsoon.

6

What do all the towering poems of a certain time try to do if not create an environment?

Four Quartets have more in common, with their emphasis on an impalpable spiritual crisis made palpable through place, with *The Duino Elegies, The Heights of Machu Picchu, Briggflats, Mercian Hymns, The Morning of the Poem,* and *Baltics* than with the more empirical "place" epics such as *The Cantos, Paterson,* and *The Maximus Poems.*

I like to think of Eliot as sandwiched between Beethoven and Robert Smithson, both their time periods, past and future, their arts, their projects. Eliot would not let his poems flow over into the environment; *Four Quartets* are an environment: "Burnt Norton," "East Coker," "The Dry Salvages," "Little Gidding." Has anyone remarked the inestimable value of those place-names, as if imbued with magical properties?

The Book of Samuel

Eliot created environment through absence. This is what sets the *Quartets* apart from more empirical long poems.

I happened to catch *The Petrified Forest* on TV the other night, and what does Leslie Howard refer to in a diatribe against the modern spiritual condition if not "the Hollow Men," and that was in 1936. A mere epigraph to that poem from Conrad ("the horror . . .") has become an iconic phrase! And what is Conrad's work if not an environment, rampant in visual rhymes?

> The Tropical Belt Coal Company went into liquidation. The world of finance is a mysterious world in which, incredible as the fact may appear, evaporation precedes liquidation. First the capital evaporates, and then the company goes into liquidation. These are very unnatural physics, but they account for the persistent inertia of Heyst, at which we "out there" used to laugh among ourselves—but not inimically. An inert body can do no harm to any one, provokes no hostility, is scarcely worth derision. It may, indeed, be in the way sometimes; but this could not be said of Axel Heyst. He was out of everybody's way, as if he were perched on the highest peak of the Himalayas, and in a sense as conspicuous. Every one in that part of the world knew of him, dwelling on his little island. An island is but the top of a mountain. Axel Heyst, perched on it immovably, was surrounded, instead of the imponderable stormy and transparent ocean of air merging into infinity, by a tepid, shallow sea; a passionless offshoot of the great waters which embrace the continents of this globe. His most frequent visitors were shadows, the shadows of clouds, relieving the monotony of the inanimate, brooding sunshine of the tropics. His nearest neighbour—I am speaking now of things showing some sort of animation—was an indolent volcano which smoked faintly all day with its head just above the northern horizon, and at night leveled at him, from amongst the clear stars, a dull red glow, expanding and collapsing spasmodically like the end of a gigantic cigar puffed at intermittently in the dark. Axel Heyst was also a smoker; and when he lounged out on his verandah with his cheroot, the last thing before going to bed, he made in the night the same sort of glow and of the same size as that other one so many miles away.

(*VICTORY*)

The Heart of Darkness may take colonization and savagery and the destructive element in which we live as its subject; it connives through context, setting, jungle, and vegetation to take more than a leaf, and his leave, from Darwin.

Eliot wants his environment to be on the level of music: this is astonishing—and yet despite this abstraction he conveys the sense of a particular climate with greater acuity than more empirically minded poets. Yeats's tower-world is far more archetypal than Eliot's. And poetry, if it is to have a future, will have to create an environment.

> Where you lean against a bank while a van passes,
> And the deep lane insists on the direction
> Into the village, in the electric heat
> Hypnotised. In a warm haze the sultry light
> Is absorbed, not refracted, by grey stone.
> The dahlias sleep in the empty silence.
> Wait for the early owl.

> ("EAST COKER," I)

7

There's an element of guesswork in beauty. I don't like a lot of makeup on women, and Eliot's *Quartets* are very elegant and spare in this way. (Even though his biographer Peter Ackroyd claims that Eliot had a period when he wore green eye-makeup on his face.)

Not knowing anything about the why or when of "Little Gidding" imbues the poem with an element of elemental mystery that is followed up with its litany elements.

> This is the death of air.
>
> . . .
>
> This is the death of earth.
>
> . . .
>
> This is the death of water and fire.

The Book of Samuel

➤

Do Beethoven's late string quartets have followers?

The limitations imposed by the instruments—wood—are part of an environment too.

➤

My cousin has done nothing to embellish the porch rail on which I rest my legs. Whatever paint the porch rail once had has been worn away by time, exposing the beautiful, smooth graininess of the wood. I think my cousin has devoted far more time to making honey than attending to the aesthetics of his farmhouse, which is his summer retreat from Montreal, where he teaches international law at McGill and travels the globe to keep the whales from being machine-gunned by the Japanese.

Jean-Luc Godard (who quoted from Eliot's essay "Tradition and the Individual Talent" as early as the language school scene in *Band of Outsiders*) demonstrates the importance of the instruments in *Prenom: Carmen*. Godard shot this film when he was around the same age as Eliot when he wrote the *Quartets,* fifty. In *Prenom: Carmen,* a group struggles to play Beethoven's late string quartets. Godard shows us the players in counterpoint to the actors going through the torments of playing his intensely sexual—and naked in all senses—*Carmen*. Nakedness is no shield here. There is a tacit allusion to the attention needed to elicit sounds from the stringed instruments. The cellist, violinists, and violist try to render Beethoven's exacting late string quartets in a room outside of which there is mayhem. Godard stresses physicality, the exertion required by the players to draw the necessary resonance from the wood.

Eliot's places are subsumed, atomized, illuminated by the sounds that come from four stringed instruments. Like Beethoven, he will take the concept of chamber music to another astral plane.

The price for continually taking into account the nature of reality is pain. Eliot's pain results from the acuity of his perceptions. John Berryman categorized Eliot's career as "a pure system of spasms."

"Astronomers say they have heard the sound of a black hole singing . . . [in] B flat—or B flat 57 octaves lower than middle C. The black holes play the lowest note in the universe" (*New York Times*, September 16, 2003).

Eliot is far more interested in Beethoven's deafness than Milton's blindness. He was a student of deprivations. (Montale has a line, "where depraved spring. . . .") His philosophical training may have inclined him to regard writing poems as solutions to problems. He sets out to solve the problem of time as space. In a note he proposed: "To get beyond time and at the same time deeper into time."

So that each line that Eliot writes takes its place before or alongside the line that preceded it.

> The way up and the way down are one and the same.

>   ("EAST COKER")

> The same road goes both up and down.

>   (*HERAKLEITOS AND DIOGENES,*
>   TRANS. GUY DAVENPORT)

Eliot found the gaiety and quickening of the Quartet in A Minor, op. 132, an inspiration while he was composing his *Quartets*. I hear echoes in the indelible lines:

> Often together heard: the whine in the rigging,
> The menace and caress of wave that breaks on water,
> The distant rote in the granite teeth

>   ("THE DRY SALVAGES," I)

It was the Quartet in B-flat Major that Eliot identified as the locus of Beethoven's struggle to express the inexpressible.

Four Quartets is infused with the torments of tenderness—a tenderness so immense it lacks no boundary: we can always take the measure of lust. Tenderness knows no bound. And it is tenderness that torments the quartets of Beethoven as well as those of Eliot.

W. H. Auden answers the questions sounded by Eliot's instruments in one of his later discursive and tonally rich landscape poems, "In Praise of Limestone":

> . . . when I try to imagine a faultless love
> Or the life to come, what I hear is the murmur
> Of underground streams, what I see is a limestone landscape

8

There were other minor drawbacks to our stay in the Gatineau, one of which, with my professed love of solitude and the country, I am loath to admit: boredom. This would never have been the case had we not just spent six weeks at a cottage on Lake Muskoka, where the only event of note was a hurricane— after which my girlfriend jumped into the murky, turbid, and contagious waters in her two-piece to right the family outboard. I wouldn't have gone into Lake Muskoka right after that hurricane for anything. The hurricane had stirred up everything that had ever been deposited in the lake; it was rife with disease. But as Camus said in *The Plague,* only the people who feared the plague got it. Earlier in the summer my girlfriend had seen a canoe topple over half a mile from shore, ran down to the dock, and paddled out to help. I chalk this sixth sense up to her Indian blood and find her lack of self-concern beautiful.

One of Armand's friends showed films in his barn, and one night he screened his favorite film to see stoned: *Stairway to Heaven* (or *A Matter of Life and Death*), directed by Michael Powell. It must have been my least favorite film to see stoned because, though craving distraction, I dozed through most of it. You know the feeling when someone else's idea of heaven is your idea of hell.

Twenty-five years later, Michael Powell's autobiography appeared; I rented *Stairway to Heaven* and again fell asleep. His autobiography was compelling, and it inspired me to rent other films of his, all of which I liked immeasurably more than *Stairway to Heaven,* and several of which blew me away: *I Know Where I'm*

Going!, Black Narcissus, The Red Shoes (which I'd refused to see before due to the look that came over my mother's face when she mentioned the movie, and the nightmares I had about red shoes that were possessed), and, it goes without saying, *Peeping Tom,* the film that ruined his career, and which I had seen in the interim.

And shooting on location on the island of Mull in the Hebrides lent a kind of genius and magic to *I Know Where I'm Going!,* a film I watch in amazement, with moments unlike anything else I have seen on a screen, moments that could have been out of *Macbeth* or *The Tempest.* It is reminiscent of the beach scene in Antonioni's *Le Amiche,* his adaptation of Pavese's novel *Among Women Only,* and the astonishing sequence he shot on the barren, rocky, windswept Lisca Bianca in *L'Avventura.*

Like Eliot, Powell didn't make a fetish of environment: half of the film *I Know Where I'm Going!* was shot in the Hebrides and half at Pinewood Studios. And sometimes they were magically mixed together. One of the things that Michael Powell was most proud of was that no one could distinguish between the male lead, Roger Livesey, who never came within five hundred miles of the island because he was acting in a play in London, and his double. The values of the Scots islanders moved me too.

> "People around here are poor."
> "No, they just don't have very much money."

As soon as I have some money I plan to go to the Hebrides.

I find film terms very useful to describe poetic effects. Since Eliot's procedure was to create maximum resistance, obstacles and difficulties, it brings to mind a comment by Powell's cinematographer, Erwin Hillier, that he used the vibrant effect of shooting against the light instead of with the flat light in the studio: the contrast "brings to life the story in a more exciting manner." Powell said Hillier spent his life waiting for the right cloud to give him the cast of sky—the *clair-obscure*—he wanted.

The day after I watched *I Know Where I'm Going!* for the first time, I received an e-mail from the Scottish novelist Alan Warner, which had a passage that went something like this: ". . . and last night Hollie and I rented a wild weird and surreal film: *I Know Where I'm Going,* which was shot on the same island in the Hebrides on which *Morvern [Callar]* takes place."

Morvern Callar is among the most original novels I've come across in years; I'm especially drawn to the section that takes place on Mull (annoyingly reduced to a ten-second gaze of longing by actor Sam Morton in the BBC's film of the novel), which is a kind of cross between Thoreau and J. G. Ballard. This passage is in the voice of the nineteen-year-old wild girl, Morvern.

> From up there you could see all that land; from the Back Settlement westwards where the railway moved into the pass, following the road toward the power station, the village beyond where the pass widened out toward the concession lands. Birches clustered in sprays where the dried-up burns dipped into the streams. One stream ran under the concrete bridge by the sycamore where sweet primroses were spreading thickly. Flickers were coming off the loch and the massive sky seemed filled with sparkling dust above those hot summer hills, fattened with plants and trees. You could hear the waterfalls down in the gulley. They would be spraying onto ferns there and drops of water would be hanging from their tips. I looked out at the landscape moving without any haste to no bidding at all.

9

Eliot's spiritual aspiration, to transcend, to get "beyond" time—and yet retain the element of space!—were destructive to the future of his poetry. He wanted his poems to distill the wisdom he had assimilated, the wisdom of our collective past, but wisdom—conceptual as well as embedded—does little to create the friction necessary for poetry to exist. Wisdom is best discovered en route.

> It would be the same at the end of the journey,
> If you came at night like a broken king,
> If you came by day not knowing what you came for,
> And turn behind the pig-sty to the dull façade
> And the tombstone. And what you thought you came for
> Is only a shell, a husk of meaning
> From which the purpose breaks only when it is fulfilled
> If at all.

> ("LITTLE GIDDING," I)

Eliot's calculated gestures, though minimal, have titanic effect. A parallel might be how much a poet can get out of the linguistic equivalent of an actor's shrug or sigh. A parallel might be Bogart's acting. There is little that method actors, like Dean or Brando, offer that Bogie hadn't initiated and expressed with a split-second of delay or sudden burst of aggression as when, in *The Maltese Falcon,* his sudden volatility, a verbal lashing that ends with his smashing a whisky glass in the fireplace—impossible to have foreseen a moment before—leads Mary Astor to respond with such breathlessly quick phrasing that the sentence sounds like one word: "Why you're the wildest most unpredictable man I've ever met." Bogart, like Eliot, uses the most minimal means possible to express the desolation that he feels: note the look that crosses his face in *Casablanca* when he discovers Ingrid Bergman with Sam at the piano, or the way he crumples a napkin when he's alone and nobody's watching.

One feature of modernist novels, from *Ulysses* to *Mrs. Dalloway* to *Under the Volcano* to Wolfgang Koeppen's *The Hothouse,* is a time frame limited to a day in the life. Has anyone suggested that *The Waste Land* was an instance of what Eliot experienced emotionally every day?

There is little doubt that Eliot suffered from an excess of emotion, an intolerable burden. He did his best to appear unruffled—sometimes an umbrella *isn't* an umbrella. (A mackintosh and hat sufficed for Graham Greene.) His reticence—armed with his umbrella in the London fog—is like a reversal of Melville's exuberant phallicism. In the realm of magical thinking, this is an antidote to the threat of embarrassment and shame.

The reason for Eliot's authority is that his work existed at the site of art. In his essays, especially those on Elizabethan dramatists, he works as a kind of archeologist on a salvage operation, because it was there that he discovered poetry from a welter of words in those plays; to dig out meaning from a nest of conventions.

Eliot's mimicry of the touchingly inept voices in *Sweeney Agonistes* is pitch perfect. He is not afraid to stand on the brink of absurdity. He has given me the courage to go on with my work in times when self-doubt might have paralyzed me. I embraced the conclusion from "The Blank Verse of Marlowe."

But the direction in which Marlowe's verse might have moved, had he not "dyed swearing," is quite un-Shakespearean, is toward this intense and serious and indubitably great poetry, which, like some great painting and sculpture, attains its effects by something not unlike caricature.

He is getting away with murder, but murder at the remove of a murder story, of which he was a fan. His allusion in "East Coker" to being lost in a dark wood is not to Dante but to Conan Doyle. "Grimpen" is derived from *The Hound of the Baskervilles.*

> In the middle, not only in the middle of the way
> But all the way, in a dark wood, in a bramble,
> On the edge of a grimpen, where is no secure foothold
>
> ("EAST COKER," II)

Imagine the copyeditor's query to these lines (with their oblique homage to Pound's "The Seafarer"): do you mean "where *there* is no secure foothold?"

And yet without a secure foothold, he knew that poetry had the power to unleash destructive forces as well as to make him more vulnerable than he had bargained for, as in the final scene of Robert Aldrich's cautionary and apocalyptic *Kiss Me Deadly,* when the androgynous, unreadable, blonde femme fatale opens the Pandoran lead "box" whose radioactive light sears her eyeballs. "Looking into the heart of light, the silence." Empty and blank sea.

Eliot seems to have been stoical with regard to the day to day, so stoical that he forced himself to become poetically impervious to the instant. Poetry, he said, is a form of punctuation. The pain of life's beauty and fleetingness was something Eliot longed to put on hold. His poems are an almost military strategy to not feel, to prevent himself from feeling, from being overcome, even taken aback, by tenderness and lust. Where are the girls in their summer dresses? Death has taken their place. (After the brief cameo of the hyacinth girl.) But the very idea of a strategy not to feel contains its opposite: the fear of being overwhelmed.

But when, if ever, was Eliot caught off guard?

Last winter I went to see a highly touted production of *Medea,* with the risk-taking actress Fiona Shaw in the title role. After Medea killed her children and came out in a sheet covered in imaginary red gore, electronic music started up in an attempt to parallel the horror of the event. There was a sudden hush: the actors stopped moving, everyone in the orchestra began to look upstairs, and word began to get around that someone in the theater had died at that instant. For some reason, everyone assumed it was someone very old, who had decided to continue venturing out into the world, rather than have their last years defined by age. After a few minutes, I got up to investigate and discovered that no one had died, that a young man had had an epileptic fit and was to be carried downstairs by paramedics; the hunky actor playing Jason told the audience that the play would resume in fifteen minutes. I felt as if chance, once again, had thrown up a truth, if only I could unearth it. Then I began a poem, "Cutting Edge Production," that re-creates the scene in a way that uses the seizure as a kind of primal inheritance that everyone has within them—this "seizure," this terrible potential for ultimate collapse in a dreaded public place.

The young man reminded me of a neurasthenic in one of Eliot's poems.

Imagine Eliot, then, as the villain in a murder mystery. He aligns himself with evil wishes. Unquestionably part of Eliot's allure is that he assimilates the methods and tones of great literature I hadn't read when I first read him, like Dante, or hadn't remembered, like the book of Ezekiel. By "hadn't remembered" I mean I was taken by surprise by the lines in a new—and dangerous—context. This arrests attention; it doesn't necessarily lead to art. It seems a strange association except that Eliot is in the wood, "the grimpen."

The names of the places in *Four Quartets* bring to mind enclosures, places with severe definition and limits.

10

Eliot's language is as unconventional as his dress is conventional. It is no accident, then, that one of Eliot's most sympathetic critics, Ted Hughes (another original, and therefore more likely to risk going out on a limb for Eliot and whose greatness, as a poet, incredibly, has been obscured in America by notoriety from the never-ending controversy involving Sylvia Plath), would attempt, some fifty years after what William Carlos Williams called "the disaster of *The Waste*

Land," to create, in collaboration with Peter Brook, a language of pure expressivity called Orghast. Hughes devised sound clusters like "lohorn" and "stch chchchcroooar," which the actor intuits isn't a declaration of love. Margaret Croyden interviewed Peter Brook on the project:

Q: I'm interested in what happened when you played *Orghast* in a village in Iran. How did the people react to the sound and to the language? How were they affected by it?

PB: They were enormously gripped and impressed at the very beginning by the strange, powerful primitive sounds of Orghast and the coming of the fire. It at once caught their imaginations. They didn't know what it was about, but they liked it. They were held by it.

Hughes's translation of Seneca's *Oedipus* is an unremarked landmark. Not Orghast, or a new language, but a breakthrough none the less that identifies the strains. This is a book that must find its way back into print immediately.

> a horseman coming breakneck past us   but the
> plague caught him up   it caught his horse   mid-
> stride   head over heels   full tilt   down
> the rider beneath it
>
> everything green has withered   the hills that
> were cool with forest   they're dusty ridges
> deserts of brittle sticks   the vine's tendril is white
> it crumbles when you touch it
> where are the gods   the gods hate us   the gods
> have run away   the gods have hidden in holes
> the gods are dead of the plague   the rot and stink
> too
>
> there were never any gods   there's only death

11

I think it was our second night in Brooklin, Maine, seven years after the ring-worm incident in the Gatineau. We had barely unpacked when a friend called to ask if we wanted to hear a harpsichord concert on Deer Isle.

It was an impossibly foggy night in the future. A hush had descended. I felt muffled and comforted in the awesome blankness. We arrived at the church on Deer Isle. Thirty or forty people in the pews. I couldn't believe how the space swelled with sound as Louis Bagger lit into his harpsichord. This was the sparest and fullest sound imaginable. The sharp notes of the harpsichord were given richness in the fog. I didn't want it to end. I had never felt more suspended, the notes carried; they penetrated, they were not swallowed by the fog. I felt in touch with hundreds of years of history and solitude.

It chokes me to remember. So much has changed. So much beauty and sadness. My beautiful friend, married to a novelist, blessed with two daughters, was stricken with MS. And now at fifty-four, it's an arthritic effort to rise and search my musty shelves for a CD of Bach fugues to put me more deeply back into the moment. Gustav Leonhardt will have to do—though he hasn't the flair of Louis Bagger! Perhaps there is an inherent sadness in the passage of time—I wish I could transport myself to the church in Deer Isle at this instant. And find a harpsichord at the altar.

12

You have to look at the *Bhagavad Gita* to find a book that expresses the conflict of being and nonbeing as well as Eliot does in *Four Quartets*. It is almost impossible to get at the axis of being and nonbeing, "the brief transit where dreams cross." *In Transit* might be a good title for the soul's next book. Or would Shambhala insist on a title more like one by Pema Chödrön, *The Wisdom of No Escape*? *Four Quartets* exists in antithesis to poetry in the sense that poetry registers temporality, and Eliot wants to get beyond that perspective. Poets as apparently different as Emily Dickinson and Robert Lowell are consumed by and obsessed with temporality—Lowell to the point of temporicide—which includes the moment of composition. And the indelible aspect of dailiness is imperfection, fallibility. Poetry exists at the axis of being and nonbeing. But language is a prisoner of temporality.

Eliot strives to depersonalize the psychological struggle. The result is a success that in some sense defeats fallibility—and simultaneously annihilates itself. Eliot's poems are instances of consummate expression that defeat futurity. The

The Book of Samuel

pleasure of reading Eliot is in itself almost inexpressible. And part of it is a delight in his naughtiness. Its deep appeal is to childhood.

> Here we go around the prickly pair
> Prickly pear prickly pear
> Here we go round the prickly pear
> At five o'clock in the morning.

("THE HOLLOW MEN," V)

Eliot's authority was his consummate mask. But all masks are only partial aspects of possibility. Eliot's may be the canniest mask ever constructed. Ted Hughes phrases it impeccably in "The Poetic Self."

> The quality that we feel to be his "greatness" is there in each passage of
> the verse, and usually in each line. But even in these minutiae of verbal
> tone, cadence and texture, it is "greatness" of a densely characteristic and
> consistently blended sort. The notable distinction of it is that it stands
> slightly outside, a reader sets it automatically slightly outside, what we think
> of as the "literary." To compare it in this respect with the work of any other
> poet in English throws this peculiarity into relief. In all his poems up to
> the end of *Ash Wednesday* the poetry lacks that provisional air of "licence," a
> sense of liberties taken, such as pervades even the most solemn moments of
> any other major poet. Usually this licence, of word, metaphor or whatever,
> is the very wings of their flight, the improvisatory genius that lifts them
> over gulfs. Contingent struggle, expedient means, exuberant freedom from
> all sacred control, the fluidity of extempore solutions, for almost all poets
> these are the stuff of invention. Eliot eschews them utterly.

Eliot's poetry came to mark an impasse; the road stops after Eliot, and in this sense he is not a generative poet. He consolidates, cannily using contemporary materials with unsurpassed deftness. That's why when *The Waste Land* was published William Carlos Williams in his *Autobiography* howled that it set us back twenty-five years. (In response, Allen Ginsberg would write "Howl.") It would take another twenty-five years—or more—for readers to learn to quicken at the astonishing hybridity of *Spring and All* and *Descent of Winter,* where Williams, as Shakespeare did before him, sometimes proves that the highest poetry may be the lowest poetry, something even more guttural and strangulated and ineloquent than Eliot had ever contrived.

To freight cars in the air

all the slow
clank, clank
clank, clank
moving above the treetops

(WILLIAMS, "10/30,"
DESCENT OF WINTER)

Now what sense is there in striving toward the inarticulate?

Generativity is its own criterion. In contrast to Eliot, I consider D. H. Lawrence the quintessential generative writer, with an almost unthinkable amalgamation of potentials in a staggering variety of forms. Lawrence sought anxiety, rupture; Eliot sought escape from rupture, anxiety. Eliot's greatness turned poets as different as W. H. Auden and Charles Olson into counterpunchers in their desperate struggle not to merely replicate his manner. I love it that Eliot could polarize people the way he did. Touching nerves was his specialty, which is why he was not so interested in *drugs,* but in—of all things!—anesthesia.

> Or as, when an underground train, in the tube, stops too long between
>   stations
> And the conversation rises and slowly fades into silence
> And you see behind every face the mental emptiness deepen
> Leaving only the growing terror of nothing to think about;
> Or when, under ether, the mind is conscious but conscious of nothing—

("EAST COKER," III)

13

In the history of poetry, there is no case as curious as Eliot's, no one whose power is so difficult to define beyond its sheer presence. It's the difficulty of not settling for anything less than expressing the inexpressible. The case of Paul Celan is not that far removed, and neither is the case of Donne (John).

> Oh, to vex me, contraries meet in one:
> Inconstancy unnaturally hath begot
> A constant habit; that when I would not

I change in vows, and in devotion.
As humorous is my contrition
As my profane love, and as soon forgot:
As riddlingly distempered, cold and hot,
As praying, as mute; as infinite, as none.
I durst not view heaven yesterday; and today
In prayers, and flattering speeches I court God:
Tomorrow I quake with true fear of his rod.
So my devout fits come and go away
Like a fantastic ague: save that here
Those are my best days, when I shake with fear.

(DONNE, "HOLY SONNET 19")

They work in a language whose enemy is their own literacy and fluency. Only the inexpressible needs to be expressed, addressed. A cry in the desert. The desert is the home of the inexpressible. With only the rare threshold. The threshold unifies everything that surrounds it, in earth and air, with life. The poet is a thresholdologist, and *Four Quartets,* more than anything else that Eliot would write, is his poem of the threshold.

Is there any question that Eliot desired grace? What interests me is the desire to touch something undeniable. An unrefuted paean to existence: "There they were, dignified, invisible, / Moving without pressure, over the dead leaves, / In the autumn heat, through the vibrant air" ("Burnt Norton," I). Something that withers under too hard a pursuit, or refuge in theory. No line defines the desired condition better than "And the unseen eyebeam crossed, for the roses / Had the look of flowers that are looked at" ("Burnt Norton," I). Do you like these roses? Would you like to have been looked at in this way? I would. And since being, like the poet, is on its way, arrival, despite its brevity, is dependent on there being a threshold. It's from there we cross over into the interior, from dwelling to tomb.

Eliot's poems represent what is withheld from knowing. There is something enchanting about their stinginess, their fracture, their brokenness.

There is nothing mannered about the twistedness of expression; it's not something to be settled into. It is poetry mostly in an elemental sense. "This is the death of air." When he felt that he had exhausted the means available to him as a poet, he became a playwright. His manner never overtakes the matter. Eliot never becomes Eliotic in the way that Pound becomes Poundian. The mad seek restrictions, since the internal limit is so ill-defined. Why else would Robert Lowell, for example, spend the best part of his last ten years on earth stuffing everything into a fourteen-line loose approximation of a sonnet, lines whose randomness save him from dullness? Eliot's poems explode sense and appeal to intuition. He can be so beautifully vague, and vague in a way that would dismantle so much of what passes for poetry. Lowell's "sonnets" are an antonym to Eliot's practice. Maybe it is madness that sparked the rejuvenating *Day by Day* or the Payne Whitney poems of James Schuyler.

There's yet another kind of poet who longs—lusts—to use language as a thing in itself and to whom the material is more open to chance, the way Williams found himself writing *Descent of Winter* while crossing the Atlantic on an ocean liner. Subject to chance, but not inconsequential: there is a striving that leads to the necessary breakdown. And it is the breakdown where language and emotion are commensurate. The fracturing isn't part of the willful formal fracturing that accompanies the superannuated term *experimental*.

Now I wish I could have produced these sentences from the vantage point of my cousin Armand's front porch on his farm in the Gatineau, but there would be too many obvious inconsistencies; such a ruse would be seen through immediately. It turns out that my next rereading of Eliot as an entirely other poet than the one I thought I knew occurred in Bologna twenty-five years later when I had obtained a Faber and Faber edition of *Four Quartets* which I then carried with me everywhere, and read in the late afternoons while the redness spread under the colonnades and I contemplated the wreck of my life. This edition with its yellow cover with gray images and graying paper is particularly beautiful as an object in itself, like the grainy wood of the porch rail. Why a Faber and Faber edition is stamped on the back "*Penguin* Italia (20000 lire)" I do not know.

Note and Proviso

Beethoven's quartets could of course be said to have followers. I mean my statement suggestively; but in the *Times Literary Supplement* of March 19, 2004, as I was concluding this essay, Charles Rosen had something interesting to say about influence and Beethoven.

> Mendelssohn's imitation of Beethoven is flagrant, particularly of the quartet
> Opus 132, but the young composer creates forms that amazingly stand up
> on their own. (To understand the achievement, one might compare the
> efforts of nineteenth-century playwrights to imitate Shakespeare. They
> invariably made fools of themselves, and arrived at either melodrama
> or pompous academic fare, with the exception of Heinrich von Kleist,
> who learned both from Shakespeare's prosody and his sense of dramatic
> movement, and produced the masterly *Prince of Hamburg*.) Not until
> a century after Mendelssohn's youthful essays would the late style of
> Beethoven be absorbed again into the mainstream of music by the quartets
> of Bartok and Schoenberg.

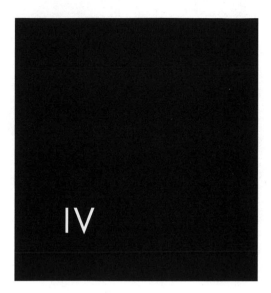

The Book of Samuel

> Poetry may make us from time to time a little more
> aware of the deeper, unnamed feelings which form
> the substratum of our being, to which we rarely
> penetrate; for our lives are mostly a constant evasion
> of ourselves.
>
> —T. S. ELIOT

1

When the time came to name my son, we chose the name Samuel. His name wasn't derived from anyone in the family. We chose Samuel because three of the writers who moved me most were named Samuel: Samuel Johnson, Samuel Taylor Coleridge, and Samuel Beckett. As it turned out, we weren't the only people in our neighborhood who had chosen to name their boys Sam. (And there is no shortage of Samanthas, which has led of late to some funny banter.) My Sam's two best friends in day care and prekindergarten (Purple Circle and the possibly disastrous Magical Years) were also named Sam. It turned out that among the handful of parents with whom I became friends—once we were thrown into what is called a "community"—two had sons named Sam. There was an actor and a writer who were also amused when we addressed our Sams in varying tones to differentiate—unless we resorted to Sam Rudman and Sam Denisov.

Imagine for a moment walking into a room full of children where parents, teachers, nannies, and other desultory characters are calling out "Sam G., Sam D., Sam R. . . ." and then three-year-old "Samantha" quips back, "Sam!" I think most of the other parents had members of their families who, in living memory, had been named Sam and chose it for its earthiness.

I, on the contrary, had rather thoughtlessly chosen the name Sam over the dead body of my beloved grandfather Abraham "Tarzan" Levy. How could this have occurred—when you consider that his brother, my uncle, was named Sam?

If I had had a special affection for Uncle Sam (Levy) it would have been one thing, but although I saw him frequently during the first fifteen years of my life, I didn't. The most notable thing about my uncle Sam was that there was nothing notable about him. He was, and I do not mean this cruelly, a shadow of my grandfather. He was probably dwarfed by my grandfather's charisma and gifts. The most notable thing about Uncle Sam was that he contributed almost nothing to any conversation, although sometimes he might tap his cane. Once, twice, never more than three times. He was no talker. He could draw out the word "yeeeeaahhh . . ." in a gravelly monotone, like Krapp relishing the syllables of "Spooooool."

In other words, Uncle Sam was more or less present in a room with other members of this often mercurial and always animated family, and that was it, amazingly, except for a mild resemblance he had to the actor Ralph Bellamy, who around that time portrayed FDR in the film *Sunrise at Campobello,* a biopic to stir the blood of the middle-aged (I begged not to be dragged to it). I hope that my grandfather hasn't been turning over in his grave all these years because I named my Sam Sam.

Not long ago Sam blew into our apartment, in the midst of a high-spirited interaction with a seventeen-year-old girl (windy hair, ash-blond, jeans torn at the knee) whom he introduced as Samantha. I didn't see her after that, and one day, for reasons too delicate and personal to mention here, I asked if he had seen her. And when he responded, "Who? Sam?" I felt the dizziness of the Sams.

2

One day, somewhere between Thanksgiving and Christmas 2004, it came to me for no reason I could identify that when Samuel (Taylor) Coleridge wrote the line "My genial spirits fail" in "Dejection: An Ode," he couldn't have meant what he said. Coleridge, despite the tragic vicissitudes of his life, never, or rarely—as when in the grip of severe laudanum withdrawal—lacked geniality, affection, the desire to be with other people in any of a number of capacities in addition to the one that required (and desired) him to hold discourse. This is because *genial* means something very different to us than it did to Coleridge. For Milton, Wordsworth, and Coleridge, genial spirits are linked to your genius, that is, your presiding deity, and produce the sexual energy for creation, for

The Book of Samuel

the propagation of children as well as poems. Since Coleridge was married to one Sarah (Fricker) and loved another Sara (Hutchinson), whose code name was Asra, his affections became paralyzed. The lack of love between Samuel and Sarah had gradually grown into a hole he could not fill, a wound he could not stanch; or a wound that he could have stanched, if he had been able to exchange one Sarah for the other.

Ted Hughes identified Coleridge's lifelong pattern of reliance on women as a direct effect of his past:

> When his beloved father died, S.T.C. being only ten, his mother sent him off to the monastic garrison of Christ's Hospital—from which, it seems, he was allowed to return to her bosom only three or four times in the rest of his school days. During this period he shifted his passionate dependence onto his sister, Anne—who then died, after a long illness, just before he left school for university. Later on, to one half-affectionate woman or another, he would say his mother never gave him any feeling of what it was to have a mother.

If Hughes was right, this would have left Coleridge prone toward emotional bankruptcy and failure. If he didn't feel he deserved to be loved, choosing the wrong wife would have been almost inevitable.

My wife and I made the pilgrimage to Nether Stowey and Hay-on-Wye in the summer of 1976. We headed, with heady optimism, to the cottage in Nether Stowey suffused with the spirits who cleared the way for Coleridge to compose some of the greatest poems in the English language. There were miles and miles of pylons, tormenting the yellow grass, bleached from the drought. The little village was white and spotless. I was beginning to get the kind of nervous feeling I like to pretend that I don't have in the vain hope that it will go away. We had arrived at the exact instant that the shops and pubs were pulling down their shutters and hanging "Closed" signs on the doors. These are the empty hours in Europe. We pushed ahead down the deserted highway. Nary a sign, a directional signal, for Coleridge's house. When we arrived, there was a sign swinging in the wind, the kind of sign that you might have seen at an inn, with a picture of the long-locked, round-faced S.T.C. We paid the nominal entrance fee to a matron who made it very clear that she had no interest or idea of what she was doing, except that it was a job that paid and that she resented having to interrupt her knitting. We walked through the display of Coleridge's letters and poems under glass and became especially involved in his correspondence with Charles Lamb. Being there made it manifestly clear how few people had created this Romantic revolution and how dependent they were upon each other's friendship. I had looked forward to seeing the lime tree bower where he composed the poem he dedicated to Charles Lamb. It was long gone. Standing on the property, idyllic but isolated, I realized why Coleridge saw fit to repeat the phrase, "my gentle-hearted Charles" three times in "This Lime-Tree Bower My Prison," as if to prove to himself that his friend was truly steadfast and constant.

What may have also contributed to the loss of his genial spirits in "Dejection: An Ode" was his awareness of Milton's copious use of the word *genial* in *Paradise Lost.* One angel brings Eve to Adam: "What day the genial Angel to our sire / Brought her in naked beauty more adorned." A line even more saturated is "satiate with genial moisture." The line of Milton's that most accentuates Coleridge's sense of sexual deprivation occurs in *Samson Agonistes:* "So much I feel my genial spirits droop."

What comes instantly to mind is an emphasis on geniality that Lionel Trilling stressed in his spirited essay on Keats's letters, "The Poet as Hero." Trilling makes a forceful and convincing case for "Keats's geniality toward himself, his bold acceptance of his primitive appetite and his having kept open a line of communication with it," and the "decisive effect upon the nature of his creative intelligence." This is a stunning and valuable insight; but it is Trilling, not Keats, who uses the word *genial*.

Now since I was long ago infected with the bracing insights in Trilling's essay and have often since then thought of Keats in connection with some form of life-enhancing geniality, I set myself up to be slightly misled, slightly off-target, when it came to Coleridge's line "My genial spirits fail." Despite the despair that it elicits, it is a more powerful line of poetry than the one Wordsworth uses in "Tintern Abbey": "If I were not thus taught, should I the more / Suffer my genial spirits to decay." Coleridge, I argued to myself, did not suffer from a loss of geniality, taking the word as I remember Trilling used it to apply to Keats, in which case geniality is what you think it is, for better or for worse. It can even mean something as quotidian as liking to be among other people, which stands in contrast to so many pernicious myths about poets, especially Romantic poets, and certain writers such as Samuel Beckett. Coleridge, I thought, must have used the word *genial* in that phrase for the sake of an assonance so delectable it would have pleased Keats, though Keats was more the priest of the open vowel rather than the dental. For all we know, Keats may have marked this line of Coleridge's for special praise in his own sonic quest.

Richard Holmes testifies in his biography, "Coleridge wrote to Estlin on 18 May: 'I have known him [Wordsworth] a year & some months, and my admiration, I might say, my awe of his intellectual powers has increased even to this hour—& (what is of more importance) he is a tried good man. . . . His genius is most *apparent* in poetry—and rarely, except to me in tête à tête, breaks forth in conversational eloquence.'" Wordsworth wasn't particularly genial except as it pertained to the higher order of functioning.

It's also possible, and we will come to this eventually, that Coleridge also may have derived *genial* from one of his fabled German sources, which he so prodigally plagiarized, in addition to Miltonic ones. But I want to stay for a moment with the more quotidian notion of geniality, and it is worth restating that for both Coleridge and Wordsworth, prior to Keats, the notion of health and well-being and Eros as the ground out of which poetry would spring was already a preeminent factor in their radical new poetics. Keats would find geniality a fundamental resource, an inroad into imagination and certain ideas—frequently misconstrued—for which he is known. For Coleridge this vein of geniality— the thrill of performance, of mesmerizing others with his monologues—would become like a drug, perhaps as much of a drug initially as the laudanum to which he became enslaved.

There is talking within the work of art and talking outside of the work in the realm of life; that is where the dangers surface. Hazlitt observed:

> I accompanied him six miles on the road. It was a fine morning in the middle of winter, and he talked the whole way. The scholar in Chaucer is described as going
>
> . . . Sounding on his way.
>
> So Coleridge went on his. In digressing, in dilating, in passing from subject to subject, he appeared to me to float in air, to slide on ice. I observed that he continually crossed me on the way by shifting from one side of the footpath to the other. This struck me as an odd movement; but I did not at

that time connect it with any instability of purpose or involuntary change of principle, as I have done since.

The sociable aspect of geniality would for Coleridge become a dark source. In some ways it would become a dark source for his namesake Samuel Johnson as well. This may seem absurd, but bear with me. To put it bluntly, they each aspired beyond anything else to write poetry. It doesn't matter if it was great poetry or not; the point is that both Coleridge and Johnson ceased to function as poets at a ridiculously young age. Pin the blame on laudanum or overwork as much as you want, the result is the same: the genius in their genial spirits had failed them. In some essential way they were no good to themselves. It's interesting to speculate on how people feel about their own achievement in light of their early aspirations.

I am led down this path by the dark fates of both my fathers.

We can't let ourselves forget that Samuel Johnson didn't write one word of the book he is best known for, Boswell's *Life of Johnson*. The fact that he was among the two greatest talkers in the history of England, the other being Coleridge, did little to curb his internal sense of failure, of disappointment. Alongside this lay the fact that Johnson was among the most sociable of men who loved nothing more than human company, who hated nothing more than being alone.

Samuel Johnson metamorphosed James Boswell. The two in one created a dialogic form that would transcend anything they would have done on their own. Coleridge remained grounded in the conversation poem. There was often talk about doing a book of conversations with Coleridge modeled on Boswell's *Life of Johnson*. He couldn't—no one has—have gone any further with the supernatural ballad that he evolved in the "Ancient Mariner" and "Christabel," and for him the conversation poem did not develop into the kind of dialogic poem that would have provoked an ongoing genre that would have sustained his poetic imagination. The idea of other people being there was far more real for Wordsworth than it was for Coleridge; just the idea that he was addressing him in *The Prelude* was enough to give that poem its own subtle internal dialogical structure. Wordsworth's imagination could encompass a dialogue with all of nature.

3

Literature is in part a story of doubles, or alter egos, and it's a sustaining trope; in Shakespeare these multiply exponentially because the drama, not the poem, is his frame. But Don Quixote and Sancho Panza, Diderot and Rameau, Jacques and his Master are among the most fruitful collaborations in the history of literature. The permutations of this are vast. This dialectical method which extends back to Plato, and runs through Hegel and Marx, and as we've established, Boswell and Johnson, is lost on Coleridge and accounts for some of his longing. Not only in "Dejection: An Ode" does he lack a spring of renewal that Wordsworth has, but he lacks the imaginative facility that allows him to create an intimate other to address. The poetry stops due to the absence of another.

Once he feels betrayed by Wordsworth cutting prize poems like "Christabel" from *Lyrical Ballads* and his marriage fails to give him the intimacy that he needs, he ceases to be a poet. And by falling in love with Sara Hutchinson he could no longer deny his sense of estrangement from his own wife, Sarah Fricker. It is as if one day the curtain went down, poetry abandoned him, and Coleridge became for the next forty years of his life a critic, a metaphysician, an autobiographer, and a legendary talker and lecturer. After reading a poem of consummate loneliness and isolation such as "This Lime-Tree Bower My Prison," we are hardly surprised that Coleridge would go on to name his magazine *The Friend*. No one needed a friend more than Coleridge at that moment. Some emptiness, lovelessness opens up inside. The idealization of solitude and nature aren't working for him; he belongs in the company of other people, much like Samuel Johnson. And Dr. Levet, to whom he dedicated a poem:

> Well tried through many a varying year,
> See Levet to the grave descend;
> Officious, innocent, sincere,
> Of every friendless name the friend.

This corresponds to one of Saul Bellow's insights about Humboldt, modeled on Delmore Schwartz, in *Humboldt's Gift*. Bellow's Humboldt imagines that he needs solitude in order to create, so he goes off to live in rural New Jersey. This decision turns out to be the beginning of his demise. How curious that it is Humboldt/Delmore Schwartz whom Robert Lowell quotes as saying "if you got people talking in a poem you could do anything." Looking back, it was almost a conspiracy between Frost, Eliot, and Pound *to get people talking in a poem:* an attempt to keep poetry contemporary with other evolving forms. And the new science.

> "My nerves are bad to-night. Yes, bad. Stay with me.
> "Speak to me. Why do you never speak. Speak."

(T. S. ELIOT, THE WASTE LAND)

Speech has its own distinctive idiom. It's historical: you know when somebody speaks what era they're from, what moment they're in. And the speaker can always be trusted to be the bearer of a partial truth.

It's surprising how many great novelists, like Faulkner and Fitzgerald, claim that Conrad's use of a storyteller within a story gave them the impetus that they needed. I've also noticed that film directors often cite Akira Kurosawa's *Rashomon* as one of the first films that attracted them to their medium. Once again, though the story is told in images, each telling of how a murder occurred is entirely different depending on the speaker whose presence dissolves as the images unfold, and we are riveted to the light on a sword blade as a man walks through a forest into a clearing where all his troubles will begin. But if anyone imagines that Marlowe and the narrators, who interrupt and embellish his versions of events concerning Lord Jim, Captain Brierly, Kurtz, and his pursuers, contribute to relativity, they've reversed the master's master: truth. The events themselves are never in question, but they provide an outlet for Conrad's range of observation, which far exceeds his capacity for invention. The only way I can read a book like *Nostromo* is in reverse; that is, I finish one page and am so intoxicated by the cadences and the audible visual reverie they induce that I then read the previous one again. Conrad tracks characters who chose darker destinies to maintain a self-image founded on romance novels. People remain mired in concepts of what it is to be who they think they want to be. And we're all subject to this temptation.

I have a long chat with Sam into the early hours. We talk about a film he could make about the rich kids he's known, the girl whose mother would phone from her limo and invite him to the Hamptons on a whim; or merely to their townhouse. We argued, warmly, about conspicuous consumption in the current war zone the world has become when his friend Carlos, a superintendent's son, arrived, and this kid who's never heard of Tolstoy or Joyce launches—after I mention Fitzgerald's obsession with the rich—into this discourse on Gatsby, and how he was no different from the drug lord in *American Gangster,* which is true.

Then the camera panned past the wall's blue screen to the party where a hundred Manhattan kids, either very rich or the opposite, piled into our apartment for the big bash Sam was about to throw after his first week at a new high school because we were off to an engagement party for Madelaine's nephew and fiancé in Connecticut; but Sam made a mistake. He saw me on the street and walked toward me, with a gait too deliberate and quick, to ask what time we were leaving. A question he never asks in an anxious tone. I knew something was up. So I stayed home. I thought about being this artist-parent who, Sam always said, "wears loose jeans," compared to other parents and neighbors "who wear tight jeans," "even though," he added, "your actual jeans are tighter. . . ."

What if there was a loose wire in the crowd? Someone Sam hadn't screened who would steal stuff or destroy it. I especially feared for our paintings. I made it a point to say hi to everyone, and then a girl, seventeen going on thirty-four, led me to the dining table where they had laid out lines of prescription meds and announced, in what would have to have been given the dubious achievement award, that the kids at Bleakmore were "the best in the city when it comes to the recreational use of drugs." I affected nonchalance and had a stiff shot of Absolut. Called a psychologist friend for advice. She said: "Mark, this is just OUTRAGEOUS, tell them all to go home, now." This must be the kind of advice I'm usually looking for. I finally got Madelaine on the line. She said "Are they harming anyone? Are they safe?" "If it's okay with you baby it's okay with me, this time." The kids would wander into my room where I had some music on and was pretending to be quietly reading. And, as is so often the case, they'd open up because what could be weirder than "being a poet"?

4

Each of the Samuels is a kind of representative figure of his era. I have noticed how often people have felt compelled to talk about the three Samuels—Johnson, Coleridge, Beckett—and the one I am now going to add—film director Samuel Fuller. It's possible that the differences between these figures have more to do with time and place than with the work they produced. Each responded to a necessity that went beyond the confines of the individual and generated a universal appeal that is very difficult to pin down. If Fuller seems a bit outranked here, we have to keep in mind his titanic effect on the imagination of the film directors who came after him.

Each form struggles to evolve as befits the medium. It might even be James Boswell who identified the possibilities of dialogue when he undertook to record his conversations with Samuel Johnson. Imagine if Johnson or Coleridge had given themselves the license to let people talk in a poem. This was a formal solution that didn't occur to these earlier great talkers who may have been distracted by the formidable example of the poetry of Elizabethan theater.

But this is the significant link between Eliot, Frost, and Pound: dialogue. And a significant moment in the evolution of the possibilities of poetry.

> "My nerves are bad to-night. Yes, bad. Stay with me.
> "Speak to me. Why do you never speak. Speak."

> He saw all was spoiled. "Don't let him cut my hand off—
> The doctor, when he comes. Don't let him, sister!"
> So. The hand was gone already.

> "I never mentioned a man but with the view
> "Of selling my own works.
> "The tip's a good one, as for literature
> "It gives no man a sinecure."

> "And no one knows, at sight a masterpiece.
> "And give up verse, my boy,
> "There's nothing in it."

Poetry and painting have followed a similar course, and each art had to wait three hundred years for its next giant step, its metamorphosis. Cubism, Apollonaire's "Zone," *The Waste Land, Birth of a Nation*. . . . There's even a dialogical element in the method of shooting film that D. W. Griffith evolved. John Boorman writes in *Adventures of a Suburban Boy:*

Before Griffith, the camera was set up on a tripod and recorded a play acted out before it. It would then be placed at another location and a further scene performed. These were cut together so the audience became accustomed to these shifts of place, but the shock of the shift was softened by a written title card, so the experience was still close to that of live theatre. *Imagine how startling it must have seemed when the camera first shifted its point of view, picking out a close-up of a character and then reversing itself to a close-up of another person. By having one look camera left and the other camera right, Griffith created the illusion that they are looking at each other.* [Italics mine.]

5

Many of us adore some of Samuel Beckett's fiction, but with *Waiting for Godot* and *Endgame,* with sparse dialogue, he pushed his art into another dimension that is equal to the highest poetry. Everyone was shocked when this most reticent and least sociable of men, though not quite the recluse some have imagined him to be, turned to an outward form like drama.

I have commented on the loquacity of the Samuels, but what connects Samuel Johnson and Samuel Taylor Coleridge is the urge to communicate. They're remembered because their primary activity of life was communication and the promulgation of that.

The forms of Coleridge's isolation led him, as has often been remarked, to "Hamletize," to think and talk too much when the occasion demanded action. This is one of the reasons that Byron made his rather gentle jibe at him in *Don Juan:*

> And Coleridge, too, has lately taken wing,
> But like a hawk encumber'd with his hood—
> Explaining metaphysics to the nation—
> I wish he would explain his Explanation.

No one admired Coleridge's poetry more than Byron, who championed "Christabel" when no one else could recognize its originality. And the "lately" doesn't include "Fears in Solitude," which is almost more about our early twenty-first-century moment than Coleridge's early nineteenth-century moment:

Thankless too for peace,
(Peace long preserved by fleets and perilous seas)
Secure from actual warfare, we have loved
To swell the war-whoop, passionate for war!
Alas! for ages ignorant of all
Its ghastlier workings (famine or blue plague,
Battle, or siege, or flight through wintry snows)
We, this whole people, have been clamorous
For war and bloodshed; animating sports,
The which we pay for as a thing to talk of,
Spectators and not combatants! No guess
Anticipative of a wrong unfelt,
No speculation on contingency,
However dim and vague, too vague and dim
To yield a justifying cause.

Within less than a decade Byron detected that the author of "Kubla Khan" was headed down the wrong path, and how does the eminently down-to-earth Byron begin *Don Juan* if not by exclaiming that he needs a form to accommodate his desire to talk for five hundred pages in octosyllabic couplets; a form to celebrate diversions and digressions worthy of more overtly digressive writers like Diderot? So many of the poets in the English nineteenth century found expansive poetic forms to accommodate their desires to talk; not Coleridge and not, in the earlier century, Samuel Johnson. One thing that all these works point to is what Donald Davie has referred to as the insufficiency of lyric. What makes this remarkable is that, with the exception of Wordsworth, Samuel Johnson and Samuel Taylor Coleridge probably had a superabundance of gifts that came closer, if not quite close, than those of any other English poets to rivaling Shakespeare.

It would be Samuel Beckett, almost two hundred years later, who would make the problem of being alone his most persistent theme. No one has explored the problem of being alone more exhaustively than Samuel Beckett. And yet Beckett, as I've suggested, contrary to popular belief, was also genial, and loved company (if he could choose it). If he didn't, I doubt he would have called one of his most lyrical and exquisite late works *Company*.

6

For Coleridge and for Beckett, the overwhelming achievements of *The Prelude* and *Ulysses* would metamorphose into a specter. They became equivalents of an unachievable height. Sam and Sam had gifts so capacious that there was no prior model for them to follow, speaking loosely, to say nothing of the conditions they worked under. Sam C. challenged the limits of poetic invention successfully until *The Prelude* began to evolve, and he ran amuck in Malta. Until the composition of *The Prelude* enters the picture, it could be said that Coleridge was as good as, if not a greater poet than Wordsworth, though certain aspects of his nature would never allow him to see it this way.

Wordsworth was Coleridge's ego ideal. If this were not the case, it would be hard to imagine why Coleridge would have endured Wordsworth's presumption in choosing to remove "Christabel" from the first edition of the *Lyrical Ballads,* and compose "Michael" to fill the gap. And there's an odds-on chance that Wordsworth did see the leap that Coleridge made in the prosody he devised for "Christabel," as he makes clear in his preface, and that he was determined to suppress it, using "the supernatural" as a smokescreen for his jealousy.

> The first part of the following poem was written in the year 1797, at
> Stowey, in the county of Somerset. The second part, after my return from
> Germany, in the year 1800, at Keswick, Cumberland. It is probable that
> if the poem had been published in the year 1800, the impression of its
> originality would have been much greater than I dare at present expect. But
> for this I have only my own indolence to blame. The dates are mentioned
> for the exclusive purpose of precluding charges of plagiarism or servile
> imitation from myself. For there is amongst us a set of critics, who, seem
> to hold, that every possible thought and image is traditional; who have no
> notion that there are such things as fountains in the world, small as well
> as great; and who would therefore charitably derive every rill they behold
> flowing, from a perforation made in some other man's tank. I am confident,
> however, that as far as the present poem is concerned, the celebrated poets
> whose writings I might be suspected of having imitated, either in particular
> passages, or in the tone and the spirit of the whole, would be among the
> first to vindicate me from the charge, and who, on any striking coincidence,
> would permit me to address them in this doggerel version of two monkish
> Latin hexameters.

'Tis mine and it is likewise yours;
But an if this will not do;
Let it be mine, good friend! for I
Am the poorer of the two.

I have only to add that the meter of Christabel is not, properly speaking, irregular, though it *may seem so from its being founded on a new principle: namely, that of counting in each line the accents, not the syllables. Though the latter may vary from seven to twelve, yet in each line the accents will be found to be only four. Nevertheless, this occasional variation in number of syllables is not introduced wantonly, or for the mere ends of convenience, but in correspondence with some transition in the nature of the imagery or passion.* [Italics mine.]

Coleridge was heartbroken, but deep down some part of him must have believed that Wordsworth was right. If he admitted to himself that Wordsworth had been unscrupulous, he would have had to give up his fantasy of their bond. He was adept at internalizing accusations. Many of us are ready if not eager to assume the worst about ourselves because it relieves the burden of success, or the responsibilities that come with the realization of dreams.

If Coleridge felt inadequate in the face of Wordsworth's looming achievement, Johnson felt basically checkmated by Shakespeare. His play *Irene* is not one of his better efforts. The thick and riotous nature of his writing wasn't born to fall into heroic couplets. Johnson was unburdened in prose and at the dinner table. Boswell and Johnson managed to recapture some of the spirit of the dialogues between Falstaff and his mates, and look forward to the dynamic of Diderot's *Rameau's Nephew*. The important thing to remember here is that a certain imbalance is necessary for these dialogues to breathe.

Coleridge's problem ultimately was the failure to find a form—and recognize it for what it was. His extravagant use of laudanum gave him a sense of boundlessness that may have taken the shape, for instance, of the entire ocean in "The Rime of the Ancient Mariner": "Nor any drop to drink." But poetry, maybe verse, is not an art of boundlessness. There is no such thing as a boundless art. And if the desire for boundlessness becomes too strong, whether or not it is inflamed by alcohol or drugs, art will always languish.

Orson Welles incorporated this boundlessness into his own body. Boswell's *Life of Johnson* might have been a formless, boundless work, but it had its terminus in the death of Johnson. So it's possible that when Coleridge says that his genial spirits fail, insofar as "genial" refers to genius and the capacity for poetic invention, he also means in some way that he can no longer think in numbers, in meters, and he does not have an eye toward inventing a new form, the way an artist might decide to forgo easel painting and create earthworks or works that use the gallery space.

I am thinking most immediately of Christo's *The Gates,* which, like his *Running Fence,* draws our attention to what is between the gates in Central Park: grass, rambles, ponds, and people whose colorful garments enrich the eye. All we have to do is imagine an alternative life for Christo during which he fulminated and foamed at the mouth over the limitation of easel painting. Hybridity was latent in Coleridge's writing a hundred years before modernism, but he didn't avail himself of its potential; his poetry and prose remained strictly separate. His journals, often punctuated by dashes, could have served as a springboard for a new kind of poetry. In Emily Dickinson's case, her letters were an inroad to her broken poems. Coleridge was stuck in a mind-set, trapped by the demands his reputation as a speaker and talker enforced. His real achievement, as you would expect, is immeasurable. Despite Coleridge's disclaimer and his history of drug addiction—much tempered by the age of forty-eight—Coleridge remained far more genial than the prickly Wordsworth. And while Coleridge's "failure" has been infinitely lamented, it is only because he set the stage for that judgment; his openness drew attention to his disappointment in his achievement, which is something that no one can judge for himself. His overall achievement is uncannily parallel to that of T. S. Eliot. It is always startling to remember that poetry was more or less done with Wordsworth once he had completed *The Prelude* by the age of thirty-five. Paradoxically, he was able to merge his method of composing while walking with his job as a postal inspector, walking and walking in the open air, but this did not rekindle his spirit. Wordsworth's response when he sensed competition was: attack. At a gathering, Wordsworth asked the twenty-two-year-old Keats what he was writing. Keats obliged by reciting his recent "Hymn to Pan," and was mortified when his hero peremptorily responded with this cruel riposte: "a very pretty piece of paganism." Whether or not it was intended as cruelly as Keats received it and as it is often taken, this in no way diminished Keats's admiration for Wordsworth's poetry.

It is the counterpoint between the whirling fervor of the parts of *The Prelude* that embodied childhood and the sections, such as the ones set in the French Revolution, bordering on reportage, that imbues the book with a dialectic. The absence of real dialogue is replaced by the internal dialogue between the twelve chapters which are so different from each other. In ecstasy, we stand outside ourselves. It's possible that the ecstatic sections of *The Prelude* are instances of "not I." And it's possible that this order of perception is simply fleeting, and resists integration into our overall sense of ourselves beyond the moment when we're writing from within an ecstatic experience whose memory we can inhabit for the duration. Without duration, no ecstasy. No transport out of self. Wordsworth creates an air mattress on which his friend can float for years, attempting to sustain the ecstasy through the proximity to—total immersion in—the author's words. Coleridge's problem: my greatest highs now come when reading *The Prelude*. Coleridge's solution: maybe I can sustain the elation if I write about it; I can think of no subject more worthy of my attention, at present. Coleridge writes, and then hears, imagines he hears, the people who've hired him to talk about . . . , or about . . . , Shakespeare? Reform? The Dream Life of Language? And sees the scraps of paper in disarray around the room and hears a door slam. Footsteps echo in the corridor. Asra, he sighs. But it is the other Sarah that he sees, and he sees the criticism in her eyes. Despair. And another talk to prepare before the carriage arrives.

Wordsworth goes on walking; he walks everywhere he can—this is what he does—and passes veritable replications of the settings in which his memories took place, including Eakins-like stills of boys adrift in rowboats through long afternoons, unfettered, and untethered; and crossing the Alps again where the weather goes down about fifty degrees in what seemed like a minute, he grips the hand of both his sister and his wife to help still the tremble in his legs when he beholds a solitary boy skating on the ice below ringed by mountains, only this boy calls out "Echo!" And William and Mary and Dorothy can hear the reverb and turn to watch—hear—"echo echo echo eeeeeccchhhhoooooo . . ." somewhere close to the spot from which they departed. Mary says, "I'll bet we could get some skates!" William: "Skates! What do we need skates for? We're already . . . close to . . . an hour late. . . ." Dorothy: "Since when have YOU attended to the lateness of the hour, you who've always found roads that delayed our arrival; remember that freezing night when we emerged from the pitch blackness and the moon appeared so close to the frozen lake we all thought we could almost reach out and touch it and then we saw its reflection and looked back and it had reassumed its position while the lake still held onto its reflection for an unnatural . . . ?" Mary: "Supernatural . . ." Dorothy: "It was . . . it made me wish Samuel could have seen it. . . ." "Why supernatural? Why not just subjective? Who can measure the keenness of our senses after walking all day in and out of forests, and only at times church steeples to remind of a town's nearness . . . ?" "Maybe you can." "I think I can. I'll make a first-rate postal inspector. If it isn't too late I could maybe change the appointment to land surveyor for the Lake District." "It doesn't matter, you're still the poet of the north country." "Still a poet." "How many people have traveled for days just to meet the author of . . . ?" "I didn't count." "But you did note their sympathy with your views, about the common language." Silence. Blankness. "And look, on that ridge, and there below, and . . . people coming up behind in our footsteps!" The scenes he's rendered over the past two years are so remote; they were written by someone else. "But who could that be?" Mary to Dorothy: "He doesn't seem to take pleasure in small things anymore, all these walkers, out here walking under the inspiration of his poems. I am trying not to think now about what he might have done without your love, then mine, from which he partakes equally." "But Mary, you're his wife." "And you, Dorothy, name one sister who's a sister in the way you are. . . ." "I will, if I could find one with a brother to compare." "I fear the easy flow of love between you and me does not extend as naturally to him. . . ." "Like breath . . ." "As it once did." "Maybe he's just tired and doesn't want to admit he's human!" "Still, his intolerance toward Samuel . . . and when you've read what he's written about William's poem . . . is there a more generous act in human history?" "Umm . . . and the poem is addressed to him." "And to think that Samuel overcame his rancor about William's excision of 'Christabel' enough to return to the poet who resided in the man." "Who resides, dear; his best work is still ahead of him. . . ." "Let's continue our excursion."

7

Both Sams, Coleridge and Johnson, were eventually consumed by a disease: the disease of talking. Talking became a substitute for creation. In this sense, their genial spirits had failed. And talking had many pleasures. They had rapt audiences, immediate gratification. I repeat, this talking was a disease to the extent that it usurped an energy that was essential for an imaginative work that they wanted to be doing, that they initially envisioned as their destiny. And in another way the profusion of prose that flowed from their pens with an almost

inconceivable fluency had a dark side as well, insofar as it occluded the possibility of poetry. So much of poetry is about resistance to flux, not the dissipation
of tension in discourse.

Another moment such as the one in which I thought Coleridge couldn't have
intended the word *genial* came to me when I read a passage in Walter Jackson
Bate's biography of Johnson. Bate observes that Johnson had composed an essay
about a book of some length at a speed that even modern technology could
not reckon; when questioned by Boswell on his opinion of the book, Johnson
said he never considered reading it, that he had just let his pen fly after assimi-
lating the implications of its rather copious title. Boswell thought Johnson's riff,
written without revision in one setting, was an excellent piece of work, far
superior (does that go without saying?) to the book he was reviewing. I'm sure
he did honor to the author. Samuel Johnson makes the epithet *quick study* seem
euphemistic. It's crucial to note that Johnson was writing this essay purely for
money, and often after he completed one of his multitudinous pieces he forgot
that he'd written it—a sort of selective amnesia, like P. T. Anderson must have
practiced writing sketches for late-night television after the box-office failure of
Magnolia. This is why Johnson was happiest when tethered to such monumental
and rewarding projects as his *Dictionary of the English Language,* the *Lives of the
Poets,* and his edition of Shakespeare. In T. S. Eliot's judgment in "Johnson as
Critic and Poet":

> Originality is found, here, in a "mode of thinking and of expression." But
> the thought itself does not have to be novel or difficult of apprehension and
> acceptance; it may be, and for Johnson most often is, the commonplace,
> or a thought which, when grasped, is so quickly admitted that the reader
> wonders that he never thought of it for himself. Originality does not
> require the rejection of convention. We have grown accustomed, during
> the last century and more, to such a riot of individual styles that we may
> forget that originality is as significant in a settled period as it is in one of
> constant change; we have become so accustomed to differences of poetic
> style recognizable by anybody, that we may be less sensitive to the finer
> variations within a form, which the mind and ear habituated to that form
> may perceive. But originality, when it becomes the only, or the most prized
> virtue of poetry, may cease to be a virtue at all; and when several poets, and
> their respective groups of admirers, cease to have in common any standards
> of versification, any identity of taste or of tenets of belief, criticism may

decline to an advertisement of preference. The originality which Johnson approves, is an originality limited by the other qualities which he demands.

I've just concocted a fantasy of an essay by Edmund Wilson, an essay much in the same vein as his utterly absorbing takes on Michelet and Pushkin, reimagining the drama of Samuel Johnson writing his dictionary.

As Bate points out, "Like nothing else, the daily sight of this [his wife Tetty's disintegration] impressed upon him his failure to live up to what had been expected, the ironic unpredictability of life generally, and the remorseless speed with which time was moving through their lives." This was immediately after Johnson had composed his greatest poem, "The Vanity of Human Wishes," which he would not have begun if its source were not in the Latin of Juvenal's classic satires.

> Yet Reason frowns on War's unequal Game,
> Where wasted Nations raise a single Name,
> And mortgag'd States their Grandsires Wreaths regret
> From Age to Age in everlasting Debt;
> Wreaths which at last the dear-bought Right convey
> To rust on Medals, or on Stones decay.
>
> On what Foundation stands the Warrior's Pride?
> How just his Hopes let Swedish Charles decide;
> A Frame of Adamant, a Soul of Fire,
> No Dangers fright him, and no Labours tire;
> O'er Love, o'er Force, extends his wide Domain,
> Unconquer'd Lord of Pleasure and of Pain;
> No Joys to him pacific Scepters yield,
> War sounds the Trump, he rushes to the Field;
> Behold surrounding Kings their Pow'r combine,
> And One capitulate, and One resign;
> Peace courts his Hand, but spread her Charms in vain;
> "Think Nothing gain'd," he cries, "till nought remain,
> "On Moscow's Walls till Gothic Standards fly,
> "And all is Mine beneath the Polar Sky."
> The March begins in Miltary State,
> And Nations on his Eye suspended wait;
> Stern Famine guards the solitary Coast,
> And Winter barricades the Realms of Frost.

8

Coleridge would cease to compose poetry, but he would become the most sought-out lecturer in England during his lifetime. Johnson turned out inconceivable amounts of prose for hire.

Johnson's *Dictionary of the English Language* is his principal opus, his great poem. He always wrote to an effect.

> He had another fault, easily incident to those who suffering much pain think themselves entitled to whatever pleasures they can snatch. He was too indulgent to his appetite: he loved meat highly seasoned and of strong taste, and, at the intervals of the table, amused himself with biscuits and dry conserves. If he sat down to a variety of dishes he would oppress his stomach with repletion, and though he seemed angry when a dram was offered him, did not forbear to drink it. His friends, who knew the avenues to his heart, pampered him with presents of luxury, which he did not suffer to stand neglected. The death of great men is not always proportioned to the lustre of their lives. Hannibal, says Juvenal, did not perish by a javelin or a sword; the slaughters of Cannae were revenged by a ring. The death of Pope was imputed by some of his friends to a silver saucepan, in which it was his delight to heat potted lampreys.

It's not a far leap from Johnson's dictionary to the consuming encyclopedic projects that characterize the twentieth century. People have come to crave information more than the ambiguous twists and sudden revelations that were offered by poets like Pope or Coleridge or Wordsworth. The closest thing to Johnson's dictionary in the twentieth century is Walter Benjamin's *Arcades Project*. The latter is something to experience; in time, it becomes like an arcade that you can stroll through. *Ulysses, The Cantos,* and Louis Zukofsky's *Bottom: On Shakespeare* are nothing if not encyclopedic. But while these works are unquestionably substantive, the inspiration for a book that contains everything that is worthy of being included in its Ark owes its impetus to Flaubert's hilarious *Bouvard and Pecuchet*. From another perspective, Flaubert's satire of two men who set out to record all knowledge in one volume might also have shown that it was no longer necessary to carry out such an absurd project.

But what remains modern is the physicality of these projects—the dictionary, the *Arcades, Ulysses,* and *The Cantos*. All four are like environments that human beings might be able to inhabit if they were more than books bound by covers and made of words, container and contained. All these projects are salvage operations. I wonder if Johnson could have completed his project with a language that was less variable, restless, and acquisitive than English. Joyce invited the reader to reconstruct Dublin from his careful reconstitution of it in *Ulysses.* Don DeLillo's reconstruction of the historical contexts of *Libra* and *Underworld* evolves out of the same project. These are sharp-edged, scrupulous works, like Cubist paintings, that cut through the pileup of lies and fraudulence—the toxic overlay that blocks our view of history itself. Since the invention of the airplane, Johnson's hard-mindedness is rarely acknowledged as a source of this valuable aspect of twentieth-century skepticism, and that's because it's such a deep source, and like the purloined letter in Poe's story, it's right in front of our faces all the time, and we never think to look at it. It's right in front of our faces, but as an example of a psychic, not a physical, problem.

Arcades are memorable in themselves, and while a lively controversy has surrounded Eugenio Montale's jackals in his *Motetti,* no one has remarked that the setting, the environment, brings its own form of engagement. I've always felt drawn to the galleries in Modena where Montale espies his notorious jackals. The simple place-name itself made me want to go there, and whenever I found myself in Italy, to stroll through any kind of "galleria," which is, okay, an elegant old-world version of our shopping malls . . . or is it? I can tell you where shopping malls are glamorized and the site of possible romance: in Phoenix, Arizona, and Greenville, Mississippi, and Florence, South Carolina. In my youth, I was surrounded by people who were over-concerned with typology. People who were more concerned with being known for the wrong thing (what they considered suitable) than with the vital process of creation itself, people who had never, I'd wager, stepped foot in Bergsonian duration.

9

If I make the mistake of letting it leak out that I'm working on something called "The Book of Samuel," there are people who can't refrain from asking if I've considered Samuel Pepys or Samuel Richardson, as if such a concept was capable of infinite expansion, whereas I have a definite target in mind, and my goal is to get there—but not by flying above the clouds and getting above the turbulence, no—over rugged terrain. Here again so much hangs on the balance of one word, or a word and phrase.

10

Both Johnson and Coleridge suffered from what I have chosen to call an "everything-nothing syndrome," a term I came up with when I was thinking about Cesare Pavese's narrator of his novel *The Moon and the Bonfires* and that narrator's relationship to another character, Nuto, who functions as a kind of ego ideal. Throughout most of the novel the "I" is like a shadow of Nuto, who possesses a stability and wholeness the narrator can only dream of: that is, this is the way the narrator sees it; it isn't an accurate reflection of reality. As for Johnson and Coleridge, they imagined themselves as nothing in comparison to Pope and Wordsworth, respectively, who were everything. Johnson and Coleridge lived their lives in the shadow of how they conceived of the greatness of their—of these—contemporaries. This idealization of the other was inextricable from their greater sadness and sense of disappointment. I didn't light on this idea while thinking about literary works; I noticed it in the way people talk about each other. There are people who, as everyone knows, know they exist mainly through their sense of a certain connection to someone else. How this may be understood in a romantic relationship is another matter entirely. I'm talking about friends, contemporaries, peers. When I listen to people going on in this way about whoever has slipped in as their ego ideal, I want to intervene. I also feel slightly sickened, not to say bored. What a terrible way to go through this life, selling yourself short in exchange for the comfort, the umbrella, of another person's imagined wholeness.

In time, of course, this wholeness is transformed into achievement, and the syndrome is concretized so that A can talk about B's accomplishments and somehow objectify the inflation. I'm not trying to get at anything so profound; I'm saying that it depresses me. And it depressed Johnson and Coleridge. It didn't depress Samuel Beckett, who functioned as Joyce's secretary for a short time and worked his way through the master's overwhelming achievement by creating his own entirely other overwhelming works. But it's not comparable because Joyce and Beckett weren't contemporaries. And underneath a certain "I"'s overestimation of the other, there may lie an egoism so outsized that it dare not declare itself. Johnson and Coleridge handed over the mantle, the baton, of poetry to Pope and Wordsworth. Coleridge is the far more depressing case; sometimes listening to his praise of Wordsworth at the expense of himself brings one to the brink of tears. How could it not? There was no one around to recognize the far-reaching possibilities of what Coleridge had done in his poetry, only his "brother," Wordsworth, who did his best to make sure that the attention was focused on himself: from vision to venality in no time at all. In the years during which Braque and Picasso created the cubist paintings that represented the most singular revolution in the visual arts since the Renaissance, Braque characterized their collaboration as "two mountain climbers roped together." But here again nature took its course and fulfilled itself in the case of both artists. Braque was Braque and Picasso was Picasso.

This puts the vanity of human wishes in another light. Human wishes are vain if disappointment is inevitable. Juvenal and Johnson have a different concept in mind when they probe human failing in "The Vanity of Human Wishes." For Wordsworth, Whitman, Hopkins—and Freud—human wishes are not vain. Or is the real difference between wishes and wishing, conscious and unconscious wishes? The more I write the word *wish,* the more ghostly it sounds, like *wisp.* Hushed voices, whispers, don't dare to say the wish aloud. And then there is the bond between wish and will. Wishing is prelude to willing. It is the wish that gives the impetus to the search. And if a wish connects to desire and desire to imagination, the result just might be art.

Freud is responsible, but not to blame, for the radical shift in the sense of "wishing." Hardly anyone now can think of wishing without assuming that it refers to a leakage of unconscious desires that Freud pinpointed in *The Psychopathology of Everyday Life.* It is time that we took another look at this and the unexamined assumptions that we now live by as if they were facts, or part of nature. Freud's patients were not only revealing their inner lives through the proliferation of slips of the tongue, to which everyone is continually susceptible, they were also victims of distraction: their misreading of signs, for instance, might cause them to get off at the wrong stop—or more importantly not to get off—because it was the fate of many of these patients not to leave Germany in time to avoid being thrown into concentration camps. Freud detected the dangers of being un-conscious, out of tune. The people's ignorance of their own wishes was inextricable from their denial of the social and political reality that was threatening to engulf them. This reinvention of the wish is vastly more profound than anything that preceded it, but Freud's project didn't include the practical application of these realizations, and he died shortly after Germany invaded Poland. What Freud meant by *ego,* in which the unconscious and conscious are meshed so that a person proceeds as a whole, is very similar to what used to be thought of as a function of the will. The will was evidence of connectedness: union of body and soul. It was the "idea" that could direct this will, this energy toward one thing or another. It's the idea and not the will that supplies the intention. Today we think of the will as supplying intention, and intentions are—I mean who gives a fuck about intentions? (The title of an essay I read in my early twenties by William Gass has never lost its bite: "The High Brutality of Good Intentions.")

11

I want you to imagine a film of *The Canterbury Tales* in which a falcon lifts off from a pilgrim's glove and climbs into the empyrean to the top of the screen; in a split second, it morphs from falcon to Spitfire in mid-flight alone in the sky; cut to the pilgrims now transformed into soldiers holed up in a small village, who will eventually make their way to Canterbury.

The other night, Mother's Day Eve, I had a chastening experience. My son Samuel had asked me what he should get Madelaine for Mother's Day. He suggested a book. I asked him to let me think about it, and then I had this inspiration that if Sam wanted to do something for his mother on Mother's Day that would really please her, he could accompany us that night to the Walter Reade Theater where a Michael Powell film festival was just kicking off. That night Thelma Schoonmaker, who was married to Powell toward the end of his life and was Martin Scorsese's longtime editor, would be speaking. Sam didn't thrill to this idea, but since he wanted to be a filmmaker and his favorite director was Scorsese (we caught *Casino* the day it opened, and it remains an indelible film for him), he consented and even administered smelling salts to help me recover from the shock, since I knew how much he dreaded the idea of being seen in public with his parents on a Saturday night. I really anticipated that Thelma Schoonmaker was going to take us through Powell's films in an exhilarating way and that Sam would be captivated, swept away. The evening was an immense disappointment. She stayed mainly with Powell in the years after he had been barred from making films, after the scandal of *Peeping Tom,* and what we saw on the pristine screen at the Walter Reade Theater were not brief scenes of his films but slides of him walking the Scottish countryside in kilts with his friends or riding a horse while holding his young son on his lap. I took enjoyment from Michael Powell's enjoyment of life, but there was little to interest me and almost nothing to hold Sam's attention. In fact, the only reason I'm mentioning this at all as I make various transitions, from century to century and concern to concern, has to do with Schoonmaker's focus on Powell's disenfranchisement; his ruin. The director of some of the most inspired films ever made, like *The Red Shoes, A Matter of Life and Death,* and *I Know Where I'm Going!*—the first nondocumentary shot on location in the Hebrides (a place Samuel Johnson had little use for)—was reduced after the debacle of *Peeping Tom* to living in such a hand-to-mouth way in a small cottage in the Cotswolds that for five years he couldn't afford whisky. This connected in my mind to the somewhat parallel fate of Samuel Fuller, who wasn't able to get a film made for five years between *The Naked Kiss* and *Shark!* and, as I've said, had to fight like hell (excuse the Fullerian diction) to get *The Big Red One* made, only to have it taken out of his hands and butchered. What took place brings up the line in *King Lear:* "who's in, who's out." But underneath these associations, there began to form a connection between the fates of Samuel and Michael and those of my own fathers, Charles and Sidney.

It's dawning on me now that many of the men who have entered "The Book of Samuel" were the victims of not-so-simple twists of fate.

And then there is Michael Powell's own film (his favorite—many people's—not mine) about an aviator who is also a poet, *A Matter of Life and Death.* Given how these images rattle around in the collective unconscious, it's not unlikely that Powell also chose to focus on an aviator in response to the scabrous treatment the flyer gets in Jean Renoir's *Rules of the Game.*

"One year I watched a war in London," Nanci Griffith sings on her album *Flyer,* as she dreams of a rendezvous with a handsome pilot, "in the airport leaving London."

Renoir doesn't mock his aviator so much as the social nexus which has disavowed any heroism that can't be trivialized to fit within the rules of their game.

But Michael Powell didn't get the idea for this rapid transition of falcon to fighter plane from an earlier motion picture. My hunch is that this romantic, poetic, and poetry-crazed director found his inspiration in Hopkins's poem "The Windhover."

> then off, off forth on swing,
> As a skate's heel sweeps smooth on a bow-bend: the hurl and gliding
> Rebuffed by the big wind.

One distinction between Hopkins and Eliot is what differentiates a hawk and a falcon—more precisely Hopkins's kestrel and Eliot's peregrine falcon. The kestrel is in constant turbulence, like a low-flying plane, and this demands constant vigilance, as does the poet's task.

> But, as the passage now presents no hindrance
> To the spirit unappeased and peregrine
> Between two worlds become much like each other
>
> ("*LITTLE GIDDING*," II)

The peregrine, by seeing far-off distances so clearly and flying so high above other birds, may be a bit blind to what's close up, like "falcon-eyed Caesar," as Dante calls him. Maybe heights are best aspired to. The difference between Hopkins's poem and Eliot's *Four Quartets* is equivalent to the difference between a kestrel and a peregrine falcon. The kestrel flies lower to the ground than the falcon. Among birds, the falcon comes closest to getting above the turbulence. Eliot's falcon is transformed into spirit ("the passage now presents no hindrance") and can move unencumbered on condition that the spirit remain unappeased as well as peregrine. The tension and compression and torque that Hopkins wanted are inseparable from aspiration and reality. This is another way of explaining why *Four Quartets,* though incomparable, does not help blaze a trail for future poetry. It's an end in itself.

The two worlds that become much like each other are reconciled in Eliot's poem, which is based on a musical premise that keeps it weightless. It's a paean to the spirit world. In contrast, Hopkins leaves generations of poets with something to chew over, wrestle with. And the model for the sprung rhythm with which Hopkins renders the falcon's push can be found in Coleridge's poem "Christabel":

> The night-birds all that hour were still.
> But now they are jubilant anew,

From cliff and tower, tu—whoo! tu—whoo!
Tu—whoo! tu—whoo! from wood and fell!

A merging of the two impulses, the natural and the supernatural, earth and air, occurs in Robert Duncan's "My Mother Would Be a Falconress":

Ah, but high, high in the air I flew.
and far, far beyond the curb of her will,
were the blue hills where the falcons nest.

. . .

I tore at her wrist, at the hold she had for me,
until the blood ran hot and I heard her cry out,
far, far beyond the curb of her will

Schoonmaker spent a large part of the evening talking about projects of Powell's that never came to fruition, one of which was "Thirteen Ways of Killing the Poet"; his theme, she emphasized, was always the war between art and commerce. "Hollywood's a factory town," Budd Schulberg has said, "only instead of motor cars or steel, we turn out cans of film. . . . But there's nothing glamorous about it."

12   Pawnbroker Row

> Cinematography, a military art. Prepare a film like a battle.
>
> — ROBERT BRESSON

My stepfather Sidney's most profound bonding experience in Salt Lake City was with a pawnbroker branded with the inimical name Sam Sapitski. Sapitski spoke with a lisp that forced him to contort his own name and spit out the *p* with epileptic fervor: Tham Thapithki.

The pawnbroker brings to mind a shtetl. People are gripped with a shudder of revulsion, anger, and fear en route to the pawnbroker. Often the things they intend to sell are imbued with a weight of memories that far exceeds any potential measurable worth. They've been forced into a corner that demands they part with their most priceless possessions, heirlooms ("my grandfather's watch!" "my mother's wedding ring!"), and are condemned to confront the immense distance between their subjective sense of value and an objective one—an objective view that both turns the subject into an object and devalues the object. It is not only violence, to augment a sentence by Simone Weil, that turns a man into a thing, but being forced.

The pawnbroker is a living reminder that the worst, given time, will always happen. And after the worst, ashes. When you finish delivering the last of your earthly possessions to the pawnbroker, and you die, the rabbi will read kind words over your grave, if you're an affiliated Jew and can afford one.

I have no idea where Sam Sapitski lived, but his pawnshop was in Salt Lake City proper, and across the street was the theater where I saw Samuel Fuller's films *Merrill's Marauders* and *The Naked Kiss*. It was a dingy theater on a dingy street— the perfect theater to show A-films that looked like B-films. Film instilled disorientation. The fakery imbued existence with a heightened reality, drew out and deepened the colors of the real.

Sam Sapitski, like Sidney, was a kid who also grew up in a tenement in the Bronx. They often met for lunch in a coffee shop closer to the pawnbroker's store than the synagogue, since it was more centrally located; only when together could they be themselves. (When Sidney lunched with his peers or other men of the cloth, it was always at a "restaurant" or a club.) Sam Sapitski was vulgar without reservation and had no aspirations toward the veneer of culture. Sidney had few aspirations in this direction either, beyond his fine early education at the yeshiva, which led him to be ordained at the tender age of nineteen (as Sapitski would say, "Ordained? As *what*—a schmuck?" and they would cater-waul in laughter that must have roused Salt Lake City's silence police). Their behavior was outrageous, but also contagious in its hilarity. The manic laughter of the Jews has caused immeasurable resentment from humorless pedants. Sam Sapitski represented everything that my mother detested in a Jew, or, in other words, everything that the French-German snob in my mother detested. When they quarreled, she blamed Sidney's friendship with Sam Sapitski as the reason for his regression to a mean. But these were just words; in her heart, she was crazy about Sam Sapitski, and was often on the brink of falling off her chair with laughter while the two of them kibitzed. She confided in me how, against her will, she took so much pleasure in the company of the raucous "Tham." Whenever Sidney and my mother mentioned his name in his absence, they always added the phrase: "salt of the earth." My mother liked Sam Sapitski,

The Book of Samuel

but reviled Sidney's association with him. Sam Sapitski represented the lowest common denominator—and a rabbi shouldn't associate with a pawnbroker (many of the most dangerous and destructive attitudes toward Jews congregate around the word *pawnbroker*). Who could imagine that a rabbi would have pawned the watches given to him by his wife's father? Or that a rabbi would take a loan from a pawnbroker? He was another reason why Sidney's career went nowhere except to expire prematurely in Florence, South Carolina. But Sam Sapitski was the only Jew in Salt Lake City with whom Sidney could laugh and cackle. The two of them were in cahoots. They were the outtakes of Samuel Fuller's only perfect film, and one that remained unmade: "The Rabbi and the Pawnbroker" (European title: "The Pawnbroker and the Rabbi").

13

Samuel Fuller was an unnamed presence in my life. (How odd it always seems when the Museum of Modern Art or the Film Forum has a retrospective for a filmmaker whose films I routinely saw because they were the only ones showing in town. Strome and Sapitski could have been out of a Fuller film: a Fuller film of a Malamud novel: "The Kibitzers.")

Fuller's films were often the only ones playing in these backwaters. I remember taking a group of kids in Kankakee, Illinois, to see *China Gate,* playing in the town's one theater, on my ninth birthday. I felt an enormous attraction and revulsion toward Fuller's deglamorized black-and-white palette. (And how horrible to have it conflated by coincidence with the degrading *China Doll,* a film that appeared the next year to punish my senses, as I was offended by the very concept of a woman being reduced to the concept of a thing.) *China Gate* was as transparent as the poster: LOVE AND WAR IN FRENCH INDO-CHINA. The film's main stars, Gene Barry (as "Brock"), Angie Dickinson (as "Lucky Legs"), and Nat King Cole ("in his first dramatic role"), and the incongruity of the offbeat casting telescoped an out-of-joint world, demented, out-of-scale, changing so rapidly that the camera could barely keep pace. In his autobiography, Fuller recounts why he cast Angie Dickinson in her first film role: "With her high cheekbones and slanted eyes, Angie passed for a Eurasian. *And those legs of hers stretched all the way across a Cinema-Scope screen.*" Fuller's heated hyperbolism, blunt, expressive, crude, is a plunge into the unconscious. (In *Forty Guns* Barbara Stanwyck sits at the head of the table surrounded by forty men—"forty pricks" Fuller calls them, each of whom "has had her.") Fuller tracks Nat King Cole as he walks through the bombed-out building crooning these corny quasi-Brechtian "lyrics" fashioned by Harold Adamson: "China Gate . . . , / Bitter tea, / Is this all the good earth / Has to offer me?"

Merrill's Marauders was an aberration at the time for the aberrant Fuller: it was in Technicolor; it was steeped in the colors of death, and steeped in death, and steeped in the death of the manly, forthright, fortitudinous, dependable, athletic actor Jeff Chandler, who then died offscreen from blood poisoning during surgery for back pain before the film was released.

If Fuller was ubiquitous, how did I miss *Forty Guns,* my knowledge limited to the director's comments and a still from his posthumous autobiography? Why did I have to wait to see it upon its release on DVD in May 2005? It so happened that I began physical therapy for problems relating to a herniated disk impacting on the femoral nerve in my right leg ("You have no curve in your lumbar spine, your belly button is to the right of center, you're rotated . . ."), and the office was a block away from Tower Records where *Forty Guns* was on sale for ten bucks. This was more thrilling than I imagined it would be, from the syncopated cuts to Barry Sullivan's legs from the knees down ("no one else walks like that . . .") to the sudden shots of his eyes that take up the entire frame and reveal the seasoned killer's concentration and hardness that withers the courage of the punk holding a gun on him—shots from which Sergio Leone is said to have derived the entire concept of the "spaghetti western" and its mix of silence and violence.

Fuller's films often provided a grisly counterpoint to my moods. I found it hard to understand, as a child, why these small local theaters featured films that offered so little comfort—the very opposite of escapism. In retrospect, it fascinates me that Fuller's frontal and bravura style became so noteworthy. When Fuller tells the mod French reporter his definition of film, more succinctly than I have ever heard it said, "In a word: emotion," I didn't at first take him at his word. Catching *The Naked Kiss* some ten years after I had seen *Pierrot le Fou,* I learned never to assume anything about something I haven't experienced. The opening sequence of *The Naked Kiss* has more shock effect than *Shock Corridor.* A beautiful woman, elegantly attired, is attacking a drunk, who we later discover is her pimp, with athletic grace, but as the staggered man reaches for her throat, his hands find her hair instead and when he gives it a yank—it comes off! And now the camera rises out of the gray-black shadows and is placed right in front of her face the instant her wig comes off, revealing her bald head. Fuller's characters (actors?), none more piercingly than Constance Towers in *The Naked Kiss*, were consumed with longing and raw emotion: they wore their inner lives on their faces; the physicality—embraces and blows—that corresponded to duress! How strange it was to see these things that were so peculiarly affecting, without having been clued in to the idea that Fuller was making art. He divested himself of the methods of classic cinema. "Film," as Fuller immortally announced while being interviewed in flashing pink lights at a party in Jean-Luc Godard's immortal (despite the ephemeral nature of the medium itself) *Pierrot le Fou,* "is a battleground. Love. Hate. Action. Violence. Death. In a word: emotion." (The antistrophic French translation by a miniskirted assistant makes these pronouncements sound, if possible, more portentous.)

The heightened unreality of Fuller's assault on the viewer's emotions put me in touch with an unfamiliarity that I later came to recognize was a primary definition of art. He put a barrier between actor and audience that blocked any romantic identification. Fuller's art is to have the battle continue inside the viewer long after the film's conclusion.

The French appreciated Samuel Fuller because they knew that a work of art must be considered as a totality, even if, to borrow a phrase from Jean-Paul Sartre, it's a detotalized totality.

There is another telling small detail in Fuller's cameo in *Pierrot le Fou.* When asked to introduce himself, he says, "My name is Samuel Fuller," but he pronounces all three syllables in no uncertain way; almost as a phonic version, Sam-u-el. When most Samuels pronounce their names or, like Coleridge or Johnson, have their names pronounced by others, the second syllable is slightly elided, so it sounds like Sam-yul. This bespeaks the enviable fullness of Samuel Fuller's sense of himself. I would go so far as to say that Samuel Fuller's personality had distinctive, positive aspects that would have helped all the central figures I've been talking about here. Fuller's temperament was like a counterforce to depression. He was always a writer, and long before he entered the wars of Hollywood, he had any number of novels rejected. And what was his response? To begin a new one the next day. There's the famous story of how the studio cut

Orson Welles's *The Magnificent Ambersons,* the successor to *Citizen Kane,* from 133 minutes to 88 minutes, and the unused footage was lost. In a way, Welles never recovered from this barbarous ruining of his brilliant second film. After biding his time through the late 1960s and '70s, Fuller had to wait to shoot the autobiographical war film he had wanted to make all his life, which would tell of his experiences in the infantry and, as we would expect, war as it really is. Essentially the same thing happened to Fuller as happened to Welles; his three-hour film was reduced to two hours, and he had no say in it. As far as he knew at the time of his death, no one would ever see *The Big Red One,* his magnum opus, as he had intended it.

In a documentary on the restoration of *The Big Red One,* the actors seem to have been more devastated by the adumbrated version that was released in 1980 than Fuller was. And when casting the lead role of the sergeant for *The Big Red One,* Fuller went for an actor whose life had been scarred, unutterably altered by his experience as a Marine: Lee Marvin. Lee Marvin spent his life after the war trying to cope with, if not erase, as John Boorman attests, his "guilt at surviving the ambush that wiped out his platoon." His antidote, his form of self-medication, was alcohol. Having taken John Boorman as a worldly, trustworthy, and insightful guide into human character, I feel obliged to let him finish his meditation on Lee Marvin. Forgive me if I close my eyes and hold my ears.

> In one sense *Point Blank* was a study of Marvin, and I saw it as an extension of my documentary work, the studies I had made of individuals. The young Marvin, wounded and wounding, brave and fearful, was always with him. The guilt at surviving the ambush [I began to type "anguish"] that wiped out his platoon hung to him all his days. He was fascinated by war and violence, yet the revulsion that he felt for it was intense, physical, and unendurable. . . . His power derived from this. He should have died, had died, in combat. He held life, particularly his own, in contempt. Yet he was in possession of a great force that demanded expression. So *Point Blank* begins with a man shot. Lee knew how to play a man back from the dead.

It is fitting then, in retrospect, that I should have, at the age of ten, days before the Colts would play the Giants in the NFL championship game, met Lee Marvin at the bar in the Royal Emerald Hotel in Nassau. He was an unmistakable, stark presence. He sat on a bar stool with his back to the bar looking at other elegant men and women drinking together at the small, shiny tables. He wore a blue blazer and gray slacks and brown penny loafers. He had the initials L.M. emblazoned in red on his socks, cuff links, shirt cuffs, lapels, and blazer breast pocket. Lee and I were alone at the bar in the mahogany atmosphere, where the light no longer poured through the window, but suffused the room. In the photographs I've seen of myself in that period, except for the monogram, he and I wouldn't have been dressed all that differently.

"Are you——" I began to ask.

"Yeah, kid," L.M. muttered from the left side of his mouth while looking straight ahead at the whispering couples. At the time, he was more familiar as the star of the weekly TV show *M Squad* than for his roles in films I probably hadn't seen like *The Big Heat* and *The Wild One*.

"Can I——."

Now he swiveled to look at me and spoke in a low voice.

"Why don't we have a drink together, kid."

My excitement knew no bounds. L.M. was an extraordinary, labile creature who moved with fluid grace.

"On one condition."

"Sure."

He leaned forward and whispered conspiratorially, "Don't tell anyone else I'm here."

I felt the delicious burden of an immense secret.

"A martini for me and—what—for my . . . young friend?"

"How about a 'Roy Rogers'?" the bartender threw in.

"How does that sound, kid?" he asked in his baritone.

"Good!"

"You don't look like a 'Shirley Temple' kind of kid," he said, winked, and smiled. "I don't want anyone to know I'm here," he added. "I want to be anonymous for awhile."

I gave him a nod that was meant to convey an understanding. He knocked back his martini in one gulp and let out a sigh. I hoped he would order another, but before I had finished my "Roy," two blonde women and a silver-haired man in a gray suit entered the bar, and the man addressed L.M. with annoying familiarity. "Let's go, Lee. Our table's ready."

"Sure, Ed. Let me just say goodbye to my friend."

I pointed to my unfinished drink. He chuckled. "Remember, it's our secret."

14

This is what all the people suffering from depression and related mental illnesses need as a mantra: a shot of Samuel Fuller's unshakable resilience. Every once in a while, when down, I force myself to remember Fuller's attitude, which is creative and survivalist. This is the lure of Fuller's films: survival.

I was more familiar with Samuel Fuller than I had any right to be. Why? Because on a Wednesday afternoon at 2:00 P.M. in Salt Lake City, you might find me in that dingy theater watching *Merrill's Marauders* from the twelfth row (for optimal viewing, as Ingmar Bergman recommends in his autobiography) instead of attending History, English, or ROTC.

Not until this instant did the reason for the impact of Fuller's films dawn on me; he's the visionary angel behind such honest, diagnostic films as *Fight Club* and *Three Kings*—films that reveal an awareness of the global predicament. It should come as no shock as to why Fuller was revered—and in a sense rediscovered by directors like Godard, Scorsese, Jim Jarmusch, and Tim Robbins. But more peculiarly, and more importantly, than the generation that championed his films and publicized his persona, is Fuller's perhaps more direct and unconscious effect on filmmakers like David Fincher and David O. Russell. Fuller's films provide this generation with the tools they need to deal with the tectonic shift in the world that occurred on September 11, 2001. We were already living in a global situation that was crystallized for all time on that day. I can't think of a passage of English poetry that reflects this ongoing condition more than this one from Coleridge's "Fears in Solitude."

> and forth,
> (Stuffed out with big preamble, holy names,
> And adjurations of the God in Heaven)
> We send our mandates for the certain death
> Of thousands and ten thousands! Boys and girls,
> And women, that would groan to see a child
> Pull off an insect's wing, all read of war,
> The best amusement for our morning meal!
> The poor wretch, who has learnt his only prayers
> From curses, and who knows scarcely words enough
> To ask a blessing from his Heavenly Father,

Becomes a fluent phraseman, absolute
And technical in victories and defeats,
And all our dainty terms for fratricide;
Terms which we trundle smoothly o'er our tongues
Like mere abstractions, empty sounds to which
We join no feeling and attach no form!
As if the soldier died without a wound;
As if the fibres of this godlike frame
Were gored without a pang; as if the wretch,
Who fell in battle, doing bloody deeds,
Passed off to Heaven, translated and not killed;
As though he had no wife to pine for him,
No God to judge him! Therefore, evil days
Are coming on us, O my countrymen!
And what if all-avenging Providence,
Strong and retributive, should make us know
The meaning of our words, force us to feel
The desolation and the agony
Of our fierce doings?

15

Samuel Fuller, like Samuel Johnson, began as a journalist and in many ways remained one: a journalist with a camera. What Fuller offered and what remains of Fuller's legacy is not the propaganda of his mythification, but his engagement with reality. I'm saying that David Fincher in *Fight Club* and David O. Russell in *Three Kings* were in some ways enabled in an instinctive way to reach this pitch of outrageousness, clarity, and brutality by something in Fuller. In a similar way was Boswell perhaps drawn to document Samuel Johnson. The word *document* is the key. *True Detective.*

When Fuller went into decline, it was partly because the system had changed and partly because his films lost focus. At some level, loosely speaking, Samuel Johnson was part of a collectivity like someone working in the Hollywood system. Allow me this somewhat far-fetched metaphor to get at a larger point. In comparison with Johnson, who edited Shakespeare's plays to meet Augustan tastes, and wrote the dictionary and *Lives of the Poets,* Samuel Taylor Coleridge and William Wordsworth were independent contractors, having to start from scratch. The new reality that the Romantics confronted resisted systematization. Fuller's films were prophetic of an ensuing collapse.

This idea of document is integral to reclaiming the importance of art. The question is how to find identity and direction in a world so radically changed that it scarcely recognizes itself.

While I am writing these words in my Moleskin notebook, I am listening to an album released by Aimee Mann, *The Forgotten Arm*. I have listened to her for ten years, since I happened on a live version of "I've Had It" in 1995. *The Forgotten Arm* is in touch, like *Fight Club* and *Three Kings*. It's a concept album about a boxer. Having just written the number 11 several times, I catch these lines as they pass in the song "Video" and I wonder if she was thinking what I think she was thinking: "Like a building that's been slated for blasting, I'm the proof that nothing is lasting . . . counting to eleven as it collapses."

Aimee Mann became intrigued when a boxer friend told her what the forgotten arm means in boxing: misdirection, get them on the ropes, keep one arm low while you're hitting them with the other arm. I don't think it's far-fetched to see that her use of this boxing metaphor also pertains to the way that America was hit on September 11, 2001, because our attention was elsewhere, "distracted from distraction by distraction."

My mother's family had certain connections with Hollywood, and my uncle, Herbert I. Leeds, went from cutter to editor to director before he was twenty-five. He then directed a flourish of B movies and sequels—some of which are beginning to appear on DVDs, like *Mister Moto on Danger Island* and the *Michael Shayne, Private Detective* series—that were shot in about ten days, which led the critic Mike Nevins—professor of law, biographer of Cornell Woolrich, and chronicler of the metamorphosis of the Cisco Kid from O'Henry's story to the hero played by Warner Baxter in four of Leeds's films—to observe that "a Leeds film is cut in the camera." I grew up in the shadow of his suicide, a shotgun blast to the chest in the Blackstone Hotel in 1954. The survivors—my grandfather, his second wife (to all effects my grandmother), and my mother—talked about my uncle Bert a lot. When I noticed back issues of detective magazines, like *True Detective,* strewn around their apartment, Grandma Tatiana told me that Bert always read them. I, as a way of getting to know my vanished uncle, read them too and later became addicted to genre fiction, mysteries. The reason that I introduce my uncle at this moment has to do with one of my mother's more pungent reflections on his suicide—her statement that "Bert was never the same after the war." And his one war film, *Manila Calling*, is the most memorable. My uncle, like Lee Marvin and Samuel Fuller, witnessed a lot of death and destruction, unlike the majority of the people in Hollywood, even those who saw action. But Bert wasn't in the infantry; he was a commando. I think he became a commando for the same reason that he was asked to direct a film about the Dionne Quints in Montreal: because he was fluent in French and competent in German. He fought and filmed. He took photographs of the Remagen Bridge when it blew.

16

Madelaine and I were getting a jump on Thanksgiving's restful postures as we sat together, thigh to thigh, on the couch, and read, a rare quiet and intimate moment since our son wasn't home. It was the Wednesday before Thanksgiving 2003. There was a PBS special on Freud, and we decided to leave it on while we read, just in case we detected something new. Then the call came. It was my wife's brother. Their mother had died moments ago.

The call came just as the discussion began to falter, over the matter of Freud and his mother, whose imposing face and "take no prisoners" expression now flashed on the screen—the problem of Freud's disregard for the pain his mother caused him, while he kept his eye trained on the Oedipal and Electra conflicts between father and son, mother and daughter.

In between the memorial on Sunday and Thanksgiving itself we had tickets for *Medea*. Strange, we're not frequent theatergoers, but the day after my father died we had tickets for a play by Simon Gray, *The Common Pursuit*, about the founding of Ian Hamilton's journal *The New Review*, and my desire to see it increased a thousandfold. It would be my only "break" between the unavoidable realities surrounding my father's suicide and his memorial service on Sunday, at which I feared I might need more than moral support.

The discussion on the PBS special on Freud turned to his domineering mother, whose hero he wanted more than anything else to be. I began to think about what the future of psychoanalysis would have been if Freud had examined more closely the son's relationship to his mother, as opposed to the aggressive instinct of the Oedipal conflict with the father. I've often thought that Freud was also wrong in not emphasizing the father's hostility and jealousy toward the son. When I ran this by a friend who is a Freudian analyst, he stunned me by responding, "Nobody's perfect."

This problem extends toward my own father, who lived on the Upper West Side of Manhattan and went to Brooklyn every Sunday to visit his mother. Of course, since I was so rarely in his company, I don't know if he actually visited his mother every Sunday when I wasn't there or if this was in part a performance. But my father was definitely obsessed with his mother. He talked his mother up to his young wife, my mother. He wanted to bring his mother along on his honeymoon. My mother couldn't fathom why. Were these mothers the one unequivocal love for these men in the unpredictable mess of their affections? I jotted down a few sentences during the PBS special: "If a man creates an ideal image of his mother, chances are he'll never look very carefully at another woman either." Not that there isn't a price to be paid by taking another route. I think I separated from my mother at a relatively early age, but the cost of pushing her away, to stop her from suffocating me, was her unflagging anger.

It wasn't clear from the PBS special or the Peter Gay biography I quickly consulted if Freud was aware that he had hostility toward his mother, whom he definitely went to see *every* Sunday. He did know that he went to see her to bathe in her unqualified acclaim. But he didn't seem to want to analyze the ache in his gut that doubled him over and made every Sunday of his life hell. I had just finished a volume of poetry called *Sundays on the Phone,* whose title puns on my mother's phone call every Sunday at a metaphorical 10:47 A.M., a classically inconvenient moment for a couple whose romance is still alive. This was her right. And she would enact it. She couldn't wait to call us two hours later—that would have put her out. She couldn't wait for us to call her then, or in the evening, because other people's children attended to their mothers on Sunday, during the day. But I was truly dismayed by the question of whether or not Freud was aware of the importance of his ambivalence toward his mother. How could a science and mythology that have taken such a hold over Western civilization proceed with such confidence when something so central, so essential, was left unexamined?

The Book of Samuel

I consulted the work of Wilfred Bion, who had been Samuel Beckett's psycho-analyst and friend. It is well known that Beckett's major works began to pour out of him when he was in his early forties at the time his mother died. The first book in his prose trilogy, *Molloy,* begins with him in his mother's room and speaks of his frenzy to find his mother without quite knowing why. Both Beckett and Beckett's character have problems with "mother." She had quite a grip on his soul.

17

I thought poetry had abandoned Coleridge, but apparently the decision was, to some degree, mutual. I don't think that he intended to stop writing poetry, but I imagine he approached the prose he would write, like the *Biographia Literaria,* as if he were embarking on an adventure, taking flight.

Coleridge identified his postpoetic phase as that of inserting *The Prelude* into the universal mind. He intuited that people were not ready to take in, absorb, the violence of Wordsworth's insights without an interlocutor. (Perhaps there is, in the universal unconscious, a kind of oscilloscope. Proust and Freud would rework, conceptualize, and extend Wordsworth's recovery of the memories of childhood.) In some way, *The Prelude* was a collaboration between Wordsworth and Coleridge. This shouldn't be underestimated.

Poets are always in dialogue with other poets, and poetry. The letters that Coleridge sent Wordsworth, including the sublime Cumberland skating winter-lude, are in places almost identical.

> In skating there are three pleasing circumstances—the infinitely subtle particles of Ice, which the Skate cuts up, & which creep & run before the Skater like a low mist, & in sun rise or sun set become coloured; 2nd the Shadow of the Skater in the water seen thro' the Transparent Ice, & 3rd the melancholy undulating sound from the Skate not without variety; & when very many are skating together, the sounds and the noises give an impulse to the icy Trees, & the wood all round the lake *tinkle!*

And then we return to further inexhaustible ground.

> . . . The precipices rang aloud;
> The leafless trees, and every ice crag
> Tinkled like iron, while the distant hills
> Into the tumult sent an alien sound
> Of melancholy, not unnoticed, while the stars,
> Eastwards were sparkling clear . . .

The Prelude demystifies material that for thousands of years had been part of myth, the supernatural. The magic occurred on the roads Wordsworth walked, the frozen lakes he skated on, the outwardly modest mountain he climbed, Snowden. Madelaine and I, along with a hearty crew of disparate walkers, climbed Mt. Snowden uneventfully. On the way down, she and I paused to read the mist-clearing passages from the twelfth book of Wordsworth's poem in the 1805 edition and, as we rested our backs against ergonomic rocks, watched the elderly sidle down on knobby canes. A visit to Tintern Abbey was more solitary. We had the afternoon to wander in the reeds along the river, the two of us alone together in nature. This immersion in the reeds gave me what I needed to complete a line from Pasternak's poem "As With Them" I had been unable to get right until I turned away from his text: "It's hard on eyes sheaved like eaves."

A stop at a pub in Hay-on-Wye was not uneventful. A couple's quarreling was about to boil over. When the pub closed, they took the argument into the parking lot. Here nature was defaced by concrete and roadside litter. A thuggish young man with dirty blonde bangs was berating a dark-haired woman, calling her a "fucking cunt," a contradictory epithet that has always made my stomach turn over, as does everything that implies hatred for women together with a threat of violence. That came next. She matched him shout for shout, and as her shrill voice rose, he resorted to his fists on the edge of the now-deserted lot; yet despite my concern I reminded myself of an inviolable adage: never interfere when a couple is quarreling because they'll both turn on you. And now, a quarter of a century later, in parts of the British Isles the word *cunt* as a slur is applied to men and women equally. That's progress.

Coleridge embraced spreading the word about *The Prelude* as his mission much in the way that Boswell set himself up to be in Samuel Johnson's company. Neither Boswell nor Coleridge made these decisions: the decisions were made for them. I'm thinking that Coleridge's skating letter to Wordsworth is transformed into Wordsworth's indelible skating scene and is then appropriated by

Hopkins in "The Windhover" in his close-up of the kestrel at a moment of peak tension. If I press "pause" amidst the rapturous and rapid whirling of this passage from the first book of *The Prelude,* I can isolate the connection.

> , then at once
> Have I, *reclining back upon my heels,*
> Stopped short; yet still the solitary cliffs
> Wheeled by me—even as if the earth had rolled
> With visible motion her diurnal round!

> As a skate's heel sweeps smooth on a bow-bend: the hurl and gliding

Later Robert Lowell brings the skate back to Earth with a nicely perverse twist, a sadomasochistic glint in "Between the Porch and the Altar": "As the Norwegian dancer's crystaled tights / Flash with her naked leg's high-booted skate / Like Northern Lights upon my watching plate." We are witnessing the conflation of the palpable and the impalpable, the kestrel's motion connected to the skater, then a kite given a power and a volition of its own that look forward to aviation.

> At this hour
> The heart is almost mine with which I felt,
> From some hill-top on sunny afternoons,
> The paper kite high among fleecy clouds
> Pull at her reins like an impetuous courser.

Lowell's fascination doesn't end there; the kite hasn't yet run out of energy and is hardly prepared to land.

> Or, from the meadows sent on gusty days,
> Beheld her breast the wind, then suddenly
> Dashed headlong, and rejected by the storm.

Ever since there have been images of men, they are always searching the sky. I ask myself, why do we look up? What do we think we'll see up there? Why is God in the clouds rather than on the ground? Our associations with vision have to do with ascension. These poems and films have taken the vagueness out of the visionary quest.

18

Gentle as falcon
Or hawk of the tower.

— JOHN SKELTON,
"MY MISTRESS
MARGARET HUSSEY"

Falcons were often part of the trappings of poetry, the way that certain objects and possessions find their way into Renaissance paintings. Falcons have what men need and often lack—the ability to bring things into focus and proceed forward almost instantaneously.

We'll ee'n to't like French falc'ners, fly at anything we see.

The spirited use of falcons in the taut, pellucid sentence in Hamlet's greeting of the players is an instant call to action, a call that sets the players in motion. How quickly this sentence moves on your tongue when you say it aloud. Shakespeare takes the falcon out of the medieval tradition and brings it into the world of action where risks need to be taken, and precision is required.

When the wind is southerly I know a hawk from a handsaw.

I know what you're thinking: *North by Northwest.* What does Hamlet mean? What are the implications of the juxtaposition between directions? What could be more north-northwest than Denmark? Yet this solves nothing, because it is the southerly winds like the sirocco, *tramontana,* and the mistral that are known to drive men mad. Normally the line is interpreted as a testimony to Hamlet's ultimate sanity—and maybe it is. But more intriguing is its ambiguity. He's saying, against nature, that when the wind is southerly, he's completely lucid. I have a friend whose daughter is in distress; I might have said that I hope "the wind is southerly," if it weren't already too southerly and if southerly weren't also the wrong word to invoke a sanity-enhancing temperature. The heat is far more relentless than it was in any of the previous three summers in a row I have spent in the city; it strains our sense, shortens tempers, impinges on patience. The only thing I can rely on to help is water, drinking water continually as if hooked up to an I.V. Cool, clear water. Because, I learned belatedly, our body doesn't announce when it's dehydrated. (Excuse me while I take a break and pour a glass of New York City tap water, which they say is purer, and richer in minerals, than any of the available bottled spring waters.) Dehydration takes place subtly, insidiously, when you're not doing anything, such as exerting yourself, breaking a sweat, and so the symptoms appear to have appeared out of nowhere, and they are disconcerting—nausea and dizziness—and it takes time, no matter how much water you now imbibe, for your body to regain its balance, its—equilibrium. There's also an unstated but implied similarity between the hawk and the handsaw; they seem congruous rather than incongruous. Isn't the location of every line I've quoted closer to north-northwest than southerly? And yet, the aerial imagery in Duncan and Hopkins and Powell and Wordsworth has an exactness that testifies to a kind of clarity. This ascension and aspiration take place in heights where the air is bracing. Otherwise it's too darn hot; nothing wants to fly too close to the sun.

One scene stands out above—and below—all others in *North by Northwest;* it is when a small, single-engine plane disguised as a crop duster but equipped with machine guns attempts to put an end to Cary Grant, who at first dives behind a rock and, after a ricochet, runs and hides in the cornfields. This keeps him protected from gunfire, but not toxic spray.

There was no peregrine falcon at the helm, no decisiveness, no precision in this airplane cum bird of prey. A more skillful pilot could have gotten the job done and made *North by Northwest* the same eighty-eight minutes as the abridged studio version of *The Magnificent Ambersons.* I myself spent many an afternoon hiding in cornfields, or pretending to hide from an imaginary pursuer while I daydreamed or read and worked my way through the provisions, most likely a few pieces of Wonder Bread, a slice of processed cheese, and a handful of M&Ms with their magic coating.

> Crossing
>
> another State Line
> surrounded by Illinois cornfields
> where I used to hide in childhood foxholes,
> it all comes back—twenty years ago
> the stalks were pliant, stiff,
> rough green fibers, unwoven,
> and winds that chafed my face
>
> and dazed me. Now
> harvesters groan to the edge

("LOG," BY CONTRARIES)

It's maddening to be in the dust and heat, and the only reason the wind isn't southerly is because there is no wind, only absence, desolation, and dust.

But what if I take another step backward and consider questioning Hamlet's sanity as much as we would that of the poets whom I've represented? Prior to his directional signals, he says to Guildenstern, "My uncle-father and aunt-mother are deceived." The use of these compounds shows that he has a grasp of an ungraspable situation. There's a disease in the statehood. Sound familiar?

Hitchcock's crop-dusting scene isn't that far from the sort of footage that we see in the "desert wars" where Blackhawk helicopters threaten and impinge, skim the ground, against a palpable, shimmering heat.

My analogies are never far-fetched enough. I have no sooner attempted a preemptive strike against my own intuitive method than I receive a letter from a friend, the poet John Kinsella, who is back home on his rural turf in Australia, but being attacked, bombarded, by none other than the culprits I've just introduced: crop dusters, maniacal aviation.

> herbicide and poison spraying is rampant everywhere, but york is a
> disturbing case-study. sometimes we have three different people spraying
> the same patch of ground. at this very moment our house is basically
> being dive-bombed by a crop duster (it passes over on its way to paddocks
> down the road—very very low)—this stuff is done right up to the town
> limits. some here think that it has brought major health problems and
> even behavioural problems at the local school (though i am sure the school
> would deny it)—but this comes straight from various teachers over the
> years . . . at a famous old property a friend of mine (an artist) was waving
> his hands telling a cropduster to move away from his property and the
> plane aimed for him and literally cropdusted him . . . the boutique town
> of horrors. it really is a catastrophe. link that with the unbridled aviation
> in the district (it is selling itself as a place of leisure aviation), and there's a
> disaster waiting to happen—we have, often simultaneously, skydivers, small
> aircraft, ultra-lights, hang gliders, gliders, crop dusters, and high-flying
> commercial aircraft over york. i have spoken with aviation authorities and
> even the health dept over the years—all recognise issues, but none can do
> anything about it. post 9-11 the aircraft industry was supposed to be more
> regulated—not in york. it's a cowboy scenario.

I would suggest that John arm himself with rakes and golf clubs, but those are useless once these planes pull back the lever and go back up, with the same brio as the kids on strips who burned rubber when they pulled out in their souped-up GTOs, Corvettes, and Shitmobiles with zillion-horsepower engines under the hood, good for mountain driving around Denver, Salt Lake, Albuquerque, L.A. (the "mountains" becoming hills but still good if you're skillful at the wheel, watch out for oncoming cars at turns, tread carefully after dark when the cautious slow-moving vehicles weave back and forth, like a man slurring his words, over the dividing line). It is posthumously rumored that James Dean may have had a death wish, but he was holding firm to the wheel of his Porsche 550 Spyder when it crashed into the side of a black-and-white Ford Custom Tudor Coupe, whose driver had run a stop sign, and crushed the life out of him after just completing *Giant.* Two years later almost to the day, a poet who was nothing if not self-aware was wrestling with his darkest urges and introduced a Tudor Ford in a poem called "Skunk Hour."

> One dark night,
> my Tudor Ford climbed the hill's skull

He concludes:

> My mind's not right.

I concur.

I turn back to the crop-dusting sequence in John's new book, *Arcadia,* where a plane has just swooped within fifteen feet of his windshield: life imitating art. "There's no getting away from them. / Spray-drift sensurround, surround sounds / but furtively sibilant, odour-ploy" ("The Shitheads of Spray"). Hitchcock's scene has been replaced by a far more dangerous and sinister thing against which John recounts his outrage in poem after poem. Hitchcock's scene ends. John's travails continue. John's travails—I mean the travails of the place. He is being threatened by greed and leisure. It's difficult to imagine that people are so desensitized, that they can be so frantic in their pursuit of thrills in order to feel alive. Arrogance used to be flying too high, now it's flying too low.

19

Around the time that Michael Powell was concocting his images to bring high romantic longing and aspiration into the mechanical art of cinema—which he called "the mythology of the twentieth century"—and not that long after Stephen Daedalus picked up where Daedalus left off, Samuel Beckett's characters begin to test the limits of immobility. You can see him now, Molloy, crutches and all—to compensate for a stiff leg—setting out on a long journey on a chainless bicycle. He can still find rapture in the motion that crutches give, "a series of little flights skimming the ground. You take off, you land, through the thronging sound in wind and limb, who have to fasten one foot to the ground before they dare lift up the other. And even their most joyous hastening is less aerial than my hobble." So much for aspiration, heights: the entire debased rubric of the Romantic walker/sightseer is reduced to a man who is reduced to an essential, irremediable problem—an aching leg. Pim crawling through the mud in *How It Is* is almost a colossus. Suddenly we are reawakened to the magnificent usefulness of bicycles and crutches. Samuel Beckett's role as part of the Resistance, holed up in the French countryside, required silence and stealth, for which a bicycle was safer and more useful than a faster mode of transport with a motor. Beckett forces us to think about what it is to be human from the ground up—to clear our minds of notions. Beckett's reductions, his flight from fantasy, from living a concept, provokes us to reevaluate art. Post-Romantic poetry is inclined to begin with unexamined suppositions, assumed truths, including certain subjects, certain settings, which are inherently more poetic than others, as if we are closer to God in the air than on the ground.

The artist is the one who identifies the task.

The rest, that which simulates art, is superfluous.

The new road, but not Whitman's open road, was the one that Frost identified as the one that only had at heart your getting lost.

The dark road which we've been sent down as the new millennium is launched is the road of fraud. And it's as difficult to identify as a virus.

20

Robert Frost was the first poet with whom my son Sam became acquainted, when he was ten. In the summer of 1996, the three of us rented a house beside the Battenkill River in Vermont. It had actually been a bed and breakfast and came equipped with cable television in the living room. Sam and I sometimes shared a bedroom so we could listen to music and talk late into the night. Until, night after night, we were inflicted with a sudden profusion of bats. I knocked two down while they hid in back of the window curtains after they had whirled, swooped, and dived around the room, and I delivered the death blow with the heel of my cross-trainers. Now Sam, who had gone upstairs to "get something," came down having sighted yet another bat. Madelaine figured out that the closet in "the Captain's Room" (of the B & B) led to an attic which led to the eaves where there could very well be a bat cave. We made the by-now ritual trek upstairs. Nothing in the room. Nothing in the alcove. And there, on the bathroom ceiling, hung a bat, huge semi-human face, round belly, wings outspread. The idea of smashing something with such a human face with the badminton racquet I was holding in my right hand suddenly appalled me, and Madelaine suggested a remedy: turn on all the lights, take out the screens, open the windows, and let the bat fly out. We executed the plans, finished at the moment in *Giant* just before James Dean was about to strike oil, got into the car, and drove to the Dairy Bar in Arlington and asked the owner what he would do. "Light some bombs."

Sam didn't want to sleep in that bedroom anymore, after the second bat, and now the fifth—they could appear at any time during the night. Channel surfing now around the Olympics, he asked if he could watch *Live and Let Die* and I said okay but by midnight I suggested we take our bitter medicine now, go up, listen to our new CD of *Negotiations and Love Songs,* and read. I started to thumb through my new Library of America edition of Frost's collected work.

"Are you going through the whole book that fast?"
"Yeah. But I'm not reading, I'm just skimming, to get a feel for it."
"I know. What's that one?"
"It happens to be a poem about a boy who gets his hand cut off."
"Can I see?"
"Let me see if I can find some of his short poems."
"How short?"

"Very short."

"The one about the boy didn't look very long."

"Here's a short one I like, 'Fire and Ice.'"

"Okay."

I read.

"I agree with him. I'd take fire too."

"But he says ice would work just as well. But if you think about how enraged and fierce James Dean was, you get a good picture of the kind of energy he's talking about."

"Read the one about the boy."

"Okay."

"What's it called?"

"'Out, Out—.'"

I read.

"That wasn't so long. The doctor killed him when he cut his hand off."

"Not really. It's unclear to the boy what's happened and what's going to happen. He's in shock. But it is a shocking poem."

"Can I see the book?"

"Sure."

"These pages are flimsy, but nice. Can I read you 'Dust of Snow'?"

"Sure."

He read with great gusto, then asked the right question: "What's 'rued'?"

I tried to explain how Frost uses an intentionally short but unusual word to give the poem its character. Sam seemed satisfied. Big yawn.

"Shouldn't we go to the bathroom before we go to sleep?"

"Okay."

"I really like Frost, even though I don't like to rhyme in my own poems."

"I know what you mean."

Long pause. "Frost is cool."

Sound of toilet flushing.

The Book of Samuel

21

There's something prelapsarian about *The Prelude*. This was possible for one reason, in addition to Wordsworth's native genius: Dorothy, before the fall. The immersion in water makes me think of woman; I am beginning to think of Dorothy Wordsworth as a waterfall with more than enough warmth and depth and wet to go around.

A waterfall pours over rocks scored with ridges, clefts, and declivities. This rocky precipice has a certain female aspect that is easily overlooked because it is impenetrable; hard. The profoundly porous qualities of hard substances are often overlooked; unnoticed; denied by men for fear of being overwhelmed, engulfed, absorbed. The counter-stress to the depth of this pleasure is not pain; it is fear. The fear that men have of the power of women, which Rilke locates in a phrase he copied from a papyrus of the sayings of Ptah-hotep around 2000 B.C. ("We have to die because we've known them"), is preternatural. Dorothy Wordsworth had a subterranean power like this. Given how Coleridge dried up as his marriage to Sarah Fricker became sterile indicates how central Dorothy's presence had been in Wordsworth's life, but he wasn't aware that it was she that was filling the need.

It has been justly noted that Coleridge's failure to do whatever it would take to marry Sara Hutchinson was one of his greatest mistakes.

Language unties the very soul of thought. I had always thought that Coleridge bought into the notion of his so-called failure. I had always conjectured that Samuel Johnson must have felt more than a little disappointed in himself for his failure to write many good poems, poems to rival his prose. In that way he is like my fathers, who really talked away their lives. My real father, later, in silence, living to be alone on his boat, *The Unbelievable,* could carry on relationships on the mainland at a distance he preferred, with water in between, and report the variegations in the weather on his ship-to-shore radio to his second wife, Merrill. But certain information, certain documents have entered and now fly about the house, and I find that Faulkner's aspirations, once he dubbed himself burnt-out as a writer, to live for fox hunting, to actually move to Virginia where the fox hunting was better than in Alabama, weren't that different from my father's at exactly the same age.

Faulkner and his foxes. Hemingway and his boat.

And it has taken me until now to see that, while he only once in earshot mentioned Hemingway's name, my father gravitated to a boat as his floating castle because of Hemingway's example. And there were many years, before he lost his job and drifted into madness, when his looking forward to being on Long Island for the weekend where his boat was moored wasn't that different from Hem's looking forward to his Sunday marlin expeditions.

He talked more to us from his ship-to-shore than when we were in the same room together. One summer, we went to California because Madelaine had a grant to look for signs of life in outer space. He sent us numerous tapes complete with instructions on what to do while listening to them—mainly humorous asides.

If he hadn't had his boat he wouldn't have had the accident that in some way severed his connection to sanity, threw him off. What happened? His friend carelessly slammed his boat into the dock, and my Dad went flying. He was never the same afterwards. He had diffuse pain and trouble with his balance. And his rage at the man who caused the accident played no small part in his being thrown off course, defenseless against the demons he had fled, self-medicated, and lucked his way out of facing.

It's just strange to piece together these connections, that like Faulkner and Hemingway, my father loved to ride and fish. There's something beautiful about these escapes that occur within reality.

But there's more. William Faulkner was also an aviator. He flew every chance he got.

He wrote *Pylon* in no time while taking breaks from *Absalom, Absalom*. *Pylon* is rampant with anti-Semitism because he now identified the enemy as the Hollywood Moguls, the Jews who raked him over, exploited his talent, wasted his time, during his forays as a screenwriter. How strange that the writer I hadn't thought to introduce into this falcon section was the only one whose actual name, Faulkner, was derived from Falconer. He's also the only one who was an avid flyer. And knew his way around the flying scene just as Hemingway did around a bullfighting ring.

The Book of Samuel

And me: I write a book called *Rider* but I don't ride. I rode with my father a few times. Once in open country he gave his horse the go, jumped the fence, and disappeared, and I mean disappeared, gone, no trace of him or his party in the distance and no sign that any of the riders thought: what happened to Mark? And when my father returned, pleased with his own prowess, smelling of stables and leather, from this afternoon speeding through the open spaces on an animal's back, and he saw that my face was scrunched up in distress, he said nothing. He was on to his next "men's" activity. Now I was hurt and my voice broke when I asked why he hadn't come back, or sent someone, or checked. Long, boring afternoons are longer and more boring when you're ten than when you're fifty. "Mark," he said in a voice that was frequently, no pun intended, hoarse, "you told me you knew how to ride."

And that, I wanted to scream, meant "don't look back"? I knew how to mount a horse and move at a trot, but my knowing how to ride was derived from the ease in the saddle I noted in the cowboys on TV and in the movies. What was there to it, riding, once you got on the horse? How much harder could it be than riding a bicycle? To backtrack: he didn't abandon me in a wilderness; he'd taken us to a dude ranch for a long weekend. I had water, comic books, *MAD!* . . .

This little scene, little phrase, *in nuce,* would exemplify why my father sent me to psychiatrists, as if it were abnormal, in a clinical sense, for an imaginative ten-year-old boy to pretend, but not really believe, if he thought there were anything at stake, this was ostensibly a protected environment (with paid helpers), that he knew how to do something he didn't know how to do and that looked easy. To leap ahead, other times come to me when I said I knew how to do something I didn't know how to do and made a fool of myself, without complaining, enduring, and in certain cases, over time, mastering this activity in a shorter time than might seem possible. There may have been a subterranean logic to this wishful thinking: that if I said I knew how to ride a horse or a motorcycle or play golf or "whatever," then I would acquire the ability to do so rapidly. The central obstacle to this method is something called: the physical world. It is here that my mimetic capacity got me into trouble.

Now everything's upside down. People don't believe me when I tell the simple truth and do believe me when I invent outrageous exaggerations. More and more. Inside out. Because more than anything else, more than injuries to the body, people dread being caught out as fools. They dread making mistakes. In every walk of life. And their mistake is that the courage to continue to make mistakes is their magical connection to invention; their shot at originality. I see them every day on my daily round, multitudes crippled by the fear of being wrong, making mistakes; the fear, I am forced to add, of being caught out in having been wrong. It's no accident that the phrase "being wrong or right" lends itself so easily to reversal, as Robert Frost definitively demonstrates. Frost's "Acquainted with the Night" has a sincerity and authenticity that all but a few villanelles lack because the form is an extension of content, the interchangeable, reversible nature of words doomed to imprecision in their application. I could just quote the lines from memory, "the time was neither wrong nor right," but I am lonely for Frost this early Saturday afternoon, partly due to my unforced confinement after the epidural injection I had into a herniated disk a few days ago; I could count the days, but the phrase "a few days" puts me in contact with a poet, James Schuyler, whose work I loved, and whom I introduced at his last reading, which was one of his first readings, despite his age, sixty-seven, because mental problems had prevented him from venturing before audiences, and now "mon hypocrite lecteur, mon semblable, mon frère," together we have entered a poetic space, which is where my heart is today, but that for *Practical Reasons* (a book I. A. Richards didn't write but one both of my parents would have read and begged me to read), I have not gone there. I have gone: here.

> And further still at an unearthly height,
> One luminary clock against the sky
>
> Proclaimed the time was neither wrong nor right.
> I have been one acquainted with the night.

After typing those lines, I come upon my Library of America edition of Frost with a shiver and part of me wants to imitate John Lennon's strategy in "God." After he sings, "God is a concept by which we measure our pain" he says, "I'll say it again," and he does.

Frost and loneliness. I am lonely for Frost today, I mean I am not lonely for Frost today, I am lonely for an event I missed Wednesday in which a certain special friend of mine, whom I don't get the chance to see often enough, read all of *Mountain Interval* aloud at Columbia (with two other people, one of whom I had seen two nights prior at a memorial service). Correction: I missed having the chance (scratch out) to see her, due to an engagement made months before with a friend with whom I've canceled too many engagements, and it's possible

The Book of Samuel

that my nerves, FOR ONCE a reference to a physical nerve, the femoral nerve, running (scratch that), extending through my lumbar spine down the front of my right leg into my ankle, couldn't have endured that much stasis—sitting. I might have listened to a poem I went to hear for pleasure in pain.

Not that I wasn't tormented by the thought of a wrong conception. Because that would mean throwing out months of mental preparations and months of work, and I had deluded myself that I was on something of a smooth track with the prose I was trying to write, the same "prose" I have always feared would interfere with my muse, with the composition of poems, the new kind of poem I had begun to write since I finished the fifth of my quintet of long or book-length poems interspersed with interconnected sequences that looped back to the beginning in *Rider* and forward to the end in *Sundays on the Phone,* the fifth of the five. This decade-long project served many purposes; it kept me, like a rider, on course. It allowed me to create an imaginary world and an environment, insofar as the latter is possible in a literary art. And my friend grasped this when she wrote me a letter saying that she'd been "living in *The Millennium Hotel.*"

I like to imagine receiving that letter after the physical Millenium Hilton hotel was disabled in the attack on the World Trade Center on September 11, 2001. In an ad the hotel has taken in a magazine, it now offers "exciting views of the rebuilding of the WTC."

I am once again contemplating the possible meanings of the missing *n* in its name—Millenium Hilton.

22

I receive an e-mail from a friend who knows I listen to Sam Phillips, and not Sam Phillips, the "Father of Rock and Roll." It said that she was performing at Zankel Hall, and asked did I want to go.

I thought that Zankel Hall, a recent addition to Carnegie Hall, was for classical music, and that intrigued me as well. I assumed the concert would be sold out, as everything wonderful is in New York City these days, but we miraculously found aisle seats in the eleventh row. Sam Phillips, a beautiful blonde woman with a spiritual air, and to my surprise, backed by an orchestra with violins and cello, in addition to bass guitar and drums, appeared with a handheld recorder through which she transmitted the background music to a song she then sang. After this, she retrieved her guitar and began to strum it sparingly, and said, in a way that was both dramatic and self-effacing, "I've been going through a difficult period. For the last year and a half, I've been separated from my husband, T-Bone Burnett, who produced this album." Hearing this transformed her for the audience into the image of an exceptional woman, stripped of everything, and trying to maintain dignity after having been discarded, probably for a younger version. Sam sang for about fifty-nine minutes, keeping us entranced and tense, when she announced that the next song would be her last. There was something shocking about this early terminus, and from her tone you knew there would be no encore. It was painful to think of being released from the tension that she contained and contained us. She wasn't embarrassed about her image—the image of an afflicted woman—heightened by the contrast between her white blouse and her stark black floor-length A-line skirt. The final song was piercing as she sang it, her voice melodious and grave: "After you've given up and all is gone / Help is coming." Long pause: "one day late."

23 *"Like a Bird on a Wire"*

Hemingway often described competition among writers in boxing terms. He felt he'd been "sucker punched" and knocked to the canvas by the critics of *Across the River and Into the Trees,* but as if he'd been saving it for just such an occasion, he believed the fish story would allow him to regain his position as "champion." But underneath Hemingway's bravado, the emptiness had grown, and now it would swallow him up: his genial spirit failed.

Never mind that a good half of *Across the River* contains some of his best writing; the fact that critics leapt to the attack when the book shifts from his evocation of Venice before and after the war to his infatuation with the young Countess Renata . . . consumed his combative, pugilistic, and unstable mind. The criticism of *Across the River* is so uniformly negative that many people have read everything Hemingway wrote except for this book. This is a dark fact. It is the rarest of critics who can judge a work of art until it's been approved by literature's higher court. Several exceptions that come first to mind are Denis Donoghue, Christopher Ricks, Susan Sontag, and Edmund Wilson, each of

The Book of Samuel

whose best essays are works of art in their own right. There are bad books that make valuable reading, and so-called good books that are enjoyable and fun to read but sidestep all the difficulties and obstacles that come into play in the creation of a literary work of art. Artist-critics, or what Wilde called *The Critic as Artist,* usually make the effort to bring out any excellence in a book by a good or greater writer who has strayed off course. Today Martin Amis, Julian Barnes, Elizabeth Hardwick, Robert Hass, William Gass, and, of course, Susan Sontag are among those who have adopted that role. One great novel by Peter Handke never came within a fraction of reaching the public it deserved. German writers I met were negative about it for "being exactly 1,000 pages in the German edition." I found it as rewarding in its own way as *Walden.*

In September 1952 *The Old Man and the Sea* appeared in *Life* magazine, selling over five million copies in a flash. The next week Scribner's rolled out the first hard-cover edition of fifty thousand copies, and they too sold out quickly. The book was a huge success both critically and commercially and, for the first time since *For Whom the Bell Tolls* in 1940, Hemingway was atop the literary heap . . . and making a fortune. The Pulitzer Prize he won for *The Old Man and the Sea* in 1953 was the prelude to the Nobel Prize that would be awarded to him in October 1954.

Flush with money from *The Old Man and the Sea,* Hemingway decided to exercise his wanderlust, returning to Europe to catch some bullfights in Spain and then to Africa later in the summer for another safari with his wife Mary. In January 1954 Hemingway and Mary boarded a small Cessna airplane to take a tour of some of East Africa's beautiful lakes and waterfalls.

"I'm back in the Cessna again."

To a writer like Hemingway, whose depression continued to deepen, and could only be alleviated by distraction, the Pulitzer reawakened his mania; and now that he was high he wanted to fly, and experience another signature Papa Hemingway adventure. He would never publish another book in his lifetime. And yet his unfinished, posthumously published books proved that his imagination was keen, ripe, and wise.

The pilot, Roy Marsh, dove to avoid a flock of birds and hit a telegraph wire. The plane was badly damaged and they had to make a crash landing. The group's injuries were minor, though several of Mary's ribs were fractured. After a boat ride across Lake Victoria, they took another flight in a De Havilland Rapide, this time piloted by Reginald Cartwright.

Don't think twice: it's not all right. In a fever to reward the author with the Nobel Prize as back pay for his early indelible contributions to the art of prose for a book that the young Hemingway would have written in ten pages in *In Our Time,* fate, looking for someone on high and damaged by hubris, like Malcolm Lowry and Jackson Pollock, found the victim who was right in front of its featureless face the whole time. Fate has no mind, but it can follow orders, and was rewarded every time it made a serendipitous choice. And what could make a greater scoop in the underworld than the Death of Hemingway soon after he received the big one? I only wish Buddy Holly and the legions of others who've crashed in small planes had made a note to "watch out, and trust your nervousness." Now you can think twice. Hemingway's plane had already crashed before it crashed. The pilot, diving to stay clear of a flock of birds on a telegraph wire, could not get it back up into the air and a crash landing was the only choice. Hemingway pretended to be unfazed, just "all shook up." And Mary was too tough to let a few fractured ribs deter her from Destination Uganda. At first relieved to catch a De Havilland Rapide, the Hemingways sighed with relief—but the plane had hardly lifted off the runway when it went down, catching fire. But the true hero is roused by danger, and Hem, after the other passengers had escaped through an exit at the front of the plane, broke through the main door by turning his head into a battering ram. The press ran with it: Hemingway Indestructible Again! Image, image, image. But the images on the X-rays showed: fractured skull; spinal disks, two, cracked; right arm and shoulder, dislocated; liver, right kidney, spleen: ruptured; sphincter muscle, paralyzed (by compressed vertebrae on iliac nerve); head, face, arms: third-degree burns; hearing: "impaired"; vision: impaired.

Summary: crash victim survived. Minor injuries sustained.

But there is no sign they ever departed. And the multiplicity of drugs required to treat each injury in its turn over the next six years further dislocated the already fragile, unstable, and increasingly disoriented writer. Writer? Or boxer. *Wanna fight kid, I'll knock you on your ass. You don't think I can? I knocked Tolstoy on his ass with* For Whom the Bell Tolls, *you bet. That's real war, war I took part in, like the war before that; not something I reconstructed from books. Willa Cather, poor woman, got her "war" from watching . . . film. So who's the champ, huh, who, who?*

The Book of Samuel

Faulkner, his best books out of print until Malcolm Cowley assembled the Faulkner reader with its map—requested by Cowley—of Yoknapatawpha County, also felt the ground underfoot give way. He'd hoped the symptoms would stop after, finally, his gift was recognized for its true worth when he was awarded the Nobel Prize for Literature in 1950. He couldn't have been drunk because he was never not drunk. He wrote on alcohol. A small amount in a tall glass of water sipped at intervals throughout the day had always steadied his hand and focused his imagination. He's the only writer on record of whom it could be said that alcohol worked, in the way he used it; that alcohol helped his writing. Another half-truth in a world of half-truths. It did, and it didn't. It did during the ten years in which he wrote the great books that made him the greatest American novelist. Even Hemingway rated Faulkner highest. Who did Faulkner rate highest: Thomas Wolfe. Because he reached higher.

Faulkner knew Hollywood, including stunt men. And actors who could ride, like Hemingway's buddy, Gary Cooper. But I doubt there was an actor who could ride like William Faulkner, who, as they say, "grew up on a horse."

But Faulkner knew that nothing he wrote in the future could measure up to the decade-long run that produced *The Sound and the Fury, As I Lay Dying, The Wild Palms,* and *Absalom, Absalom.*

The first thing my father did when he was flush in his late twenties was to buy a horse, which he kept in Claremont Stables, and rode every morning before work. The Claremont Stables, a New York City landmark, shut down within six months of this writing. I'd ridden there too, as a young tyke and, once freed from practicing inside the stables, was sent out with a group of children to go, at a trot, around the reservoir. I heard a man's voice, "Hey, you up there, did I say you could break into a canter?" "But it feels so good." "It'll feel better if you don't get thrown." "Yes, sir." And he was right; cantering was like that other inestimable pleasure I hadn't experienced yet; the stop-go rhythm threw me into reveries. My intoxication as we rounded the path for the third time turned to anxiety when my mind began to wander as, with heightened senses, my eyes were enraptured by the colors of the trees that had burst into blossom, and by the girls, ranging from my age to twice my age, in skirts that ended just below the hip joint, who flooded the park, and my passion switched from riding to meeting one.

When in his presence, I could visualize the fall that severed my father's connection with reality's solid, insoluble, and inexorable presence; reality, that like a wall, didn't care how you arrived at this gate without a ticket and with a shoulder bag to hold all you would need on the trip. But inside reality, chaos runs wild, and with delight runs from one strictly regimented location to another, which is why, in the years when we traveled together, my Dad refused to leave for an airport if there was a chance it'd leave more than a ten-minute gap between our arrival and the plane's departure because "Mark, it's not going to leave without us." "Mark, always pack light." And he was right to take no more than two of anything and to wash it in the sink every night, whether you were in Chicago on business or Mazatlan on mischief: in quest of the marlin. I guess I should have told him about the girl I was in quest of who'd gotten off the plane with us and was staying on the next floor, alone, in the Hotel del Cine. I was sixteen.

I didn't understand why you'd want to follow someone else's tracks. To that extent. In another ten years, I had to get to Keats's house on Hampstead Heath. Then, after I read *Prometheus Unbound,* I had to get to the Baths of Caracalla, where Shelley wrote the entire poem, forging an impromptu study in whatever space he could clear, what rocks he could requisition, what imaginings he could conjure in the Roman distances, out of the ruins in the fields, out of the dissonance he knew was in the uncertain clasp of present future and past, that roused the few animated objects that the wind had let stay overnight in the ruin. Returning is never. Underneath the protective patter of social discourse all my subjects knew there was nothing to go back to because they were already in the future, and it was best to attend to that now; now: no matter what the costs. Giacomo Leopardi, who hardly went anywhere, except to his father's library, had figured this out too; but by then he'd been condemned to a life of inaction. Leopardi hit on the word *noia* that, without acknowledgment, without even any recognition of the source, became one of the few concepts to hit the street as "nothing," or "nothingness." As the observant "rascally young Prince" Hal chides his fearful retinue and its Lord of Misrule, with this aphorism worthy of William Blake: "for wisdom cries out in the street and no man regards it."

24

The *New Yorker* on April 25, 2005, published Saul Bellow's sentences from an account in progress, which he had addressed to Philip Roth. They expressed precisely how I have felt through March and April 2005. Something else happened to Bellow in 1949 that also struck home. "In 1948, I went to Paris to write a third novel. *But by the winter of 1949 it became miserably—hatefully—apparent that I was once again on the wrong track. I fell into a depression thicker than the palpable soddennesse of Paris. . . .*" (I have added the italics and *e* in homage to Chaucer; I like the look and sound and feel of *soddenness* with an *e* at the end.)

And when Bellow writes about the failure of his first marriage, and the loss of his beloved son, I am disturbed to see the straightforward parallel between the inestimable Mr. Bellow and the—ultimately—misunderstood Charles Rudman, who went through the identical experience at the same time. I have compassion for my father and what he must have felt at that moment when he arrived home to find that the apartment had been emptied (I imagine she left the crib). My affiliations were always split, torn, rent, sundered by the drama that followed, my mother running to the airport with me bundled under her arm, and I was forced to listen, time and time again, beginning long before I knew what the words meant or the meaning the sentences contained, that my mother left in this manner to punish my father for bad behavior—his jaunt to Virginia Beach with his pals was the last straw in a series of selfish and irresponsible misdemeanors. My father was paying for his way of going about things, of acting as if it were beneath him to explain anything he wanted to do and to act in even a mildly conciliatory manner, the way husbands do when they're going somewhere with the boys to have fun. My father didn't know how to say things like: "I'll make it up to you when I get back, and I'll spend more time with Mark." I have to emphasize again that I don't know the truth of anything that happened between my mother and my father and the families before I was about five, but I imbibed the venom, hatred, contempt, and disgust in the company of my mother's family, since all his actions in their narrative confirmed that she had married beneath her—and part of that was true. But this is only half of one side of the story—less than is offered in *Rashomon*. And a simple true word like *incompatibility* was never used. This was Blame City. And now a phone call from a close family friend telling me that my mother had planned this departure long in advance, not on angry impulse, combines with Bellow's comparable anguish. It has taken me days to try to find again the other passage in Bellow's

"Reflections" that is so eerily close to my father's experience, his father having died several years before I was born.

> Those years were the grimmest years of my life. My father had died, a nephew in the Army had committed suicide. My wife had left me, depriving me of my infant son.

(NEW YORKER, APRIL 25, 2005)

25

All dark and comfortless.

—King Lear

This is what America has refused to accept: vulnerability. Basically, everyone in this "Book of Samuel" has been thrown for a loop. Nothing has turned out smoothly. It's only in an empire that a large part of the population ever thought things would turn out smoothly; that everything was under control. "Kubla Khan" is in some sense the consummate colonial fantasy—no wonder it was interrupted even as it was being written down, and the flow stopped as ancestral voices were prophesying war. The barbarians were at the gate. There is something colonial about Coleridge's supernatural poems. "The Rime of the Ancient Mariner" has aspects of a parable of empire. America is very much like the ancient mariner himself. Until now, Americans haven't really feared the consequences of having their wishes gratified; they assume that they will be appreciated for their underlying goodwill. Retribution puts America in shock. Retribution for what?

I have a friend, a historian, Alexander Stille, who has written with an almost uncanny sense of awareness on these vague and perilous aspects of history. In his book *The Future of the Past:*

> Although we pay lip service to living in a global, interdependent world, Americans are, in many ways, becoming more insular. . . . The terrorist attack of September 11, 2001, exposed how dangerous this cultural neglect could be. Intelligence reports sent by foreign governments to the FBI and the CIA were ignored because almost no one at the agencies read foreign

languages. A quite specific warning from French police on the eve of the attack went unread and untranslated.

Alex's larger awareness could not protect him from harm.

On a Monday in late January, I checked my e-mail before leaving to teach my first class of the spring semester and discovered a ragged communication, asking if I were friends with "Lexi/Alex." This was followed by some reference to death. I rode the subway in anguish at the thought that something terrible, something as terrible as death, had interfered with Alex. It made no sense. I had seen him several months before carrying his three-week-old son Sam in a Snugli at a book party for a mutual friend. He was with his lovely young wife, whom I hadn't really met, although we acknowledged each other with glances. All that afternoon I assumed or half-assumed that "Lexi" was one of Alex's nicknames. I didn't know how to reach the friend who had e-mailed. In desperation, I resorted to Google.com. What I found was shattering. Alex was alive, and I took a deep breath to celebrate that, but something terrible and even more unimaginable had happened. What I found was a notice that Lexi Rudintsky, his wife, had died a few days prior at her family home in Massachusetts. Alex, Lexi, a vertiginous combination when you add the dimension of tragedy. Now I was forced to assimilate, to let myself believe, that Alex's wife, Lexi, who was thirty-two, sixteen years younger than Alex, was no longer among us. I kept seeing her standing next to him in the hot room at the party, looking happy and confident. She had had a baby three weeks before, and unknown to me at the time, she was about to have her first book of poems published in the coming year. And there, in the middle, the sleepy, dark-eyed baby: Samuel.

CODA

A Garland for Nicanor
Parra at Ninety

(On the occasion of *Antipoems: How to Look Better and Feel Great,* antitranslation by Liz Werner, New Directions, 2004)

In the fall of 1972 I sat with a group of students at Columbia University's watering hole, the West End Tavern, drinking watery draft beer across from the Chilean poet Nicanor Parra. I had made sure to get a seat across from Parra, whose *Poems and Antipoems* had been a source of delight and inspiration to me. I didn't intend to write dramatic monologues, like Parra, but I was in agreement with his implicit critique of modernism and neo-Romanticism. The political edge to Parra's poetry was, up until this point in time, completely internalized. He was wearing a heavy suit and tie and blocky shoes—conservative garb for a poet at that time, but not perhaps for a poet of Latin culture. He was also affable and warm. I overcame my shyness and told him how I felt about his work, and then recited a good part of one of his poems, "The Viper," in an animated and slightly exaggerated way, which suited the bravado of the poem.

> For years I was doomed to worship a contemptible woman
> Sacrifice myself for her, endure endless humiliation and sneers,
> Work night and day to feed her and clothe her,
> Perform several crimes, commit several misdemeanors,
> Practice petty burglary by moonlight,
> Forge compromising documents,
> For fear of a scornful glance from her bewitching eyes.
> During brief phases of understanding we used to meet in parks
> Or we would go to a nightclub
> And fling ourselves into an orgy of dancing
> That went on until well after dawn.
> For years I was under the spell of that woman.

She used to appear in my office completely naked
And perform contortions that defy the imagination,
Simply to draw my poor soul into her orbit
And above all to wring from me my last penny.
She absolutely forbade me to have anything to do with my family.
To get rid of my friends this viper made free with defamatory libels
Which she published in a newspaper she owned.
Passionate to the point of delirium, she never let up an instant,
Commanding me to kiss her on the mouth
And to reply at once to her silly questions
Concerning, among other things, eternity and the afterlife,
Subjects which upset me terribly,
Producing buzzing in my ears, recurrent nausea, sudden fainting spells,
Which she turned to account with that practical turn of mind
    that distinguished her,
Putting her clothes on without wasting a moment
And clearing out of my apartment, leaving me flat.

(TRANS. W. S. MERWIN)

I think I had long sections of several of his poems by heart, "The Trap" and "The Tunnel" among them, and I had made no attempt to memorize them. Parra, who was one of the best known and most intriguing poets in the world at the time, responded with immense warmth and said, "I can't believe that a young American poet knows a poem of mine by heart. I am moved." This spontaneous act on my part, this sharing of my enthusiasm with this wry and ebullient man opened the door to further conversation. I asked him what he thought about his compatriot, Pablo Neruda, knowing that his work was a direct rejoinder. "Neruda is a great poet, no question. His poetry may be as great as poetry gets. But he is a nineteenth-century man."

It is hard for me to convey how shattering I found that sentence. Parra was saying that the cosmic repertory, the full orchestra of the poetry of the past, was no longer viable or possible. I wasn't at the time familiar with Adorno's now over-flogged dicta about the impossibility of poetry after Auschwitz, but I was acutely conscious of the necessity for poetry to respond to a new reality. It is also shocking to consider that Neruda, who does have the characteristics of that grand nineteenth-century sensibility, was born, not in 1899 like Hart

Crane, but in 1904. It seems incredible that Neruda is only ten years older than Parra because he does seem like someone from another era, more like the contemporary of Rilke.

This erasure of the nineteenth-century sensibility still informs poetry in a significant way, with regard to what I consider a viable neo-Romanticism. One way to look at this has to do with a rejection of the concept, dubiously derived from a phrase that John Keats used in a letter, of "negative capability." For Parra, in his vision of the future, poetry would not be about the sensitive receptivity of the poet as an individual, a lyrical self; a different identification would be called for. Poetry would have to respond to what Donald Davie would later call in his important, compelling, and little-known book, taken from the Hodges Lectures on Czeslaw Milosz, "the insufficiency of lyric." (Davie's book on *The Poems of Doctor Zhivago,* translation and commentary, is one of the great quixotic acts of critical/imaginative writing, structured very much like *Pale Fire* but endowed with an incisive mind rather than a lunatic scholar.)

> We thus come round to press again the insufficiency of the lyric mode
> for registering, except glancingly, the complexity of twentieth-century
> experience. Since I have invoked, as spokesman for the lyric voice, a figure
> so illustrious and never to be discounted as John Keats, it is worthwhile
> pointing out that in our time an anti-Keatsian position is to be found
> articulated by persons not much less distinguished. Here for instance,
> surprisingly, is Pasternak, writing in his own English to his American
> translator Eugene Kayden, in 1958. "You say I am 'first and last a poet, a
> lyric poet.' Is it really so? And should I feel proud of being just that? And do
> you realize the meaning of my being no more than that, whereas it hurts me
> to feel that I have not had the ability to express in greater fullness the whole
> of poetry and life in their complete unity?"

I was twenty-three years old, and I wanted to write poems in the spirit of Keats, as expressed in his letters. Instead I was to translate poets who required me to stretch beyond any perception I might have had in regard to the limits of the English language. Part of the attraction of poetry was its difficulty.

I didn't want to go straight to a postmodern aesthetic on the basis of some external objective doctrine. As Keats said, "that which is creative, must create itself." I also believed what Keats said right afterwards, that by leaping "headlong into the sea . . . [I had] become better acquainted with the soundings, the quicksands, & with the rocks, than if I had stayed upon the green shore, and piped a silly pipe, and took tea & comfortable advice." I'm willing to embrace Keats as a model for the development of a poet's imagination—push yourself, fill four thousand lines of blank verse at the rate of fifty lines a day, as he did when he wrote *Endymion*—but I cannot take the concept of negative capability at face value.

The poetry of Brecht, eastern European poets Miroslav Holub and Janos Pilinsky, Polish poets such as Zbigniew Herbert and Czeslaw Milosz, these and others had already predicted a poetry that severely and definitively rejects this notion of negative capability, which is still a kind of raft upon which much American and English poetry attempts to float.

The later works of Parra are far more critical. If I put quotes from Brecht, Milosz, and Parra side by side, you'd see what I mean. Keats's letter, which was not initially intended for public consumption, is quoted flagrantly in almost everything written about poetry, without thought, as if it were now part of nature, and not a phrase snatched from a letter written by a twenty-three-year-old English poet.

I had a lot of growing to do and was still willing to try to imitate Neruda's largesse. I would have given anything to have written a lot of the poems in *Residence on Earth,* as would most of my friends. "And the names of the months sound to me like threats / and the word winter is like the sound of a lugubrious drum." And then we discover that he means the next lines quite literally: "Later on you will find buried near the coconut tree / the knife which I hid there for fear you would kill me . . ." ("Widower's Tango," trans. W. S. Merwin). Parra said that he no longer wrote poetry. I smiled. "I don't believe you," I said. "Poetry is all around us," he said. "It is in the graffiti on the walls. I walk around and write down the graffiti, and those are my poems." I wasn't quite sure how to respond to his slyly humorous tone. I was interested in approaching poetry as a series of signs. Whenever I could, in a poem, I would use the equivalent of a found object, in the hope of some semiological revelation, but as I said, I was unwilling to limit my own practice by this kind of reduced aesthetic, even if I agreed with it in theory. I had been in continual dialogue with Parra's problem with poetry since that conversation at the West End. It was fine for him, who had already exhausted many possibilities of language, availing himself of *endecasilado,* the Spanish equivalent of iambic pentameter, to limit his imagination so severely, but for me at the time it would have been a form of amputation, a serum that prohibits growth.

In Paris the summer after the conversation with Parra at the West End, my girlfriend and I visited a relative on her mother's side, who was married to a Chilean diplomat. In the course of tea, in their airy, elegant, and uncluttered apartment in the sixteenth arrondissement, in which we had never set foot until that day, I interjected that Nicanor Parra was an important poet to me. "Why, Parra," he said, "he's very funny." "He is," I said, with a vaguely uncomfortable tingle coming over me. Santiago continued: "Everyone knows of the Parra family in Chile."

The second time I saw Parra was frustrating. It was at a crowded party on the Upper West Side; Allen Ginsberg corralled him and sat cross-legged at his feet.

(There is only one appropriate response to the literature written in Spanish in the twentieth century and that is to bow.)

Fifteen years passed. Meanwhile, a longtime friend, Kevin Mathewson, son of Ruth Mathewson, from whom we had rented a house in Brooklin, Maine, had become close to Nicanor and his sister, a well-known folk singer. At some point in the Christmas season, Kevin invited us to come over for a glass of wine and rekindle my acquaintance with Nicanor. We arrived at his mother's brownstone. Nicanor, dressed in a brown suit, was grazing the bookshelves. Kevin reintroduced us, we shook hands, and I briefly reacquainted him with our conversation. He claimed to remember it. It seemed to amuse him to no end that his ironic statement had had such a resonant effect on me. I had used it as part of an attempt at self-definition in an interview I had reprinted in my first book of poems. His humor and irony and warmth allowed for multiple tonalities in dialogue. At this point, he began to sing the same tune he had sung fifteen years before at the West End; he wasn't writing his own poetry, but he was writing the greatest poetry of his life.

How much better could conversation get? Where was he going next? I was anxious for his next sentence, but wanted him to deliver the resolution of this contradiction in his own time. Then he spoke.

"I am translating *King Lear* into Spanish for Joseph Papp. This is the greatest poetry I have written. For the first time I feel I am a great poet, while translating Shakespeare." Poetry per se was even more dead and superfluous than it had been in 1973. If Parra was a jokester, he was also making a critique of culture, like Karl Kraus. I hadn't thought of the connection between Parra and Karl Kraus until this instant, but it helps explain him to me, as it does for me to remember that he was a teacher of physics and mathematics for many years. He certainly wasn't over the top in this critique, as is Thomas Bernhard in a book like *The Old Masters* where the narrator ridicules the idea that Tintoretto is a great artist with unquenchable and delirious venom. Clearly, Parra meant and did not mean what he said. Parra, seventy-something at the time, had his finger on some kind of truth, which he chose to express in a tone imbued with understated gaiety. It was more fun to listen than to make another case. I reminded him of how similar this was to the argument he had made at the West End, fifteen years prior. This amused him. I told him my counterargument, "that which is created must create itself." That amused him further. (That was tacit, and the less I said the better.) Then he upped the stakes. "Do you know who the greatest poet in America is?" I remained the straight man. "Fredric Jameson."

I loved it. A conversation with Parra was like a game of five-card stud with a master bluffer who, some of the time, wasn't bluffing. Most of the time, you need the cards to win. I refused to give Parra further satisfaction by making the obvious protest that Jameson was a critic and theorist and not a poet.

I then apologized for not sticking with the poetry of signs. At this point, I hadn't seen any of his work in print since *Emergency Poems*. "Fredric Jameson," he repeated, "is the greatest poet of our time." This declaration is given added resonance when uttered with a Spanish accent. "This is what the young people want to read. Theory, not poetry." I resisted the childish impulse to pronounce how disturbed I was by the painfully self-evident truth of his revelation, of a reality I was keen to deny.

The key to the idea of Parra has to do with the creation of narrators who do not exist, who are part of antimatter. His is obsessed with the idea of their nonexistence and the nonexistence of the self in terms of the stable ego. That's why Allen Ginsberg, the eternal student of Buddhism, sat cross-legged at his feet.

The Book of Samuel

How strange, that no sooner should I write Parra's name than I discover that the treasured, faded, and weathered copy of *Poems and Antipoems* is missing. I have this past year lent it to one student and then another, and I don't remember who had it last. I call a friend at New Directions, his U.S. publisher, and there was some confusion as to what *Antipoems* I was looking for, because Parra's first book to be published in English in twenty years, *Antipoems: How to Look Better and Feel Great,* about whose existence I knew nothing moments before, is soon to appear in September 2004, two months from now. Once the confusion was resolved, to my surprise my friend agreed to send Parra's *Antipoems: New and Selected* over by messenger, which gave an afternoon spent indoors writing the quality of an adventure.

The fact that Nicanor taught physics and mathematics must be factored in, amid all the raillery. No matter how funny it seems to say that Fredric Jameson is the greatest poet of our time, it comes from someone who has a theoretical background and whose concept of antipoetry is so easily mistaken as a mere rebellion against certain Romantic and modernist tendencies. In reality, it's grounded in the provocative and dualistic concept of antimatter. Liz Werner comments in her incisive introduction to her translation of *Antipoems:*

> The concept of antimatter can lead us to a deeper reading of antipoetry. In 1928 a physicist named Paul Dirac came up with a mathematical equation that predicted the existence of an antiworld identical to ours but consisting of antimatter. Each particle of this world would exactly match each particle of our world, but would carry an opposite charge. Viewed through the lens of antimatter, *antipoetry mirrors poetry, not as its adversary but as its perfect complement; it is not by nature negative, but negative where poetry is positive, and vice versa; it is as opposite, complete, and interdependent as the shape left behind in the fabric where the garment has been cut out.*

(Now, trapped in Manhattan for the third consecutive summer, I am hit, forgive me, by a rush of images from summers spent in Maine, several at the Mathewsons' Red House on Naskeag Point in Brooklin, with which I will not burden you, okay, keeping an eye on my son, who is nineteen and began to drive to Maryland at midnight this July Fourth weekend to visit a friend who had just come out of a coma, and doesn't share our passion for solitude and silence, harbors and quiet coves, and eating for free on the mussels we waded out to gather at low tide, while my wife, still in her nightie, works on mathematics problems, utterly absorbed, in another world, though she did consent to watch the radiant Maria Sharapova outplay the indomitable Serena Williams in the women's final at Wimbledon. . . . Perhaps it is she who should write about Nicanor Parra, she to whom the concept of antimatter is more palpable than it is to me, who might tend to regard it as something in the vein of possibility, like negative capability.)

And now *Antipoems* (2004), whose subtitle is "How to look better & feel great," has allowed me, after a thirty-year wait, to read and MORE IMPORTANTLY SEE the outcome of Parra's laboratory experiments. These antipoems are like political cartoons Joan Miró might have drawn, which speaks to the eternal youthfulness of Nicanor Parra, who must be ninety, since he was born in 1914.

Parra, unlike his contemporaries around the world like Yehuda Amichai, Edmond Jabès, Wislawa Szymborska, Zbigniew Herbert, and, and it goes without saying, Czeslaw Milosz, did not continue to publish in English in the 1980s and '90s, and I fear he may be largely unknown to younger readers. (Define "younger.")

> just thinking about it
> makes my hair stand on end
> a lion a she-wolf and a panther
> *miserere di me*—
> gazed at me like they wanted to eat me for breakfast
>
> what luck that the great Tómas*
> came along at exactly the right moment
> otherwise I wouldn't be telling this story—

("CANTO PRIMO," *ANTIPOEMS*, 2004)

It may not be an accident, unless it is a case of supreme accident, that there is a certain consonance between Parra and the work of two great Portuguese poets, Carlos Drummond de Andrade and Fernando Pessoa. It is almost as if the birth of Parra's voice coincided with the death of Pessoa in 1936. Pessoa is more multivalent than Parra, but Parra's persona is more evocative than the persona of Pessoa's he most resembles, Alvaro de Campos. Parra's poetry pokes a hole

The Book of Samuel

in the grandiose poetry of the modernists. His goal is to unsettle, to keep the reader alert and thinking on their feet. If Rilke ("You must change your life") and Frost ("Drink and be whole again beyond confusion") and Bishop ("knowledge is historical, flowing, and flown") strove toward unquestionably magnificent and comforting forms of closure, or resolution—which over time are in danger of becoming chestnuts—Parra's endings are keyed to the next step.

> My angel! she said nervously.
> Let me sit on your knees once again!
> It was then that I was able to ponder the fact that she was now wearing
>   brief tights.
> It was a memorable meeting, though full of discordant notes.
> I have bought a plot of land not far from the slaughterhouse, she
>   exclaimed.
> I plan to build a sort of pyramid there
> Where we can spend the rest of our days.
> I have finished my studies, I have been admitted to the bar,
> I have a tidy bit of capital at my disposal;
> Let's go into some lucrative business, we two, my love, she added,
> Let's build our nest far from the world.
> Enough of your foolishness, I answered, I have no confidence in your
>   plans.
> Bear in mind that my real wife
> Can at any moment leave both of us in the most frightful poverty.
> My children are grown up, time has elapsed,
> I feel utterly exhausted, let me have a minute's rest,
> Give me a little water, woman,
> Get me something to eat from somewhere,
> I'm starving,
> I can't work for you anymore,
> It's all over between us.

("THE VIPER," TRANS. W. S. MERWIN)

Every work of art is a diary of its own creation, just as a stone, as Osip Mandelstam claimed, is a "geometer of the weather." Some art is eternally fresh, will never be dated, like that of Fra Angelico and François Villon and John Skelton and Gustave Courbet and Constantine Brancusi.

I keep thinking of Santiago's comment that Nicanor comes from a famous family of clowns. That he comes from a famous family seems undeniable. In *Passions and Impressions,* Pablo Neruda testifies that "the Parras of Chile [are] outstanding in poetry and folklore, their talent ever ripening and flowering." Parra doesn't write like nobody's listening. And when nobody listened, he interrupted a reading by the most revered Chilean poet of the time, Gabriella Mistral, by jumping onto the stage and reciting a poem he had written in her honor. This endeared him to her, and she used her influence to help get him published.

There is a reason why poets of my generation, born around 1950, have been so profoundly influenced by foreign poets, though it may be more a matter of sustenance than influence. Foreign poets don't have the feeling of writing in the gap, as de Tocqueville put it, between the void and the crowd, which he insisted defined the disorienting American spiritual condition. What was the fate of some of the most inventive and multivalent American poets born in the same year as Parra, poets like John Berryman, Randall Jarrell, and Weldon Kees? Different fates, clearly, but none as happy as they might have been. Randall Jarrell tried to address some of the problems of being a poet in America from a special angle in "The Obscurity of the Poet," as Richard Howard did in the title of his book of essays *Alone with America,* and as Berryman did in *The Dream Songs* and *Love and Fame.* Permit me to use some Freudian terms without necessarily subscribing to them, because the Oedipality of most of these poets is so overwhelming, so crushing.

To return to Parra's fabulous assertion that the theorist Fredric Jameson was the greatest poet of our time, I must now confess that I hadn't read anything by Jameson when Parra said this, although I knew who he was, and I got the drift. I figured Jameson would be a replicant of Barthes, Deleuze, Derrida, and Lacan, and I felt no compulsion to read another writer who did not generate his own ideas, but merely applied the theories developed by others to contemporary contexts. And I may not have ever read Jameson had a student not given me, some fifteen years after the second conversation with Parra, a Xerox of an essay of his on Joseph Conrad called "Romance and Reification: Plot Constructions and Ideological Closure in Joseph Conrad." I'm not sure who gave it to me, but I may have mentioned in class that I was rereading Conrad's *Victory.*

The copy of Jameson's essay, in a brown folder among manila folders, lay in a pile for about a year. When I began thinking about Conrad again I began to fantasize about rereading *Nostromo* and *Lord Jim,* but couldn't decide in which order. In the midst of this indecision, I pulled out Jameson's essay which, I discovered, is specifically on these two books, and was staggered and stimulated by its brilliance and implications. I had never read anything quite like it. Reading Jameson's essay was like reading a book. It was so profound and provocative, I could only read five pages at a time, and then mull them over. And of course I couldn't go back to Conrad's novels until I had "finished" the essay by Fredric Jameson, America's greatest poet.

I began to carry around the manila folder with the thirty-five Xeroxed pages in the hope of finding the spare time to read and digest them in between my other tasks.

I had never read a better definition of Conrad's work than Jameson's opening gambit, calling it unclassifiable, "spilling out of high literature into light reading and romance, reclaiming great areas of diversion and distraction by the most demanding practice of style and *écriture* alike, floating uncertainly somewhere between Proust and Robert Louis Stevenson."

The beauty of Jameson's essay is that it's perfectly compatible with the density and texture of these two inexhaustible novels of Conrad. Or as Jameson would put it, "the 'event' in *Lord Jim* is the analysis and dissolution of the event, . . . but we have understood very little about this narrative unless we have come to realize that even that 'real story' itself is for Conrad hollow and empty, and that there is a void at the heart of events and acts in these works which goes well beyond simple anecdotal mystification."

I think Nicanor Parra would consent.

Notes

I like to think that prose as well as poetry can have form. I decided in advance that the appropriate length for an homage to Nicanor Parra should be twelve pages. This is also because I was writing about Parra as a way of moving into other material when my inability to find my copy of *Poems and Antipoems* led me to the discovery that his new book was in galleys.

As I was finishing this essay, in July 2004, a biography of Pablo Neruda mysteriously arrived. (I had never before received a review copy from Bloomsbury Press.) While the book is somewhat disappointing for the way it stays on the surface ("but a quick read"), it had this passage from a letter by Neruda about the poem of his I chose to quote, "Widower's Tango": "Sometimes, a light would wake me up, a ghost moving on the other side of the mosquito net. It was her, dressed in white, brandishing her long, sharpened native knife. It was her, walking around and around my bed for hours at a time, without quite making up her mind to kill me" (Adam Feinstein, *Pablo Neruda: A Passion for Life*, Bloomsbury, 2004, p. 65).

This poem "Canto Primo" is graced with a curious footnote: "Tómas Lagos. Literary critic and friend of Nicanor Parra's." Here Parra is referring to the prologue to the volume *Tres poetas chilenos* (*Three Chilean Poets*) in which Lagos writes, "Hasta aquí nomas llega Neruda y después Parra." (Neruda takes up to this point and no further. From here on, it's Parra.)

What Are You?

How could they have missed the turn?

How could civilizations, isolated, divine so much of what the Roman architects
contrived and handed over to the ruling class who were moving as far away

from the divine, the sacred, the quick step of the Etruscans as they could

without falling off the earth——if you believed in a pool table planet——either way
the Roman, and Mayan, war machine ran on, until whatever it ran on, ran out

like a close-up of the last trickle of gas from the shell of a Shell station

adjacent to the inexhaustible oil reserves in Texas and——a mere 6,000
miles away, the Middle East: and the last patron, or patrone, who had a camera

on his person always, took the photo, set the Canon on flash and caught

the interminable fall of the last drop of crude oil to fall on earth,
like a bead of sweat from a lover or a boxer's brow, or liquid explosive no one

within range intuited would blast a hole where the town once lay the instant
it struck

pavement, and the concrete wall——the gas station's horizon to the East——

broke apart like pool balls at the break
and altered the events that led to the execution of the Spaniards, and Basque?——

who opposed the army of tongue-severed mutes, to whom gun, and bomb,

uniform and badge, and other elegant apparel, and all for free, carried
such instant privileges, and incentives to kill—

tore through the wall of trees that protected the trail from traffic,

once I heard the sound and saw people objects debris take to the air,
and disappear, and deemed the immensity of the hole out of sight,

and hugged a tree trunk, taking retrospective cover,

after the third party who belonged to no party on Spanish,
or Basque, soil, never thought to warn inhabitants

within range, I realized while the truth sank in

that I'd been spared and that the sound I now feared
was the pumping of blood to my own heart when

I heard the whirring of the blades and waved

to the helicopter pilot where he could set down,
where the clearing, the nearest haven

for journalists, which would never have been

approved, if they hadn't been stunned, scorched,
and stricken, by the tirade Malraux launched

when he'd stepped off a flak-stricken plane.

Sources

Since most of my sources are "the complete works" and biographies of the authors I've engaged during the writing of this prose, I am only including references to works that the reader may not know.

Adelman, Gary. *Reclaiming D. H. Lawrence: Contemporary Writers Speak Out.* Lewisburg, Pa.: Bucknell University Press, 2002.

Ascherson, Neal. "The Man in the Otter Collar." *New York Review of Books,* November 28, 1996, 4–7.

Brodsky, Joseph. *So Forth: Poems.* New York: Farrar, Straus and Giroux, 1996.

Czarnecka, Ewa, et al. *Conversations with Czeslaw Milosz.* Translated by Richard Lourie. San Diego: Harcourt Brace Jovanovich, 1987.

Ellis, David. *D. H. Lawrence: Dying Game, 1922–1930.* Cambridge: Cambridge University Press, 1998.

Holmes, Richard. *Coleridge: Darker Reflections.* New York: Pantheon, 1999.

———. *Coleridge: Early Visions, 1772–1804.* New York: Viking, 1990.

Kinkead-Weekes, Mark. *D. H. Lawrence: Triumph to Exile, 1912–1922.* Cambridge: Cambridge University Press, 1996.

Lawrence, D. H. *Phoenix: The Posthumous Papers of D. H. Lawrence.* Edited by Edward D. McDonald. New York: Viking, 1936.

———. *Phoenix II: Uncollected, Unpublished and Other Prose Works.* Edited by Warren Roberts and Harry T. Moore. London: Heineman, 1968.

———. *The Selected Letters of D. H. Lawrence, V, March 1924–March 1927.* Edited by James T. Boulton and Lindeth Vasey. Cambridge: Cambridge University Press, 1989.

Lowry, Malcolm. *Selected Letters of Malcolm Lowry.* Edited by Harvey Breit and Margerie Bonner Lowry. London: Jonathan Cape, 1967.

———. *The Voyage That Never Ends.* Edited by Michael Hofmann. New York: New York Review Books, 2007.

Magnuson, Paul. *Coleridge's Poetry and Prose.* New York: W. W. Norton, 2003.

Mandelstam, Osip. "Conversation About Dante," in *Selected Poems of Osip Mandelstam.* Translated by W. S. Merwin and Clarence Brown. New York: New York Review Books, 2004. The other excellent translations of Mandelstam are by James Greene.

Milosz, Czeslaw, ed. *Postwar Polish Poetry: An Anthology.* Berkeley: University of California Press, 1983.

———. *The Separate Notebooks.* Translated by Robert Hass and Robert Pinsky. Hopewell, N.J.: Ecco, 1986.

———. *A Year of the Hunter.* Translated by Madeline Levine. New York: Farrar, Straus and Giroux, 1994.

Pasternak, Boris. *My Sister—Life.* Translated by Mark Rudman with Bohdan Boychuk. Evanston, Ill.: Northwestern University Press, 1992.

Rudman, Mark. *Diverse Voices: Essays on Poetry and Poets.* Brownsville, Oreg.: Story Line Press, 1992. (This collection includes an early version of the Crane/ Lowry essay, "Mosaic on Walking," and contains "On Czeslaw Milosz: No Longer in Continuous Time" as well as "On Letters" and "On Notebooks" that led to the evolution of a way of writing prose that, while focused on poetry and other poets, would not necessitate excluding anything as "external" to the subject, which is imagination.)

Wat, Aleksander. *My Century: The Odyssey of a Polish Intellectual.* Edited and translated from the Polish by Richard Lourie. New York: New York Review Books, 2003.

Williams, William Carlos. *The Collected Poems of William Carlos Williams.* 2 vols. Edited by A. Walton Litz and Christopher MacGowan. New York: New Directions, 1986–88.

———. *Imaginations: Five Experimental Prose Pieces* [*Kora in Hell, Spring and All, The Descent of Winter, The Great American Novel, A Novelette and Other Prose*]. New York: New Directions, 1971.

———. *In the American Grain.* New York: New Directions, 1956.

———. *Paterson.* New York: New Directions, 1992.

———. *Selected Poems.* Edited by Robert Pinsky. New York: Library of America, 2004.